IT'S NOT ALIENS, WORSE, IT'S US
Discovering Our Lost History

Jared Murphy

Printed by

PARANOIA PUBLISHING

http://www.paranoiapublishing.com

PARANOIA Publishing
C/O The Anomalies Network LLC
PO Box 3124 Martinez, CA 94553

info@anomalies.net

Acknowledgements

There is a massive amount of details in all the subjects above that have many books, research, and investigations. The world we live in is connected and tied via our personal health and relationship to the earth, to each other and all the life that calls this home.

There are many great researchers that have been on this for a very long time all have unique insight into what is going on. I hope this list can be a start or a continued reference into your personal knowledge base.

Many of these people will have YouTube channels, websites, books and all have multiple ways to purchase material. If you find them on one of these formats, I want to encourage you to seek out their work on the other available formats.

Cover Art by Shawn Lohse
Shawnlohse.com

Illustrations by Marie Drescher
Instagram @rieinspired

Erik Von Daniken:
daniken.com
HISTORY IS WRONG

Michael Cremo and Richard L. Thompson
Forbidden Archeology

Michael Tellinger:
Michaeltellinger.com
Slave Species of God: The Story of Humankind from the Cradle of Humankind
Temples of the African Gods
Pretty much anything you can hunt down for YouTube lectures

Brien Foerster:
Hiddenincatours.com
Lost Ancient Technology Of Egypt
Beyond the Black Sea: The Mysterious Paracas of Peru
Lost Ancient Technology of Egypt Volume 2

Sylvie Ivanova:
Megaliths.org
On YouTube @ newearth (Her ancient history research videos are invaluable!)

David Hatcher Childress:
davidhatcherchildress.com
Please look for his lectures and videos on YouTube also!

Hugh Newman:
hughnewman.co.uk
Please look for his lectures and videos on YouTube also!

Ken Wheeler:
Uncovering The Missing Secret's of Magnetism
Please look for his lectures on YouTube on Magnetism, specifically

Ancient-code.com
Ancient-origins.net
Sciencedaily.com

CHAPTERS

Chapter 1

INTRODUCTION

IT'S not aliens, it's us. If you point and yell, " GODZILLA" people know what you are doing, they look and no one expects to see Godzilla, if there really was a Godzilla when people looked, people would really be surprised, but they would know what to do, they would run....well there is the selfie crowd. Seriously, if you yelled Godzilla, and there really was one, people at this point in time in history would look where your pointing and say something to the effect, " holy shit, it is real" and run. It's not aliens, it's us, what does that mean? It means that a massive base of physical evidence, including genetic information that has been found, is being found and is exponentially being put together that shows there was at least one global advanced society on Earth before the history we know. Over our modern times people have claimed Aliens helped us build the Pyramids, or helped us in our past, and visited. The physical exactness and complexity of these ancient structures made aliens an easy assumption. "They must have helped" is the assumption.

There is growing evidence being dug up that our history is way different than we Have been told or chosen to acknowledge even though the evidence is right in our face. People like Wim Hof, Stig Seversen, Mark Sisson, Rob Wolf, Ido Portal and Erwin Le Corre are rediscovering forgotten human abilities from changing our very gene expression to our breathing. Conscious control of our immune system and inflammatory response and holding our breath for 22 minutes while connecting to our quantum consciousness. These are things we once thought god like or only someone special could do. Our ancient past has a hidden history and we are finally placing the pieces back together to start answering the questions of who are we, where did we come from. The general what the hell of it.

We have to step through many pieces to create a picture we can understand and going over our history of archaeology, some very well known archaeological sites. Genetics, quantum sciences and some very recent scientific research to paint a new global picture of what was and where we might go and what we are.

The mainstream religion of archaeology requires obedience to a historical record that is at a minimum untrue and becoming more and more obviously out right lies. Michael Cremo puts it as "knowledge Filtrated" to fit the story that is told about our past by the founders of archaeology. These people lived in a time that bloodletting was still a thing and Louis pastor was coming of age. Even at the advent of archaeology there were researchers finding clear evidence that contradicted the popular theories of mans existence on this planet. If evidence is found to contradict the findings of the last couple hundred years about our established theory of the past, the evidence whether large scale buildings, statues, out of place out of time pieces or whatever, they are suppressed, hidden, made only available to "qualified" researchers, destroyed, or miss labeled. If researchers who find out of place out of time artifacts and publish their findings, perhaps indicating a new historical timeline, they are told to retract it by mainstream archaeology and academia. If they don't understand the error of their ways, they are discredited ruined or called fringe or just crazy, they are fired from their University positions and conferences are held to discredit them. It is an outright modern witch hunt and burn them at the stake. Sometimes what a researcher or archaeologist will do is renounce their find and realize they made a "mistake" in their initial observations. Sometimes when evidence is found it's called out of place out of time artifacts, it's also called an enigma or a mystery, then no further research needs to be done, it's a mystery and left to the imagination. It is a global crime that deserves it's own stage.

We are in the infancy of archaeology with barely a couple hundred years of activity in modern times if you can call the 1900's as modern, with the later half being "advanced" with the advent of us going to the moon and modern computers. The last couple hundred years have lead to a number of prominent theories, including Darwinism, Christian archaeology to justify the story of the Bible. Great efforts to establish the historical record of the Bible is made by digging up the Middle East while the Hindu religion and the Vedas are treated likely fantasies of a eastern culture. Non western history is being treated as second class information to that of the Greeks, Romans, and the Renaissance and has lead to highly focused specializations in Egypt, the pyramids, Stonehenge and Greco-Roman research as an example. Mesoamerica as one archaeologist put it is where cultures go to die(more on that later).

There are many Russian, Chinese, Indian, Japanese, and other non western archaeologists doing research that is finally making it into English language and they are all providing a more global picture of the ancient past. The alternative researchers, frequently insulted by standard academia as being labeled "pseudo-archaeologists" or "pseudoscience" have embraced a more unbiased look at our past combining all these researchers and developing new ideas. This has been met with extreme resistance by standard academia. Archaeologist stumble through the pieces of our history and have been trying to piece it together to fit an early 18th, 19th, 20th century Victorian theory. The focus on predominant theories has created such a biased to look at any other options has left the field of truth open to any researcher willing to look at the evidence and not apply a Victorian filter to it.

Theories have expanded to include aliens. There are many that believe that the gods of Sumer or in the Book of Enoch of the Bible, are clearly indications of alien interaction. The theories abound that aliens genetically modified us, or that we were created by aliens as slaves has become a widely spoken one of the many ideas amongst alternative history researchers with the gods of Sumer as a frequented pointed to reference and the Sumerian stories.

One of the other great references for alternative researchers is to the complexity of ancient constructions. There are so many from Stonehenge to The Great Pyramid of Giza that appear impossible to build today. Many theories how loin clothed slaves built them abound for standard and alternative historians and researchers. Of course there is that really cool older guy on YouTube that moves whole buildings on a couple stones with a couple poles and levies. You should look at that guy sometime, it's cool. The idea is expanded that loin clothiers had a little shove by benevolent aliens, but it is still a theory in line with the standard academic model. That we are advanced as we have ever been now.

There are sightings of UFO's in our history. The famous air battle over Los Angeles during WWII or the Bermuda Triangle and photos galore of individuals, ships, planes and you name disappearing in the Bermuda Triangle. Late night radio shows across the US and websites talk about abductions and sightings. Roswell and Area 51. We have TV show after movie of humans meeting or saving or fighting aliens. So many of these sightings now that the over all dialog for humans at least Americans is to say, " hey, I have seen an alien for real just like on these shows". Every other movie or a documentary seems to be pointing to the size of the universe and saying something else has to be out there. Right?

We have been digging more and in the last 40 or so years, some archaeologists, alternative researchers, and intelligent observers have looked at these ruins with non Victorian eyes. What they observe, even a couple Victorian archaeologist did, that the complex buildings credited to a particular known ancient society could not have built by the credited society. That maybe these are squatter cultures, that moved into the destroyed, abandoned towns and cities of a prior more advanced culture and adapted the sites to a new purpose.

What if remnants of a past human society survived and lived, retreated with their technology and are among us, they continued to advance and to us, appear alien. What if the UFO's and assorted alien experiences are really intentional and unintentional interactions with our ancient human ancestors? The idea has become mainstream that maybe aliens have visited and the signs of their visits are in our past via cultural stories, myths, religions, sightings, cave paintings, statues, etc...

It is easier to believe that our lineal history from caveman to now as it is told to us in current displays at the natural history museums with cavemen around fires and loin clothed villagers. Sitting around building grass hut houses and that maybe aliens helped build things like the pyramids, then to accept that a prior unknown chapter of human history happened, and we are the decedents of survivors. Of that great human society. We need to dissect the piles of obvious ancient technology, newly found sites, old sites and look with new eyes at a more accurate theoretical picture of our past. If there were highly advanced people that survived a catastrophe, why leave us to our own resource today?

For some people this is a new subject, for others we will be seemingly gliding over some exciting as seen on TV or YouTube details and insights on amazing and old sites and pieces of ancient technology but there is so much to cover for another paradigm shift. Taking the new research that is being done, painting a new paradigm is one of many paramount points for us to have a clean filter for our true complex past and future.

We will pull in the very real technology pieces that it would take today to build these giant structures and small advanced artifacts found and therefore the technology our ancestors would have likely had medically. We will deconstruct the urgency that needs to be in our current global research. This is a book about our past, our human past and our global human future.

Chapter 2

50,000 ft. PIN HOLE VIEWS

A picture of flying cars landing at parking lots near the great pyramid and elongated skulled humans talking to giants and aliens would be a cool visual right? Maybe a line of human cavemen being injected by alien slave masters and reptilian overlords whipping us while carrying heavy blocks up ramps, to build the pyramids and dig up gold to pimp their saucers? Maybe in more recent theories aliens forcing us to mine gold while they land space cruisers at Baalbek, Lebanon after a quick trip to Nazca, Peru? We can't do it. Our past is way bigger than was taught in a Victorian or 20th century schooling or alternatives being built on the existing storyline.

There are pyramids globally, common building techniques, shared myths, religious ideas and other indicators of a large populated earth going into at least one common disaster. There are objects, math and sciences that indicate from our soil to our construction methods that indicate an understanding we, modern man are just comprehending and in applying to our past is clarifying our understanding. To take it all in, we will drill down and up and build a comprehensible understanding of who we are and what we have been missing about who we are and were that makes this mysterious planet more so and less so.

We are going to take a 50,000 ft. view, to highlight, places just being found, sciences being applied and found in our ancient past, and objects that point to a more sophisticated global fallen ancient society. We will look at how the breakdown of that ancient society lead to it being lost in myth, legend, drugs and religion. Even further it has been blurred by entrenched hypothesis frequently intentionally hiding evidences that contradict modern academia. There is a new breed of alternative researchers doing amazing work and also creating new potentially entrenching hypothesis that are good and bad. Is it too early to mention we are going to talk math; we are gonna go quantum! That gets you ramped up to turn a page, right?

We will take a smashing look at some cool quantum mechanical and toroidal field research that has become all the rage. What is really cool is that there are some people out their talking about aliens and what aliens needs. Yeah, we are are going to talk UFO's, It's not aliens, it's us. Don't be a flip a header, there are a lot of things we will go over that some have already heard of, others not so much. Piece the puzzle of humanity, the who,what,where, and when is going to come together in a new clearer way. Like windshield wiper just wiped enough of the big bug impact away to see clearly.

In later chapters breaking into more specifics on the pieces, places, and technology of our past to rebuild a more appropriate picture and hypothesis of these things and the timeline of humanity. Yes we need a few BIG examples to understanding how far apart traditional academia/archaeology is from seeing what is laying right in front of them and all of us. We also need to have a better appreciation that it isn't all figured out for us. We actually need to help. There is such a drastic break from the evidence, the emperors new cloths story should be read at every archaeology site and ancient object studied before they make a theory on it. This goes for the exponentially growing alternative history field also.

What is standard academia? Standard academia is National Geographic, the Smithsonian or anywhere you thing Indiana Jones was a professor for some examples of "standard academia". Any magazine or institution that is perpetuating the theory that we crossed to America only on a land bridge, that Darwinism and modern humans have only been around a few hundred thousand years. Anyone that can look at cymatic polygonal construction and look you eyeball to eyeball and say, yeah, the rubble stacked on these multi ton stones was the same builder, they got tired.

If you made a pinhole in the cover of this book and went on to describe what this book is about or any of the details, your dreaming and have a closer idea of the stories of our past that are conjured by "academics" past and current. Archaeologists and scientists of the last 200 years have had to work with a pinhole view to tell us our history and create a story when they find an object, mummy, tool, or building that fits in what has to be a hypothesis to help build a picture of the past. Unfortunately they were jumping to conclusions and those early theories became doctrine instead of a working hypothesis. Degrees were made on those doctrines, some costing over 200,000 in today's dollars.

HOW BIG OF A PINHOLE DO ACADEMICS AND SOME ALTERNATIVE RESEARCHERS USE?

If you know nothing about anthropology or archaeology and have never picked up a National Geographic or Discover magazine, watched a show, taken a class on art history, or any ancient history course, then you wouldn't know what kind of jumps they make. If you have studied the past or at least have seen The Ten Commandments you have seen loin cloth slaves building pyramids. How about 2001 Space Odyssey? Or Will Ferrell in Land of the Lost? You got little furry devolved people, the classic caveman dressed in animal skins pounding rocks by a fire. As we are told about the past it is because there is a theory that is continually reinforced through schooling and perpetuated by entertainment. If it's 10,000 years ago, we are in rags, have spears and are fighting off saber tooth tigers. Very Fred Flintstone. The theory we are talking about is evolution, and Darwin put a date on it, the working theory that we are the most advanced as we have ever been is now and as you go back you get less and less advanced technology, ideas, simpler people, etc. Bigger more carnivorous animals and plants but the picture is set. 50,000 years ago we were still banging rocks and kinda getting the idea of farming. When archaeologists and anthropologists find things, they take the working template of that theory and apply it to what they find. We are going to break it down that we got it wrong. The reaction sometimes is who cares? We got it basically right.

That is at a minimum wrong. We got it way wrong and that is hurting us. To understand how wrong, and to understand that we need to get it right, we have to look at the evidences of our mislabeled past, why we have and how we perpetuate those paradigms. There is such a filter on archaeologists and anthropologists, that for the laymen I want to give you an example of how badly interpretations are used to label, people, places, technology, everything based on the Victorian researchers that developed our template for history. Whatever is dug up a story is told with the assumptions that the standard theory is true. So whatever is found a story is created around it. If it's an artifact, it's value is for worship, most buildings are temples, ruling class buildings, sacrificial alters, etc... You find something and it gets put into a slot.

I hated economics for their abstract examples so although this is abstract, it illustrates the stories paleoanthropologists and archeologists use to tell you about a site.

So here is an accurate punch at the kinda of leaps and assumptions that are made...

WORLD WAR TWO

If you took Berlin, Germany and only had the Reichstag, and the ruins of it, a 1000 years from now, could you tell me about WWII?

The Reichstag Is the German parliament building in Berlin built in 1894. It had a massive fire in 1933 because Bolshevik communists tried to insight a communist uprising like they had in Russia. The National Socialists used it for propaganda and military purposes during WWII. Could you tell me about that? In 1000 years?

The German Reichstag after a long restoration process. Nothing would give you the impression that this was a major symbol of victory for the allies in World War II.

The German Reichstag after a long restoration process. Nothing would give you the impression that this was a major symbol of victory for the allies in World War II.

How about Hiroshima or Nagasaki? America drops the first nuclear weapons in modern time on the Japanese cities inducing a surrender. Now lets imagine the cities are nuked, then immediately buried in a volcanic eruption in our hypothetical situation. Could you tell me about that world's war in 500 years or 1000 years ? About the millions killed on the Russian side of the conflict.

In Stalin's time it is estimated that 60 million were killed. These included Poles, Ukrainians, Germans, anyone opposed to Bolshevik communist rule. The party starved and killed native Russians and the Americans and British supported this monster. Hitler couldn't come close to the numbers that Stalin managed to kill, starve and imprison. As a side note there is a common perpetual statement of 61 million dying, this is a valuable rabbit hole, just saying Here is a perfect example of history writing itself slowly over. As far as digging up Hiroshima and Nagasaki in our hypothetical archaeology site, could you tell me about Pearl Harbor from that excavation ?

Archaeologists like to dig up an object, and you don't need to know a lot about history to know they dug up a fertility goddess, a scared temple, or the first and only and one of a kind object. Jumping to decide the social structure of a entire society from a couple hundred, or a couple thousand of graves, could not give you a global picture of that society.

This jumping to conclusions about our past is really, really bad and can't be described enough to explain why we can stare super advanced ancient construction in the face and say it isn't. Where's Shaggy, "It wasn't me!" For those that don't know the song, he's a 90's rapper, rapping about a guy caught by his girlfriend with another woman in the act. He asks Shaggy what to do, he in turn tells him to tell the girlfriend, "it wasn't me".

The view from the Reichstag as the Russian Army mounts the building in victory and to change the flag in the last days of WWII in Europe. There is no moment in history that any historian or storyteller can reveal what the details were like unless they were there.

Establishing that we were wrong, great, seeing past it is to see the emperor naked. The emperor has no new clothes. There are many smart, open minded people that aren't ready to pigeon hole history to the solved basket. There are others though that have thrown our very history away when it didn't fit the accepted paradigms. It was easy to miss and here is a great example of the scale we are missing about our past global populations. Or at least 60 million other people that could still be remembered in just World War II that the allies let the Bolsheviks kill.

HOW OFF COULD POPULATIONS IN THE PAST POSSIBLY BE

Archaeologists create ideas about society structures, war, religion, trade routes and exploration and expansions of ancient societies. They do this by finding evidence of buildings, farming, earth work walls, burials and pottery. A society based on how big or small may indicate how they influenced other cultures, tribes, or countries. Take South America and Guatemala, the thought was maybe at its height the Mayans had approximately 5 million people. Minnesota US of A has about 7 million now. You can imagine how light the development would be if you have a whole continent with about 5 million people.

National Geographic on Feb. 1., 2018 published about a research project in Guatemala. There is a new project to LIDAR map the jungles of Guatemala and search for lost buildings and structures. LIDAR means, "Light Detection And Ranging".

So far they have covered over 800 square miles of the Maya Biosphere Reserve in the Petén region. This has produced the largest LIDAR data set ever found for archaeological research. Of course that's of January 2019. Unless you want to count Sarah Parcak. She is doing some crazy satellite research. We will discuss her findings later. Using LIDAR, they have found over 60,000 buildings, roads and highways, well terraced farmland that could support millions. The highways are raised, accounting for traffic separation and flooding. There are multiple urban centers connected by these roads and quarries to build and maintain these buildings. They are saying the land was dramatically different when this society was there based on this research.

The LIDAR scans revealing these massive cities can not reveal the length of occupation or the oldest ruins and how they were repaired or maintained over thousands of years. The earliest layers and foundations could be megalithic and the engineering started with the soil for meta-structures, including trees and plants. It will take current archeology eons to put all the pots back together. It will likely take one or two acres of excavations to reveal it was all temples and constellation based worship.

Here is an excerpt from the same article:

...from the National Geographic article Dated Feb. 1, 2018 by **TOM CLYNES**...

"The LiDAR images make it clear that this entire region was a settlement system whose scale and population density had been grossly underestimated," said Thomas Garrison, an Ithaca College archaeologist and National Geographic Explorer who specializes in using digital technology for archaeological research...

"this was a civilization that was literally moving mountains," said Marcello Canuto, a Tulane University archaeologist and National Geographic Explorer who participated in the project.

"We've had this western conceit that complex civilizations can't flourish in the tropics, that the tropics are where civilizations go to die," said Canuto, who conducts archaeological research at a Guatemalan site known as La Corona. "But with the new LiDAR-based evidence from Central America and [Cambodia's] Angkor Wat, we now have to consider that complex societies may have formed in the tropics and made their way outward from there."

"Most people had been comfortable with population estimates of around 5 million," said Estrada-Belli, who directs a multi-disciplinary archaeological project at Holmul, Guatemala. "With this new data it's no longer unreasonable to think that there were 10 to 15 million people there—including many living in low-lying, swampy areas that many of us had thought uninhabitable.""

Currently it's a three-year project and this data was from approximately 800 sq. miles. They will be mapping over 5000 sq. miles; this is just Guatemala.

This find in a nutshell describes the archaeology pin hole and every problem with academic relationships to our past. "..population estimates of around 5 million...it's no longer unreasonable to think that there were 10-15 million..." "grossly underestimated"

You could plaque that, our idea of history, GROSSLY UNDERESTIMATED.

The pictures of the LIDAR imaging shows pyramids, temples, so many large buildings. It's as extensive as a large developed modern metropolitan international city. There isn't a written archaeology or anthropological observation that this was possible. Instead of making finds over the last couple hundred years and stating the facts of what was found, great conjuncture was made with fractions of finds dug up. We have now obviously found items that indicate the Mayans were here and the civilization that they had is beyond our imagination. Standard academia went with, "we pretty much are all done and found it all." This doesn't clear the Mayans as the original builders, it just means that they had more advanced structures to build on. This kind of mistake if it was in aviation would shut down the offending company faster than you could spell FAA. On top of this universities get a pass. Quick corrections are not made. This assumption about the small size of the South American populations led to to theories about the amazon forest being an untouched pristine place that simple tribes and small villages occupied with minimal impact.

The BBC did a documentary airing Thursday June 23, 2011 about the Amazon Rainforest. It's on YouTube if you want to go looking. It shows the large geoglyphs found after all the trees were cut away by loggers in the rainforest. Remember save the rainforest? Well by the 1970's, these geoglyphs, which were football field and larger in size were being seen from airplanes. They could be called earthwork cities, with a moat and high hilled walls that surround the village or city. The geographer, Alceu Randi from Brazil was seeing them while flying over Acre. The research was continued and these geoglyphs indicated city or village centers in the shapes of circle and squares and almost everywhere in the Amazon if they cleared an area. The documentary is from 2011, they estimated 5 million could have lived in the area. The BBC mentions that the estimates based on what was found at the time indicated it may only be 10 percent of what is hiding under the foliage. How could you even suggest that? Without LIDAR, or satellite you wouldn't know. It is that easy to throw out a statistic. If you add the large towns found through clearing and the LIDAR finds, are we talking 100's of millions? Separate societies?

"We have had a western Conceit " Marcello Canuto.

This is our first example to stop the presses. The template can't apply about modern theories of the land bridge route to America for one. Did they bring Terra Preta to South America or was it brought out? The conceit of population estimates is the minimum negligence. The opinions of academia that take irresponsible jumps to conclusions don't stop. The amount of people on earth, where they were and the sizes of these potential ancient societies are looking more and more to have been massive. Yes, people could have used a land bridge, someone could have used that, likely the bark eaters. Tough people, the simple human populations that lived amongst us. Estimates range today that there are still about 160 tribes we leave alone of tribal and nomadic people. How many were around post flood over the last 12,000 years?

"....we now have to consider that complex societies may have formed in the tropics and made their way outward from there." Marcello Canuto

What comes with a statement of complex societies may have formed...it's decoding that they mean, that there was more advanced societies in sciences, religion, social connections, and clearly based on this LIDAR, a massive physically built up society. This requires construction sciences. What are they doing? Who should look at those constructions, engineers or just anthropologists? Sure in many cases it could be both. The cymatic polygonal constructions, geopolymer scientists, archaeoacoustic researchers, an army of new researchers including physicists. The paradigm shift makes more sense when you think of the boots on the ground archaeologist that stops and digs up another pot or fertility goddess, and thinks, I should spend the next 40 years here when the gold is still in the woods. Gold is supposed to be in the ground, imagine it head level and in the form of pyramids and 60,000 buildings! If you don't believe they are there, it's pretty obvious now isn't it, you don't find it? The scale of how we have settled in our belief of the past in just this example is that the continent of South America is where societies went to die. The stories, movies, tv series that could be made about this 800 sq. mile location is endless. What is emerging is a continent that could have supported hundreds of millions with a super soil we can't make. Small indicators of a highly advanced society able to sustain a population of any size with nutrient rich soil. The quality of the food being paramount to the nutrients needed is a common disconnect today. Food is done on flavor, natural sourcing is becoming more important. The awareness that nutrient rich soil is still an abstract association with how good food looks. If you grow it in sand, but have a big red tomato, well it's big and red, so it must be delicious. Just about anybody can tell you growing in your own yard produces tastier food. What if you bioengineered nutrient rich soil for a planetary population?

BRAD PITT HELPS EVERYONE LINK ADVANCED SOIL TO ANCIENT PEOPLE

Who likes Brad Pitt? He isn't Terra Preta but Brad Pitt in 2016 made a movie The lost city of Z about Col. Percy Fawcett whom got himself lost trying to find what he called the city of Z in the Brazilian Amazon jungle. He left the city of Cuiaba to look for this place he called "Z" and he was never seen again. As a side point, based on those radar scans in Guatemala how does broad side of a barn apply really appropriately now? Colonel Fawcett should have fallen on a temple, but the jungle is very thick so why would an archaeologist in 1800's or early 1900's fair better? We are again making movies and telling a story about going into the wilderness of the amazon to find a society that was told to have built itself after traveling down a land bridge, from Alaska.

What is important about where the actual Col. Fawcett went was that it was through an area being researched for the terra preta soil. Col. Fawcett found pottery shards everywhere in the jungle. This could only indicate that it was once extensively cultivated for farming. For a massive amount of farming. Percy didn't understand anything about Terra Preta but he did understand pottery shards which were everywhere he surveyed.

In digging for the truth, aired 24 Apr. 2006 Lost Cities of the Amazon they stop at a mound that used to be 36 ft. High and was 7 acres in size based on their research. This was one area. One archaeological site. They stop at Asa Tuba, a tribal city.

The "modern" tribes slash and burned sections of the amazon. At the time of the airing of this episode, they walk a site and look at Terra Preta, then travel further down river, about 2 1/2 kilometers and they point out more Terra Preta. At over 8 ft. this is still part of the area they had started at over two kilometers away. The true amount of square kilometers or miles of this soil is unknown. We don't know how to make Terra Preta. There is a known slash and burn technique used by tribes in this area but they are not responsible for Terra Preta.

So let's get into what we do know and how it applies around the whole earth to the extensive ancient occupation of man.

Terra preta (Portuguese pronunciation: [ˈtɛʁɐ ˈpɾetɐ], locally [ˈtɛha ˈpɾeta], literally "black soil" in Portuguese

Terra Preta all over the earth, 12 ft thick in some places and the consistency is a matter of debate, there is not a complete record or location map for all terra preta. It is unknown how far it extends in what is now underwater lands or deserts like North Africa where it is now known to have been green and lush to even 5000 years ago.

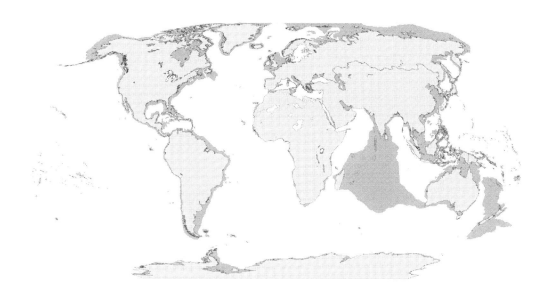

Terra Preta is now confirmed a man made product. Not as sexy as a pyramid or an alleged run way for alien ships of the Nazca Lines. If Terra Preta was sexy, there would be shows and YouTube conspiracies on it. How could ancient humans make it? The thought that the Amazon was a "wet desert" and was un-farmable beyond a small slash and burn technique of small simple people and here is square miles currently believed to be larger than the area of Spain with Terra Preta up to 12 ft. thick.

Terra Preta or Indian black earth, has been researched and to this day after almost 100 years of research they don't know how to make it. Here is a description of how much Terra Preta has been found.

"Terra preta soils are found mainly in the Brazilian Amazon, where Sombroek et

al. estimate that they cover at least 0.1 to 0.3%, or 6,300 to 18,900 square kilometres (2,400 to 7,300 sq mi) of low forested Amazonia; but others estimate this surface at 10.0% or more (twice the area of Great Britain).

Terra preta sites are also known in Ecuador, Peru and French Guiana, and on the African continent in Benin, Liberia, and the South African savannas."

Wait, it's found on all continents? No shared ancient advanced tech? Engineered soil, pyramids, shared myths? The soil you'd be standing on in all these places are the same. One more time, we don't know how to make it. Terra Preta is the best growing soil on earth. It doesn't need the fake or added nutrients the modern farm gets in fertilizers and added chemicals. It is perfect for growing. What if there were more in the world? What if this soil that can't be produced by the local tribes where they find this or modern science isn't limited to the above mentioned areas? These tribes use it, they don't make it. Who made it and if it was to be in other locations should not be looked at as a common thread? Pyramids are everywhere on earth and the oldest could be older than the last cataclysm of approximately 12-13,000 years ago, wouldn't the Terra Preta be more interesting if it showed up in Europe. Say Chernozems?

Chernozems via Wikipedia:

"The name comes from the Russian terms for black and soil, earth or land (chorny + zemlya) Or (Ukrainian: чорнóзем, translit. chornózem). The soil, rich in organic matter presenting a black color, was first identified by Russian geologist Vasily Dokuchaev in 1883 in the tallgrass steppe or prairie of European Russia.

Chernozems cover about 230 million hectares of land. There are two"chernozem belts" in the world. One is the Eurasian steppe which extends from eastern Croatia (Slavonia), along the Danube (northern Serbia, northern Bulgaria (Danubian Plain), southern Romania (Wallachian Plain) and Moldova) to northeast Ukraine across the Central Black Earth Region of southern Russia into Siberia. The other stretches from the Canadian Prairies in Manitobathrough the Great Plains of the US as far south as Kansas. Similar soil types occur in Texas and Hungary. Chernozem layer thickness may vary widely, from several centimetres up to 1.5 metres (60 inches) in Ukraine, as well as the Red River Valley region in the Northern US and Canada (an area formerly known as lake Agassiz).

The terrain can also be found in small quantities elsewhere (for example, on 1% of Poland). It also exists in Northeast China, near Harbin. The only true Chernozem in Australia is located around Nimmitabel, with some of the richest soils in the nation."

Back it up, China, Siberia, the Danube, Romania, Canada, and the Great Plains of the US, New York and Australia? Apparently there is a large black market for the soil in Ukraine. The soil is so good that it is dug up and removed by truck and sold. The sale of

15

agricultural land has been illegal in Ukraine since 1992, however Chernozem has been sold to the tune of approximately US $900 million annually on the black market.

CANADIAN AND UNITED STATES SOIL CLASSIFICATION

Chernozemic soils are a soil type in the Canadian system of soil classification and the World Reference Base for Soil Resources.

"....some very brave researchers have managed to establish the presence of "submicron remnants of burned biomass" in European Chernozem Black Soils. Here, using high-resolution transmission electron microscopy, electron energy loss spectroscopy, micro Raman spectroscopy and radiocarbon dating, we characterized the nanomorphology and chemical structure of soil organic carbon (SOC) from central European chernozems.

*We identified **submicron remnants of burned biomass** (15–45 percent of SOC), coexisting as amorphous char-black carbon (BC) derived from pyrolized cellulose or soot-BC.*

The BC was several millennia in age (1160–5040 carbon-14 years) and up to 3990 radiocarbon years older than bulk SOC, indicating significant residence times for BC in soils.

These results challenge common paradigms on chernozem formation and add fire as an important novel factor.

It is also clear that the role of fire in soil formation has been underestimated outside classical fire prone biomes.

Furthermore, our results demonstrate the importance of quantifying BC in soils because of its large contribution, longevity and potential role in the global biogeochemical carbon cycle.

Carbon Isotope Geochemistry and Nanomorphology of Soil Black Carbon:

Black Chernozemic Soils in Central Europe Originate From Ancient Biomass Burning

Michael W. I. Schmidt, Jan O. Skjemstad and Cornelia Jäger
Global Biogeochemical Cycles – Volume 16 – Issue 4 – December 2002
http://onlinelibrary.wiley.com/doi/10.1029/2002GB001939/full

But only time will tell if there are any researchers brave enough to test the other black soils[spread across the World] for *"submicron remnants of burned biomass."*

And only time will tell whether mainstream researchers are capable of recognizing the pattern formed by *Chernozem Black Soils* in the Northern Hemisphere.

Soil map of the Northern Hemisphere (Dokoutchaev, 1899) prepared by Dokuchaev for the World Exhibition in Paris in 1900.

Soil Maps of the World

Alfred E. Hartemink, Pavel Krasilnikov, J.G. Bockheim
Geoderma 207–208 (2013) 256–267
*http://www.alfredhartemink.nl/2013%20-
%20Soil%20maps%20of%20the%20world%20%28Hartemink,%20Krasilnikov,
%20Bockheim%29.pdf*

> "...But only time will tell if there are any researchers brave enough to test the other black soils[spread across the World] for "submicron remnants of burned biomass."

For all the researchers digging up bones and the millions, millions of yet to be translated cuneiform tablets, there is submicron research indicating the hand of an ancient man developing many millions of square miles of land for cultivation in areas thought never occupied. The idea that this soil is black and rich because millions of years of dinosaurs, plants and other people have died and enriched the soil naturally is looking to be wrong or partially wrong. How many soil areas have drifted, are no longer rich with Terra Preta due to it being intentionally moved or lost to the changing seas and winds? How many soils could we test now and realize they are the works of man Engineering it? If they are like Chernozems or Terra Preta or even something else, where were the fields on earth in reference to the metropolitan societies that invented them. When those societies abandoned them or moved on who came and moved into the area and cleared trees to use the abandoned soil? Twelve feet of Terra Preta or chernozem doesn't mean that the same group of people used them, or that a season of even a hundred or more years went between uses.

The Sphinx was established to be very old. This is becoming old news. The water weathering around the sphinx was noticed to be old. It took John Anthony West to get the geologist Robert Schoch to come look at the sphinx and establish that the weathering on the Sphinx could be over 30,000 years old. In fact in this youtube video, John Anthony West speaks to the first encounter with the site with Schoch. He said to not quote him about the water weathering could be 250,000 years old. Well Holy Academia and the Egyptology wing shot that idea down and tried to burn Schoch in a public debate that West couldn't participate in because he didn't have their academic credentials. Schoch went to the witch burning alone. West watched from the audience. After years of debate it is now confirmed by many researchers that it is weathering that shows aging way beyond the years

Egypt was ruled by Pharaohs. When it was tropical and rich with plants in a "pre-history."

Usually this is where a lot of conversation has happened about who came first in Egypt, the Egyptians or the pyramids? We are talking about soil, we will get back down into the Great Pyramid and Egypt in later chapters. So the area of the Great Pyramid and the Sphinx is older than the Egyptian culture we identify with king tut, Moses and the Bible. Northern Africa and the entire area was a rich tropical environment. Would the sub-micron research in the depths of the sand reveal remnants of Terra Preta or chernozem soils? Yes, annoying frustrating scream worthy, but we have no eyes on this. This pre catastrophe of 12-13000 years ago could indicate an extensive terraced, developed occupancy of Northern Africa.

Terra Preta, chernozem or possibly another advanced engineered soil could have been around the sphinx which is now desert. How many more deserts are "natural." Here we are at a big 50,000 ft view of the earth today but was it pre-flood? We can look at the maps and see that the geology of the earth has changed. The theories of tectonic plate shifting says we once had a giant continent called Pangea it slowly broke up and we see the continents where they are now. The idea that the continental drift has moved the continental land masses to where they are now is still a theory fyi. There were dinosaurs walking in the swamps of millions of miles of land that is now walkable or developed, like the Great Plains of the U.S. That was a giant swamp in Jurassic times, now it's Minnesota to Texas. It used to have pteranodon flying around. Various times in geological history the lands, mountains active and inactive volcanoes have turned the landscape in various ways.

As we delve into the more complex history of our true past, the last 20,40,60, 100,000 years may push the deserts we see as "natural" as the remnants of an ancient catastrophe or of a war. Take a picture of the earth and make sure it's in globe form, look around the earth on its rotating axis and look how it goes desert to green on the same parallel. The question, is it natural? When one desert aligns perfectly with a rich green area across the globe yet on a parallel with a desert. There is the jet stream, the earth's winds move the jet stream and the lands are said to be arid because of lack of rainfall for instance. It is hot, there is no soil, there is no precipitation because for miles and miles there is no moisture in trees plants and soil to create the precipitation. Death and dryness begetting dryness. Death is optional, maybe more precisely, very particular living environment. Mainly not a lot of water. It may not be "natural".

Satellite images can show ancient dried river beds, oceans, lakes, all throughout history the waters have shifted like sand. Las vegas has changed the temperature in and around it by human occupation occupying the soil. It has been taken back by man. Just like the amazon being a wet desert, yet engineer the right soil and it is perfect. We have a lot of developed and engineered soil from ancient times and LIDAR showing mass scale occupation.

There is plenty of Terra Preta and Chernozem not being tilled and we have 7 billionish on earth. We have enough food but we just don't seem to feed them all. We aren't using all the soil that has been engineered in the past. The amount of people could have been staggering and the quality of the highly nutrient rich food would have been amazing to eat too!

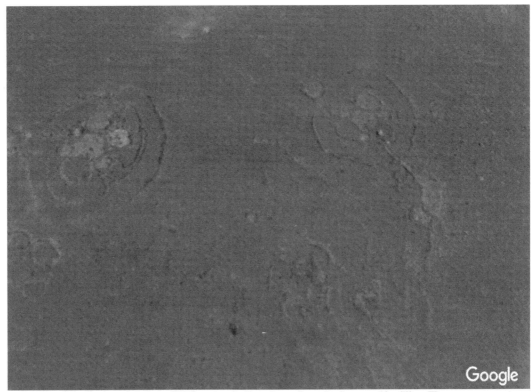

Large and small, some systems multi kilometers in diameter and numbering over 10 million. These are remnant foundations either completely abandoned or rebuilt with available material in a very simplex manor. The complexities including height, wood, metal, anything that would have composed of the original structures are long gone. There is no soil research or subterranean details for ancient advanced nano materials, earthquake and energy management.

Michael Tellinger is a South African whom noticed cattle rings. They were old. First noticed by a British explorer, he estimated them to be about 1000 in count, scattered around South Africa. Then the count went to about 3000, then 5 then around 10,000. The number was increased in modern times because they could use planes and it was added up to over 100,000. The theory was that cattle were herded into them and kept. They look like cattle rings from the air maybe?

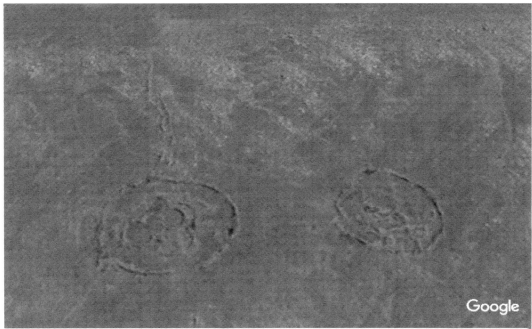

Magnetic anomalies exist in these structures. Michael Tellinger has reported extreme energy anomalies at Adams's calendar including satellite phones and geo satellite linked ground penetrating radar unable to communicate while mapping these ancient structures.

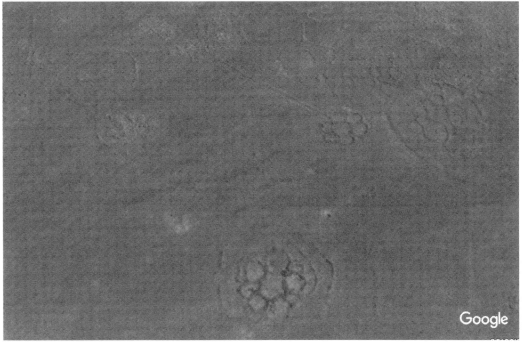

Michael Tellinger has pointed out the striking similarities of thee ancient structures and modern magnetrons. The idea of earth sized frequency and energy harnessing machines is foreign to us. The mechanics of polygonal structures tying into metamaterial engineered soil to harness waves and frequencies, then focusing them into and through a structure. Instead of applying the sciences we apply an interoperation of the past that they were simple, the most we can then theorize is what has been suggested of these structures, they are cattle pens. This is the equivalent of finding a cell phone in the future and assume it was a pocket mirror.

Tellinger found over 10 million rings. It was thought that a few tribes, a few thousand people lived in the area. Hunter gather types. Tellinger finds that after looking at google earth he noticed that there were not 100,000 rings but over 10 million. Then there was a solid indication of the whole area having over 400,000 sq. miles of terraced and terraformed land for farming. This would indicate a large human population. A researcher of any type might want to test this soil for engineering. This is still a massive amount of land dedicated to farming for a much larger missing piece of human history. Again. Including deserts that were once soil. What could you, the reader, walk out your own front door today and already have available? Every soil around you is suspect and there to study.

WHAT ABOUT THE SEA?

Oceans, bays, shorelines of all kind oh my. Terra Preta and chernozem quickly mapped shows a mass of humanity that we can't account for. In America the East and West coasts like to call middle America including Minnesota the fly over states. However, the majority of our countries food and many of the countries top medical, scientific inventions to entertainment come from the "fly over" states. If there was a rise in water and New York and Los Angeles go 100 ft deep into the oceans. Then what would the story be in 5000 years about the land mass where New York, Miami, and LA were gone? Describing our history without having a documented historical record of the lost underwater lands is at a minimum insane. I am talking about broad tools, a map, that in an instant, you dial in the year, and the earth with accurate shore lines, known population locations of the day including "suspect" sites popping up. Western Europe and American Victorian archaeology has created such a paradigm grip on our history. The story of us is the geological snapshot of what we see in every map of the world that is shown to us in school. The story of the world and anything relevant is on land IF there is a sunken city, it's looked at as a secondary prop actor in a movie or play!

Imagine going to a play, Broadway or your local community theater or to Europe for a real Greek amphitheater experience. There are characters, costumes, secondary background characters, and a set. Imagine stepping onto the stage and only describing the play from the secondary characters to the backstage. You simply tell everyone what happened from the secondary characters to the back drop. Nothing about the main actors in front of the stage telling the story perhaps of Romeo and Juliet. Go further, tell me the story of the play as you stand behind the set. Tell me about the back wall of the theatre, maybe drive 100 miles away and then tell me about the play. This is what happened to our sunken history. Cities that have sunk, dramatically sunk in the last 12,000 years were all cities attached to important people that had the center of their empires way above the seaside. The Greeks, Egyptians, Sumerians, minions, the ancients of Malta...You never hear about China, Indonesia, Japan, Russia, India in that list? We can build a whole story from Adam and Eve, the out of Africa story, not the 80's one either, to the industrial revolution and America manifesting it's destiny yet we just really don't have an explanation for the many individual genetic races of humans or their local ancient histories.

The facts of what is at the bottom of the ocean is game changing to the story of human history. This is why it is ignored. Leave it to treasure hunting. Off the coast of Cuba in 2001, a marine engineer, Pauline Zalitzki and her husband Paul Weinzweig began a survey with the Cuban government in 2001 to find all the sunken treasure ships that are known to be Cuban waters. Pauline and Pauls company, Advanced Digital Communications (ADC) were working off the tip of the Guanahacabibes Peninsula in the Pinar del Rio Province of Cuba, and they find pyramid like structures. In imaging of what they found in the deep, the footprint of a city is revealed. Yeah, there are pictures, there are experts, willing to go on record and say, they are anomalies in the shape of buildings. Where the F is James Cameron or National Geographic? The site is 2300 ft below sea level, the idea that tectonic plate shifting happened, has been ruled out, no time for details. Even for alternative history researchers, this is a pickle. There is of course a way to handle this, if "modern man" has been on the planet for a long period of time, then easy. The how long we have been here is later in the book, feel free to choose your own adventure and take a look. IF we are not sure, well here is a remains of a city. With walls. A city that would need to be about 50,000 years to be above water. That would make that area around Cuba dry. So would the Mediterranean. It would be a dry basin. There are many cities we know of that are about 300-600 ft. Deep. This city is at a whole other depth. Yes, I didn't say Caribbean, I said Mediterranean, both seas would be more lake like in that time frame than oceans. Drastically changes a map for ancient city centers.

From ancient Origins: **26 FEBRUARY, 2016 - 14:51 BRAD YOON**

Grenville Draper of Florida International University considers it highly unlikely that such an event could have occurred: "Nothing of this magnitude has been reported, even from the Mediterranean…" - referring to the idea that the continent dropped from tectonic plate shifting and a city this deep.

Imagine basing the iPhone on a rotary phone design, that is the template for archaeology. The short list of beliefs: pyramid of Egypt is about 6000 years old, cavemen were around for about 50,000 years. We have never been more advanced than now. Academia is seeing some of the work being done by alternative researchers, so they still stand on the deck of their beliefs built like a Spanish galleon and accept that they might be off a wee bit. They will sprinkle in some of what is found like Gobekli Tepe. Everything else is a great mystery. This actually gets said, you could make a drinking game out of it as you watch shows on the past, "it's a great mystery" and drink.

The alternative research crowd, that has a different timeline, the great Pyramid of Giza, Baalbek, Lebanon, the pyramid in Indonesia, Gobekli Tepe and all the stuff we are going to be talking about, show that there was a society here that is unknown and at least 12,000 to 50,000 years old. some of this ancient society have cities that have sunk prior to anything we have a written history for. This is where the tentacles of victory nightmares strangles even the alternative researchers, they look to the deep sea for aliens and Atlantis. They too believe that the majority of the world's stage is within the geological foot print that we see now. The underwater research gets another unwarranted curb stomp.

Let's look at a map of the earth 50,000 years ago. Reminders, that is the right before the dam breaks date. The flooding that would have put this Cuban site under is just around that 50,000-year date, someone built it first. They lived there. This isn't an underwater art installation.

The Taino Indians lived in this area for 1000's of years. Their own verbal traditions are about the flood that made their local mountains islands, rejoicing that they would always have fish. These local post flood myths, could be accounting for the flood in this area. How about that half full myth, we loose an advanced city but get more fishing.

There are two immediate problems we are going to encounter, over and over in our view of history, research and underwater sites. One, underwater sites are discounted. They are one offs, we will be looking at Gobekli Tepe, a site in Turkey, it's "the First" of its kind and it is being said it's 12,000 years old. It's on land, 50,000 year old pyramids and large buildings 2300 ft. underwater are not easy to get to. The vernacular is changed and we have to rewrite history because Gobekli Tepe is older than we thought primitive people could build megalithic structures. If we are relating to a theory that has turned to doctrine, that we were hunter gatherers 12000 years ago sure. If there is this Cuban city, you have to look at the possibility that this is not the only 2300 ft. deep metropolis underwater. There must be other locations, that they may be underwater, they maybe on land like Gobekli Tepe. The structures we see now, that are frequented by tourists from Mayan and Aztec to Egyptian and far eastern sites like China, India, and Japan, may be home to sites at a similar age. The constant refacing of highly advanced structures would make them camouflaged in the course of post flood history by tribal people. Not the "first" not a mystery, it's there and 50,000 years old at a minimum. Gobekli Tepe and sites like it, need to be placed not just chronologically to our new calendar but possibly on a stage that has people and props on it and a story we can't begin to tell until we build the set. Constantly handling societies in modern "country" borders is the limitation of the research of Victorian age, our imagination and an entrenched doctrine of theory. NOT FACTS.

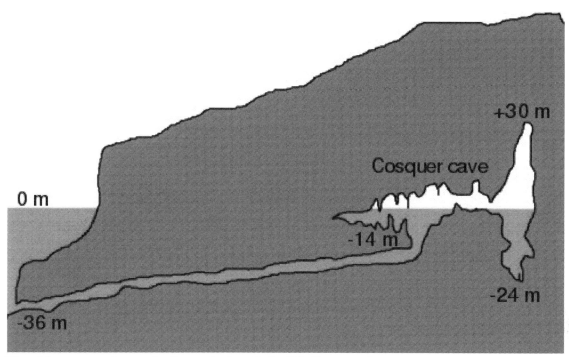

When this cave was above water, it was clearly a site for "tribal" or nomadic type humans. It is not an indicator of how advanced we were at the time of the oldest paintings. Our land masses at the time this cave was above water was miles away on some shore lines. Looking to modern shorelines and even a kilometer off shore frequently only indicates the most recent societies we know of like the greeks and Egyptian cities of the Mediterranean.

In 1985 Henri Cosquer dived and found a cave near Cap Morgiou. Cosquer Cave is located in Calanque de Morgiou in Marseille, France. The cave was sunk during the Holocene sea rise. It has many prehistoric rock art. It is over 37 meters deep. The Holocene is part of the Quaternary, it ranges from about 11,600 years ago to today. Then some of the cave art has been carbon dated to 27,000 years ago.

The Cosquer cave is located in the Calanque de Morgiou in Marseille, France, near Cap Morgiou. The entrance to the cave is located 37 m (121 ft) underwater, due to the Holocene sea level rise. The cave contains various prehistoric rock art engravings. It was discovered in 1985 by and named after diver Henri Cosquer, but its existence was not made public until 1991, when three divers became lost in the cave and died.

The Cosquer cave is important because it is cave art. It is showing that a simpler or "simpler living" human race was in proximity to the great megalithic advanced societies all around them. The first paradigm is always, oh, here is our lineal past before they all decided as a group to build pyramids. This cave, like many other rock art caves shows the very likely probability of simply living, human cultures, like tribes today, living on their own, near very advanced societies.

We consistently reference the Bible for it's accuracy in describing cities, places, and events in this continued western conceit. As western archaeologists went out and found the places of Moses, Babylon, and other biblical sites, it validates for some their faith. For western archaeologists and historians it also helps validate their belief in the greatness of western ideas, specifically the greatness of the Greeks, Romans ultimately leading to the renaissance.

The Hindu Vedas, according to western ideology, are the scribblings of a simple people. Not everyone thinks this, however the general treatment of the Hindu scripts is silence in the West unless your taking Yoga. To validate them is to validate a religion, a society, and given that these scripts discuss millions of years of history would really contradict the Bible. If validated by archaeological find, you'd have to apply what is applied to the Bible in the west. Validation of literature and the scripts represent historical truths that would help us know ourselves better just like the Bible archaeology does. Yes, many things in the Bible are argued as to fact, theological or metaphorical in nature. If you start validating the Hindu scripts, you are in the biggest Pandora's box of Western history and theological doctrine. As long as the Far East, is far from your plan to attend church, your good to study. If you want to have one idea of the deep subconscious paradigms we are going to crush, ask yourself this, who decided that it's the "Far East"? Far from....?

Religion is relevant to the deep, we were in Cuba, what about off the coast of India? There is a Gulf, the Gulf of Khambhat. There is a local legend of a city that sunk off the west coast of India that Krishna built. Graham Hanncock, journalist, went to the coast and dived it for a BBC show UNDERWORLD, LOST CITIES OF THE ICE AGE. They discuss two lost Indian cities, located approximately 2500 miles from shore, walls and plazas and man made objects at least 9500 years old. DWARKA, is on the coast of India. Krisha created a city that is now underwater, having legends that it was rebuilt many times. Pilgrims come on pilgrimages to worship in DWARKA. The flood myth got more validated because ruins were found in the 1980's.

There are pottery shards that wash up on shore, there has been dredging archaeology that has pulled up pottery shards and wood that has been carbon dated to between 7500-8000 years old.

The Harappan are now a widely recognized culture that lived in ancient India. Harappan India, the Indus Valley Civilization, bigger than Egypt and most of the ancient fertile crescent. They had plumbing, streets that ran almost perfect to the cardinal points. A well organized city layout. There is a pre Harappan civilization. The digging continues, but the off the coast marine archeology is not allowed by the Indian government. We are looking at offshore discoveries made in the 1980's and they will not allow research on them.

Jacque Cousteau made it fun to be under water, watching him go all over the world, seeing him in National Geographic, he even took a dive at the famed antikythera device ship wreck. Finding king tut is a hell of a lot more fun than getting the bends, getting eaten by a great white, or stung by a crap load of jellyfish. Getting under water to dig anything up is expensive, dirty, takes forever and almost everything down there depending on the temperature and depth is smashed, rusted, turned into a fish habitat, or perfectly preserved. You could be in a boat, with satellite gps and one swell of a wave could throw off the ship a couple hundred feet from whatever it is you even think you are going to dig up or explore in the deep. Then there are moving underwater currents, some so strong you might as well be digging in a tornado, a hundred feet in the air. Sandy, muddy ground, clouding up so you can not see your hand in front of your face. This and so much more makes digging underwater a not so fun activity. Unless, you are a treasure hunter, the idea that you could find 100's of millions in gold, silver, Spanish Doubloons! Pieces of Eight! Pirate booty! It's worth it. Or if you are one of the marine archaeologists, you could of contributed to a recent tour traveling the USA of the Sunken Cities of Egypt. The city Alexandria is exactly that, sunk, 100 ft. into the Mediterranean and they have been pulling up artifacts from gold rings to wooden statues as big as a walk in cooler. The exhibit has a video pointing out how these cities sunk due to earthquakes, and rising sea levels for various post ice age reasons like melting glaciers. They also point out how it was hard to find these cities, that there are 100's of sites around the Mediterranean that are sunken.

It's not just the Mediterranean, Indonesia, Cuba, South America, England to France and of course the new focal point, Antarctica and the NorthPole. There are whole lost continents like Lumaria, New Zealandia, the most of South East Asia, and this is the only time I am going to say these words, Atlantis. Lumaria is a sunken continent between the west coast of Australia that connected to the bottom tip of India and reached all the way to Madagascar. This continent is a potential location of Atlantis. Wouldn't it be interesting as a side note, to test the soil in Madagascar and see if there is Terra Preta or Chernozem present and India? There is terra Preta in Australia. The Atlantis myth has been chased and beaten to the ground. A story about a city that was highly advanced and the myth that it is, a place as described by Plato, may or may not have been an actual sunken city. We need to filter this over stated idea of Atlantis and start to say there is a lost ancient society, maybe it was called Atlantis. There is so much research bringing to light that we got history wrong that Atlantis is a reference of a lost high tech society.

Thee best evidence currently for that actual city is the Eye of Africa. There is a map by a greek within 60 years of Plato's death that shows the known world as the Greeks saw it, it points to the area of exactly the Eye of Africa as to the location of the city. Why is it ruled out? It's approximately 1500 ft. above sea level. Could it have risen, while shores moved, yes. Is there a significant reference from Plato's account that shows the measurements, surrounding mountains, bones found of sea creatures, elephants, the "bay" or inlets locations...just about everything seems to fit at the Eye of Africa. The math and the circles that surrounded the city center are almost spot on for the Eye of Africa being the city. There was a city in that area where pottery shards and other artifacts are found, along with fossil remnants of elephants as describe about Atlantis. We should go check this out right? Nope, it is an area of the world that is extremely dangerous. Studying it right now would not be good for anyone without perimeter armies creating a green zone. This is a problem around the world, either local warring conflict, the simple severe remoteness of sites, there are even examples of whole towns looting ancient sites and keeping anyone out because they don't want outsiders seeing what they are doing, ain't no rest for the wicked, money doesn't grow on trees.

What matters now is the 'A' word is a reference for a lost unknown culture that may have been on a lost sunken island, or continent. It is the first "post" flood myth story that I am going to tell you to filter out. No time for love Dr. Jones.

What is dangerously missing from the typical story of 1000 years ago, 2000 years ago, 5000 years ago, any time in the last 12,000 years is an assessment for sunken cities because it just might be New York, Hong Kong or the Alexandria of it's day. What was sunk we may never know. With every story that is told about 5000-year-old Sumer and that they are the first culture to have a written language discounts the extensive city line off the west coast of India and the Hindu Vedas stories of man. The ancient Indian cultures put at least a 4000 year head start on the Sumerians. If you are not looking a lot further out under the sea, you're missing it. We need to go into the deep first to find our shorelines and then our cities and past.

The map of the world 15,000 years ago, the maps of the world from 30,000 years ago. Show different climate and coastlines. Then now. Here is an accumulation of data of what the the world looked like 50-100,000 years ago. This is going to become more important as we keep digging. Look at the world stage starting with Dogerland.

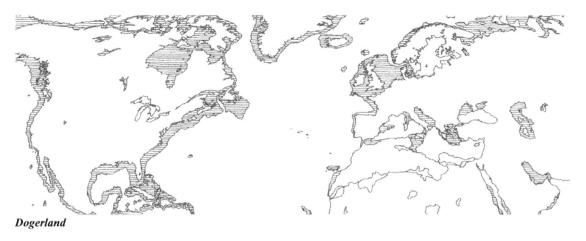

Dogerland

Let's look first at the map around Cuba. We are not telling archaeologists what to do, we will do that in a later chapter. If this city off Cuba was above water 50,000 years ago, then the area may have been a bay city possibly on a river, or a lake. Filling in other potential sites in that area would mean more sonar, solid factual guesswork and work our way out to the sea at that depth and build back a coast line that accounts for tectonic shifts, up and down and then repeat the process based on the maps of what the world looked like socio-geographically.

It doesn't matter if India has a city off the coast a couple hundred feet if the tectonic plates shift in that area meant that that was 50-1,000,000 years of movement. In other words if the Cuban city is under 2300 ft. it doesn't mean that everything is at that depth everywhere but it does mean we should look starting at that level. Then eduguess that maybe in some areas the shifting in the same age maybe more than 2300 ft deep and also up above the sea. The ideas of the 19th to 20th century archaeologists basing all their theories on what they knew is looking more and more infantile.

The rise above water brings us to Lake Titicaca. It is in the Andes. It has salt water and sea horses. I love seahorses, and sea shells and lighthouses. I love them forever. Google that digression.

Lake Titicaca is located in the Andes and is at the center of one of many ground zeroes of what is likely our great advanced ancestors. There are structures that continue into the lake and whole buildings and pyramids in the bottom. So was it always a lake, maybe a smaller one? Was it always salt water? Likely not.

In our reassessment of the world map and societies lost, we have what looks like a dry valley that we now call the Caribbean, the Mediterranean looks like it too could have been a dry valley basin in the same period, and here in the Andes, Lake Titicaca could have been part of a large bay connected to the ocean. It has been theorized that Brazil may have been lower and under water. The amount of human flood myths, is astounding for two reasons. Mainstream archaeology balancing on the insightful Victorian mind (the same mindset that thought women shouldn't vote) thinks that all flood myths are from "localized" events. Not a global event, despite common engineered soil around the globe. The more we look, it's obvious that the events could, be global, and or a local chapter of one large flooding globally with a survivor myth. If all these areas were inhabited longer and more extensively than thought, there are many geological events they would have been exposed to. Listening to these local human tribal histories with a lot more respect is necessary to understand our past.

We are only doing 50 grand view, there are many sites, specific places, that point to a more vast occupation of the earth and its chapter 2 and going at the mainstream academia is gonna just keep being fun. Like popping bubble wrap. You just can't stop.

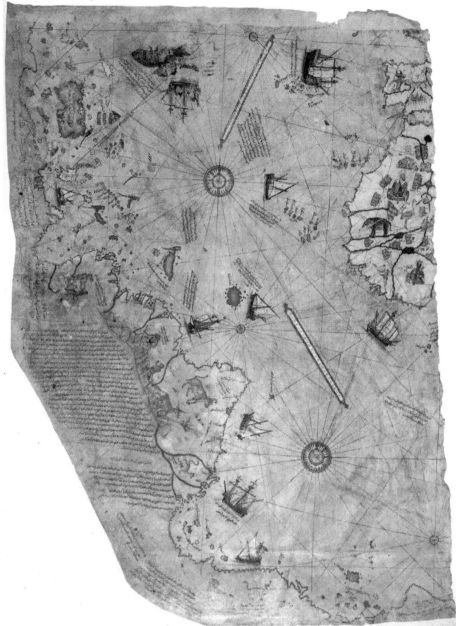

The Piri Reis map is one of many that indicate an advanced ancient knowledge of longitude, shorelines and world land masses that should not be known in the maps timeline of creation. The maps like so many other pieces of history labeled out of place or out of time are not one offs. It is sheer academic hubris to not study on the facts in the ground, anything else is not science. It's not enough to try to patch these finds into our histories. We keep finding complex pieces of technology and labeling it unique and a mystery. It is time to acknowledge that we might be missing advanced technology that we just didn't recognize because we are just catching up.

Some of what we are going over is actually being talked about so much that some people need to hear it like it's the first time, others may read some of this and read ahead. No judgements. This is coming up because I am about to discuss the Piri Reis Map.

This map is commissioned by a very famous Turk, particularly to the Turks. Admiral Piri Reis creates a map in 1513 that shows the outline of a portion of the coast of Antarctica before it was frozen over a kilometer deep in ice as it is now. On that map itself, Reis references that it is a copy of older maps, put together as an update. Like a new road atlas with the latest roads. They were updating their maps for travel and war. It is incredibly valuable to get places and cartography was incredibly important. This is one of many odd maps of the ancient past that don't fit for the technology of their day.

U.S. Air Force Captain Lorenzo W. Burroughs, a cartographer does an analysis of the iced over coast of Antarctica and the map, writes a letter to Dr. Charles Hapgood in 1961. Captain Lorenzo details that the Piri Reis map and the kilometer-deep iced coast line appear to match. Hapgood focused on geological shifting. Hapgood applies his theories and published in 1965 Maps of the Ancient Sea Kings that it does show the prehistoric coastline of Antarctica.

There are always Naysayers. There is one theory that the competing countries of the time had a binding contract that if they explored and found that a land was close to one of their already established lands, then that land is theirs. So the turning on the Piri Reis map showing it closer to africa would make it the property of the discoverers and map makers.

Therein lies the problem, the map is using Mercator Projection. This is a methodology not being used by cartographers for about 55 years after the map was made and not really well for about 200 years after that. The greeks knew that the earth was a sphere. The Mercator Projection was invited by Gerardus Mercator, a Flemish cartographer in 1569. The Mercator Projection is a map of the earth on a cylinder with the longitude and latitudes on it. On it's basics, as you get further from the equator, the map distorts latitude and all the countries get bigger. It looses its accuracy. You would need a lot of other technology and discoveries to correct that. Hapgood and his students at the University of New Hampshire really studied the map. They were able to analyze the topography of the Piri Reis map and it is accurate to the areas inland from the Antarctic coastline. As far as Prof. Hapgood was concerned, the only way this level of accuracy could be done is by plane. With a plane an ancient society would have to have intricate knowledge of cartographic and nautical sciences. Professor Hapgood and his groups assessment puts the information necessary to make what is on the map to at least 4200 BC. It was amazing enough to see a map with these details however it is possessing a science unknown. This is going to be a reoccurring problem in everything we will be looking at. Significant technology, placed, applied and used when it shouldn't be for hundreds or thousands of years.

The accuracy of the Mercator Projection was not done until the introduction of the chronometer in 1760. It took a few more inventors, mathematicians, and more to produce accuracy needed. The Mercator Projection was also on the greek radar. However it is the accuracy of the Piri Reis map that makes it so out of place. When an advanced civilization falls, the pieces of the tech could end up scattered and here is an example of that in this one map.

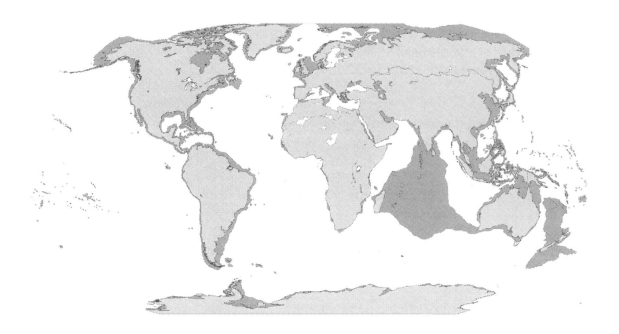

Whole continents have sunk. Here is your final world map with Lumaria. Greater New Zealandia, another of our lost continents, and one more look at Dogerland. Look over lost lands with rivers, and clearly the lost cities that lay at the bottom of the sea. Close to our shores are not the only losses as we will soon read. Many rabbit holes with these lands, where were the occupied and when and by whom? Looking at a map today and simply establishing our human story by what we see is the true fantasy. Let's start by dialing back the physical map of water ways, lakes and oceans. Lets look at where deserts were 50,000 years ago, and start raising the civilizations of the deep, including Dogerland and off Cuba.

The first place archaeology shoulda coulda been looking is underwater. This is not a fun place to start, it's dangerous, it's hard. It's where we should start to assess humanity's habitat and build the story of our past, not the last. We have been working backstage off stage and building and filling in that story by people who only heard about the play. So keep these maps in mind and lets dig through some Mad Max tech.

How many more cities lay in the leagues of the seas, sanded and buried? This site is not small. The largest buildings are towering from the ocean floor while the surrounding city grid is well covered and or un-photographed. It may say more about all of us that we are not screaming as a public for more photos, publicly funding or raising money while the news streams update on the progress of the project to explore this ruin. Instead it is sitting in whispers on the internet. It was once one or two examples that mainstream science was able to silence to maintain the "established" timeline, there are so many examples in black and white they could die in the avalanche finds now. There is a clear disconnect between the methodology of hiding the truth and the obvious truth to anyone citizen archaeologist looking at the facts being found daily.

Chapter 3

OBJECTS, PLACES, MATERIALS AND A LITTLE MATH OF THE PAST

There are ruins and impacts all over the earth indicating catastrophic events. It left pieces of ancient technology and buildings in the hands of various "squatter" cultures. They came in after the great cities were abandoned. These ancient high technology items found now are always labeled as one offs and or "mysteries". We have to roller coaster details and broad facts to get to the specifics of where humanity was. For now just image you are at the scene of a highly advanced ship crash, wreckage of a ship has scattered to earth and there are pieces spread over miles. The ship broke up high in the atmosphere and now we are going to pick them all back up and put the ship back together like Humpty Dumpty, except we are going to go one step or two further and put back a whole society, eventually. Then we are going to smash that society with war and or epic catastrophes that have god smacked earth. For now the local tribes thought, no one was going to use this stuff and they took what they could find and used it in really inappropriate ways, like jewelry and cave painting brushes. One more thing, the crash happened and we aren't exactly sure when. We are going to look at places, objects, and materials that have been adapted over time that were once apart of something older and more advanced.

The Baghdad Battery, one of a few found. It is the exception not the rule for anything to make it through history and into the hands of the discoverer. Genetic technology is laying in program as we live and breath. This is looked at historically as a confirmation of the theory of evolution. The Baghdad Battery is a remnant of a known science, there would be similar technologies available to others in the same or earlier time periods, what little would be found if the only other locations were 2300 ft. deep in the ocean or in the estimated 95 percent of Egypt that lays still under sand.

THE BAGHDAD BATTERY

Let's start with baby steps, many people have already heard of the Baghdad Battery. It is made of clay jars, asphalt stoppers and iron rods. Wilhelmina Kohn, a German Archaeologist found the battery in 1938 near Baghdad. Little known fact, he found more than one, we just have the one example apparently. That is one of the statements that you'd like to digress on but we would never get through the book. The batteries are estimated to be approximately 2000 years old. They can create more than a volt of electricity. This battery was likely used by the Parthians who lived in the area of
Baghdad. They were using it to electroplate silver.

> *"The batteries have always attracted interest as curios," Dr. Paul Craddock, a metallurgy expert at the British Museum, told the BBC in 2003. "They are a one-off. As far as we know, nobody else has found anything like these. They are odd things; they are one of life's enigmas."*

Ancient Origins Article on 17 out of place artifacts 28 SEPTEMBER, 2015 - 03:08 ANCIENT-ORIGINS

It's not standard equipment back then, ...it's an enigma ! Where is Shaggy, sing it, "It wasn't me!" This is an expert at the British Museum, maybe you should refer to it as the Holy British Museum attached to the British wing of the Religion of Archaeology. This is a curio like something you'd find at a Victorian curiosity's shop where you'd by a Mogwei. No water, no food after midnight for the Mogwei. Maybe buy a mummy and a shrunken head? If you have seen the TV show Oddities, check it out, it's about a modern curiosity shop. It's basically the porn shop version of a "respectable" museum. Leaning on the morbid, unexplainable and mostly all for sale as a centerpiece. The shops rely on shock, awe and morbid curiosity of the human soul. It was a great place in the past ages particularly for a Victorian age. The mysterious, H.P. Lovecraft sort of stuff could be sold. The curiosity shop was as much museum as it was a retail store.

This is the first time we are looking at an item that is labeled as one of a kind. Common sense about our past is thrown out of the window. When you relegate something to the trash, do you expect it to last or be able to be found in 1000 years? There are scrapers that make a living driving up and down alleys in America looking for scrap metal. There are full on hoarders that go looking for things people have set out with the trash that maybe couldn't be sold or they couldn't be bothered to sell the item. They set it out and maybe someone will take it. Here is one of the oldest true statements, "one man's trash is another man's gold". Frequently items are taken and used by others. We use Craigslist, eBay, Etsy, Amazon and even the want ads in things called newspapers to sell off our items before they hit the trash. The hardcore digger goes through the actual bagged trash.

The modern scraper takes metal to a processing plant and after separating precious metals, they get paid by weight on the rest. The items are melted down and made into something else. The Baghdad battery went missing during the Iraq war. Many antiquities went missing from the Baghdad Museum. There are many theories on where and why. It was clearly an item that could easily be in everyone's home of the day. They only found a few, so there is only a few? Is it more obvious that items of antiquity have survived only under incredibly specific, and for us lucky, conditions or there were only approximately four or five of them?

It is more theory and conjecture to believe that this was a one off. We go to the store and get a battery. It looks pretty advanced. Being made of metal and sometimes having a heavy duty plastic exterior if it is for a car or larger device. If a society was loosing the knowledge on how to make electricity, would having the elementary knowledge of the elements to make a charge result in the construction of the Baghdad batteries? In modern time the battery was crude but the elements for it being "modern looking" was there as it was "invented" in 1799 by Italian physicist Alessandro Volta.

The use for the Baghdad Battery was to plate silver, gold and other metals. This was done for coins to statues in ancient times. Of all the uses for things that we give ancient people credit for they get the electricity thing going and the only use and first use, this one time is to plate metals?

A team of researchers from the Institute of Nanostructured Materials in Rome, Italy wrote an article published in the Accounts of Chemical Research A July 2013.

> *".... the high level of competence reached by artists and craftsman of these ancient periods who produced objects of an artistic quality that could not be bettered in ancient times and has not yet been reached in modern ones"*

The Basilica of St. Ambrogio's alter. Nano coated, the thin coating is consistent, and considered unrivaled to today's technology.

The team looked at the altar at the Basilica of St. Ambrogio that dates back to 825 AD. It's a wood cased with gold and silver plated panels. It appears that mercury mixed with liquefied metal made up the plating acting like a glue as it was applied.

The team looked at a statue of a leaping lion that was made of ceramic, wrapped in a thin layer of copper and had a single layer one thousandth of a millimeter thick. This is not only incredible for a single layer, but one that was consistent all around the statue. "Artists" of the ancient world produced consistent layers of whatever metal was used. We don't know how to do it today. Let's add that one to our clue list including world wide engineered soil.

From ScienceDaily.com, July 24, 2013

> "....more than 2,000 years ago developed thin-film coating technology unrivaled even by today's standards for producing DVDS, solar cells, electronic devices and other products."

Science daily was quoting from the ACS journal Accounts of Chemical Research.

These coatings on coins and art were worn off over the ages in some cases by being thrown into privies, when the barbarians came or an invading force it wasn't uncommon for Romans and other ancient people to throw the valuable coins into the privies expecting to come back for their hoard after a passing danger. Instead, the coins would lay abandoned and urine acted as an acid bath removing surfaces. There are many other ways time and elements would strip away the surfaces leaving the lower levels of a multi coated coin or statue.

Let's start adding up the technology involved to analyze the surfaces. There is x-ray photoelectron spectroscopy and scanning electron microscopy focused with energy dispersive spectroscopy. They analyzed the surfaces and sub surfaces with these devices.

These are some of the techniques that would need to be applied at sites and surfaces of large megalithic structures. There is an assumption that these large megalithic structures were always stone. Just touching on this now, we'll discuss more during cymatic polygonal constructions. It seems that despite the amount of research into the quantum applied fields that are being done for quantum computing/spintronics we are still at the entry point of the sciences. While your standard academic thinks we have the past wrapped, if you stick with the Victorian story everything is. Don't look behind the text book, your college tuition, just do what we tell you and thank us for letting you write us a check.

Our modern cell phones and the device that your likely reading this book on doesn't use the same technology that the ancients were using to plate bracelets, statues and other objects. There is more nanotech in their ancient bracelets then we have figured out how to apply in our day to day devices. Is this the first place the nanotechnology was applied In the ancient past? Is it possible that plating was a devolving science once used for high tech equipment and as the ability to use that tech was forgotten, lost, repurposed, the application for religion and simply beautiful art was all it devolved to?

In Secrets of the Lost Races, author and researcher, Rene Noorbergen speaks to metal plated objects found from Sumerian and Babylonian sites dating 2000 years BC. That would put the Baghdad battery in the declining days of the technology. Plating in Sumerian times would have been a declining industry. Again, who introduced it in Sumer? At the point you are plating pretty objects it is a similar application than actually working on a computer motherboard. There are signs of smelting plants around the world, and we have no time to discuss them.

This one device is classically now considered a one of a kind. Prior to finding it, it was said to be impossible for the time period approximately 2000 years ago. Instead of rediscovering our past through what we find, it is wrapped into a one off category and the human timeline is maintained from loin cloths to now in our perceived advancement over the last 50,000 years. This is an impossible timeline with a city in Cuba that couldn't have been above what for at least 50,000 years.

IS THERE ANYTHING MATHY AND MECHANICALLY?

The Antikythera Mechanism is a 2000-year-old mechanical device used to calculate the positions of the sun, moon, planets, and even the dates of the ancient Olympic Games. (Wikimedia Commons) Stating further, "... it was calculating astronomical changes with great precision."

The Antikythera has been well studied and there are many TV shows and news reports on it. It is referred to as an ancient computer. It was found in a shipwreck in a rusty chunk dating to about 150 B.C. The device is held in the National Archaeological Museum of Athens. One theory is that it was on a ship of looted items from some campaign and was being transported to Rome for a victory parade of Julius Caesar.

Jacque Cousteau visited the site in the 70's and found coins that were minted between 76 and 67 BC. Pergamon is one idea on the origin of the device, it was home to the second most important library in ancient times. The Library of Alexandria being the most important. It was a scientific center and maybe the devices were housed or built there. Carmens and Evens argued that the device prescribed to the Babylonian math style more so than Greek. This is a great example that using the complexities of math itself an object could be better understood. Not entirely known, just better understood. Instead of projecting it is one of a kind and the first ever...

""If it hadn't been discovered ... no one would possibly believe that it could exist because it's so sophisticated," said Mathematician Tony Freeth in a NOVA documentary. Mathias Buttet, director of research and development for watch-maker Hublot, said in a video released by the Hellenic Republic Ministry of Culture and Tourism, "This Antikythera Mechanism includes ingenious features which are not found in modern watch-making."" -Wikimedia Commons

What did Dr. Paul Craddock say from the British Museum? One of life's enigmas?

Sing it, "It wasn't Me! " ...it's a one off, an enigma, it's the first of its kind. Just like the Baghdad Battery, it was a one off and curiosity. You can stair in disbelief that anything like this was ever possible. You can even convince yourself that your not looking at remnants of a much more advanced understanding of the world. Is this observation of the device made with a falling societal understanding of the sciences, a rediscovery or both? How do we, with a fraction of our brain in constant use, make any assessment without a consideration of our limited abilities and equipment?

This close-up of one piece shows the devastation the elements have on metal devices. Anything left of 2000 years ago, let alone 50,000 years ago or 100,000 years ago would be a miracle. Enough is left in meta-materials that the most advanced sciences can be re-engineered. If 50,000 years ago we only had loin cloths, the rope and pulleys to put the polygonal masonry together around the earth make sense, until you apply science and not agreed human morphology.

We don't have a complete fossil record or written record of this time period. More room to make allotments for devices like this or statues made from melted and repurposed machines of their day might be more helpful in describing our past.

Key point on the discovery, no one is in agreement as to what the actual device looked like. There are unfortunately fused pieces and possibly some still at the bottom of the ocean. Currently none of the models work as they should. The motion of the planets, the alignments are just not entirely accurate for some of the recreation devices. Without being able to rebuild the actual device to spec, we will not be sure of its true ability.

We have nanotechnology unable to repeat plating techniques and now we have a computer that is calculating incredibly difficult mathematics and as stated, no one would have believed it possible. If you find one, is it the first or just the lucky one that made it through time? Common sense would say there are more. Also, was it found at thee most important site thee equivalent of Fort Knox of it's day or was it found on a transport that was the ancient equivalent of Fedex shipping an Amazon order?

This tablet represents one of millions that have not been translated. It could be a lifetime job unless a computer scanner could interpret un-translated cuniforms and then verified by a humans.

THE BABYLONIAN PLIMPTON 322 CLAY TABLET, MATH MATH MATH

Dr. Daniel Mansfield, of the UNSW, says :

"Our research reveals that Plimpton 322 describes the shapes of right-angle triangles using a novel kind of trigonometry based on ratios, not angles and circles. It is a fascinating mathematical work that demonstrates undoubted genius

[...] The tablet not only contains the world's oldest trigonometric table; it is also the only completely accurate trigonometric table, because of the very different Babylonian approach to arithmetic and geometry."

The table shows, "Genius" and in the same statement, "it's the oldest trigonometry table." It's the only completely accurate table. Anyone impressed yet? Also called Pythagorean triples. Like the Greek Antikythera Mechanism, is the worlds first computer. Every time we speak and call this stuff the first, it does a couple crippling things: One- You don't look or speak of it in context that there was a larger understanding of obvious higher science and technology so you don't see it, you don't look for it at other sites or future digs. Two- If it is the first then you can keep speaking and describing an area as a stand alone isolated society and all the academics can keep all the research separate. It pounds the paradigm of every society is as described by standard academia, separate.

Technologically just happened accidentally. If it is the first computer you never need to look at a society where this machine is the one millionth computer of an ancient Apple store. Terrifying to speculate that if this isn't the first and there were more than we have been describing these societies in ways that devalue the reality of how advanced they were. These items and their math were likely survivors of a more advanced past! We don't seem to be willing to be more patient in describing our past. There are pieces that are out of place based on our description of our past not to the realities of the pieces. We have to stop creating a dialogue based on massive leaps of conjecture about any society in the past. Projecting an opinion of what the puzzle is and spend more time putting the puzzle together and letting it reveal. We have spent so much time telling our past what to be, we need to accept our true past, if we are willing to listen, we may start to see the reality.

Let's keep jammin on this exciting math, on the only one ever found...

*"Dr. Mansfield said **in a video about the research results** that the 60-base system allowed the Babylonians to have more accurate results than the modern use of base 10. The different approach used by the Babylonians to arithmetic and geometry may have "possible practical applications in surveying, computer graphics and education."*

....Scientists are now saying the content of the 3700-year-old tablet surpasses modern knowledge too."

Luis Teia wrote about the possible purpose of Plimpton 322 in a **previous article for Ancient Origins** :

"Unlike what one may imagine, the reason behind the tablet was not an interest in the number-theoretical question, but rather the need to find data for a 'solvable' mathematical problem. It is even believed that this tablet was a 'teacher's aide' for setting up and solving problems involving right triangles. This sounds like an environment not so different from our classrooms today."

The Greek astronomer Hipparchus, who lived about 120 years BC, has long been regarded as the father of trigonometry, with his 'table of chords' on a circle considered the oldest trigonometric table.

"Plimpton 322 predates Hipparchus by more than 1000 years. It opens up new possibilities not just for modern mathematics research, but also for mathematics education. With Plimpton 322 we see a simpler, more accurate trigonometry that has clear advantages over our own," Dr. Wildberger said.

If it was a classroom aid, then this is a common set of problems, it's a common taught system. How long in the working commercial environment does something have to get to end up in an academic classroom? Even in this professional speculation, the location of this Sumerian tablet isn't supposed to be a big deal. This is a tablet from one of many towns not a secret base. With access to known information and just another day in junior or senior high in ancient Sumer. Where are the cheat codes?

This is a tablet that is 3700 years old and could be applied to computers, surveying, and surpasses modern knowledge. There are tables that describe how much volume is in a cup, or a jug or a building. These tables were developed and are available in computer problems now but were originally in books, hand written and over many years by very very smart mathematicians that had to work out each problem. If there was a catastrophe it would take us, today, modern man, many years scratching out these problems to rebuild just these tables. Math like this doesn't happen overnight.

This is only one tablet. In one culture that we credit as being one of the first on earth to understand "modern" settled living with farming and higher learning. With this tablet and its applications to hexagonal and heptagonal shapes it was very helpful in pyramid calculations for instance. This would be the equivalent of saying you needed a computer run lathe to make a baseball bat.

YBC7289 is another cuneiform tablet that gives very accurate computations. **Sexagesimal (base 60)** is a numeral system with sixty as its base. It originated with the ancient Sumerians in the 3rd millennium BC, was passed down to the ancient Babylonians. This system was used by the Chinese, the Greeks, it is used in modern times for for measuring time, angles, and geographic coordinates.

Daniel F. Mansfield & N.J. Wildberger. Plimpton 322 is Babylonian exact sexagesimal trigonometry. *Historia Mathematica*, published online August 24, 2017; doi: 10.1016/j.hm.2017.08.001

Kilonewtons, developed by Sir Isaac Newton's second law of motion, one newton specifically is one newton needed to accelerate one kilogram of mass at one meter per second squared. No copy editor isn't going to tell me that this isn't the very next best sentence in this book! Kilonewtons like the math in the Plimpton Tablet represents math that is being used for many practical world applications. In safety applications for fasteners and load anchors in the construction of large buildings, like pyramids, temples, and buildings and rock climbing. This math is helpful to build ships, design machines, shear strength and tension, think ship sails to a keystone cut in a polygonal wall. Newton's law of motion covers thrust of a rocket and the motion of thrust of a launch vehicle. Kilonewtons would also be very helpful if you built giant pyramids and cymatic polygonal walls or foundations. In catastrophic events, in a society that was working for millions or thousands of years, force would be an important calculation. The building materials including polygonal blocks would reflect the ability to manage external force and internal force. Force created from what the pyramids were doing, which includes energy creation but may also have included communication management, healing and defense against war.

The credit given for trigonometry is Pythagoras of Ancient Greece. Approximately 2000 years after the Plimpton Tablet is written. This tablet, based on style of lettering and the math in it, is theorized to have been written by a scribe, administrator or teacher as a teachers aid for a math class.

Each of those applications would mean this is established math, used in those applications, taught in a school used in a government office, is math that has been developed and been around for a long time. Wither for a ratio based trigonometry or not that isn't developed overnight. Applications for Force as a factor on cymatic polygonal construction would be an interesting calculation when considering the wave cancellation factors of a cymatic polygonal wall and earthquakes. In short, modern calculations of math appear on the antiquity to be above to apply in a more complex, complementary way to an ancient high society construction and lifestyle.

PI

3.14.....whatever. It is forever currently given to the Greek mathematician Archimedes for creating an algorithm for it. PI on it's simplest use, describing a circle, is really useful to geometry and trigonometry. Specifically in describing circles, spheres, and ellipses. Therefor building things like temples and pyramids, anything with a degree of accuracy PI is your guy.

Many of the appearances of π in the formulas of mathematics and the sciences have to do with its close relationship with geometry. However, π also appears in many natural situations having apparently nothing to do with geometry. As in Eigen value problems that naturally occur in the vibrational analysis of mechanical structures. These naturally occurring eigenfrequencies of vibration appear to apply to many ancient buildings.

Eigenvalue problems occur naturally in the vibration analysis of mechanical structures with many degrees of freedom. The eigenvalues are the natural frequencies (or **eigenfrequencies**) of vibration, and the eigenvectors are the shapes of these vibrational modes.

The Great Pyramid of Giza is uncomfortably built on PI. It is officially not recognized that PI is incorporated in Giza, even though the Egyptians themselves knew of PI, the Sumerians had it down before the Egyptians building spree. We have the Plimpton tablet and other examples. The question we are going to tackle later is, is it just because the pyramid is really really accurately pointed to true north, and or is it also because if it was an energy machine, or a transmission machine, it would have some very good use to incorporate PI. PI, being infinite would easily apply for any frequencies, whether your worried about the vibrations of an earthquake or an amplifying wave from or through the earth via a man made structure like the Giza Pyramid. One of thee most famous monuments on earth, built on an equation that should not be part of their ancient construction vernacular, but it is. Whether you like it or not Pi was used in the pyramids design and with a geometric finish line with highly accurate precision.

J.H. Cole used modern survey equipment and has found the parameter is a perfect sphere. Also helps to know the Great Pyramid and Menkaure are both 8 sided.

Food spoils after awhile depending on the food and math doesn't hold well through an apocalypse. If a lot of smart people disappear, we have a general notion that math is 2+2 and it wouldn't take too long to get back geometry or trig, or PI. Well...take the tables that help mathematically describe the volume of something. Think of liquid in containers, a pile of rocks, perhaps the volume of something as simple as a sink. These volume tables give you the equations to use. Rebuilding functional industrial math would be a 9 to 5 job. A job requiring very smart people dedicating their time to building math that could be used from construction to designing machine equipment.

Back to Archimedes, he developed the first calculations we know of for volumes and surface area. These calculations were developed and used through to our modern times. Used and refined by mathematicians over a couple thousand years. If there was a disaster, clean water, food, shelter will be priority one, math is likely going to be, did you kill one deer or two? The time to build back the math and the theories and equations to build and work with the machines now is really significant. You need not look further back than the cuneiform math tablets of Sumer, Archimedes to Oppenheimer and Schrodinger to know how long it would take if our current global configuration was hit by a large meteor or a large scale nuclear war. It was only the last 150 years that we became as "advanced" to create laptops and cars and planes. Did the consciousness awaking take that long or even longer? Human consciousness, when disconnected from the full earth grid we once had maybe a better indicator as to how far we have been knocked out. Possibly how big of a catastrophic event we survived.

There are millions of cuneiform tablets that have not been translated. Along with the Plimpton tablet, there could be more that describe PI, differently and some that contain the equations for volumes and surface solutions. We haven't translated them, we haven't found everything there is to find. In saying that, the evidences for metal plating, the trigonometry of the Plimpton tablet, and PI built into the Great Pyramid and other structures, there will be more math found. Found in structures, in tablet or written form and in the buildings that have been "found" and written off as explained already.

THE GOLDEN RATION MATH MATH MATH AND GREEKS, QUASICRYSTALS ARE COOL

The golden mean, golden section, extreme and mean ratio, medial section, divine proportion, golden cut, golden number, divine sections, golden proportion, or the golden ratio, is everywhere. Mathematicians have studied this equation for about 2500 years. Some of the properties of the golden ratio in the dimensions of a regular pentagon and golden rectangle include cutting it into a square and a smaller rectangle with the same aspect ratio. The golden ratio is a basic law of all life, it is in the arrangements of leaves and branches along the stems of a plant, veins in leaves, animals down to the nerves, in the proportions of chemical compounds and the geometry of crystals.
The Rhind Papyrus shows Egyptian math didn't account for the golden ratio, so either it is coincidence or it relates to an older more advanced society that does. There are other math works, and the Rhind Papyrus is not the final point on prior math.

The Rhind papyrus shows math that really is reengineering of the existing papers.

In 2010, the journal *Science* reported that the golden ratio is present at the atomic scale in the magnetic resonance of spins in cobalt niobate crystals.

Erik Von Daniken, author and researcher, sites some very interesting facts in his book, Odyssey of the Gods about some crazy math in Greece. He meets a Greek general after a lecture in 1974. Brigadier General Dr. Theophanias Manis of the Greek Air force noticed that the air force encountered some bizarre math in the fueling of fighter jets and training exercises over Greece. They were investigating fuel fraud because all the pilot reports were coming back with identical numbers. The general further investigates, having access to the maps that the ruins below Athens, Greece are arranged in very particular ways. Specifically to the golden ratio. Von Daniken investigates further and it is completely true. The maps start showing golden ratio alignments. Dr. Manias works with the Operational Research and have established 200 geometric relationships and 148 golden ratio geographic proportions. Apparently prehistoric sites needed to be really accurate again. Of those sites, it isn't like a straight line to them across a field. They span mountains, hundreds of miles of sea, bays and waterways. This is not alignments that are coincidental or convenient to make for a wow factor. These are all holy/sacred sites that make travel and design more reliable is a possible explanation. This would discount the extreme accuracy of the alignment of the sites. If you were using highly specialized machines for sending wave energy or communications, lining all you cities up and sending and receiving structures is a better possible reconstruction.

How does it apply to an ancient lost society? In Von Daniken's book, History is Wrong, he digs in on the known stories of the gods having come before Athens as we know it of Greek history. Frequently a recurring theme in archaeology is local people and their myths are ignored. Their legends, stories, and very faith is brushed off as the musing of simple people. It's the politest way to put it. Archaeologists, come into an area, ignore or don't listen to the locals and the locals just don't share the stories with the outsiders. The Greeks have the same stories, the famed temple that King Leonidas went to to ask the sages if they would survive the Persians, the temple of Athens, it's built on cymatic polygonal megaliths. The Greeks believed that there was something built there before they built on it by the gods. This is where I want to have a lot of verbal diarrhea about polygonal masonry but we got to save it for later. Cymatic Polygonal masonry is all over Greece. What is important in our current western world history for school, is to teach the Victorian theories. It was just enough for us to dig up the Greeks for art history, pat ourselves for democracy and and love the 300. If the Greeks had some stories about building on top of other cultures, it's a story, no need to entertain that when we have so many awesome Greek god stories to go over. So it went, so it goes for Spartan movies.

...Unless a significant amount of math, like PI, like metal plating and an Antikythera device, and a Plimpton tablet come up? This would be relevant if we are talking about a super advanced ancient society that was using a network of ley lines, of earth energy. Building on a global pattern for the transmission of energy and communications that was using almost unbreakable building techniques that last the ages. We throw cell phone towers on top of apartment buildings in the city to giant super towers in a farm field and throw up signal and hope it lands on people. It is not incredibly detailed other than to overlap the signals for redundancy of "coverage". These ancient construction methods in Greece showing incredible accuracy over hundreds of miles connecting sites, if applied to communication network alone, would mean an exact location set would be used, the network would be global and it would be more efficient and effective. Of course currently we just keep adding towers on apartments and restaurants in highly populated areas and just microwave people right in the face to get them a better signal.

Side note: There is no commentary in the Egyptian papyrus that discuss why the Egyptians build anything big.

Here we go citizen scientists! Gobekli Tepe, 5% dug up, massive single piece megalithic pillars with river rock and ruble between the pillars. This is the snap shot of where the site was when buried. Specifically where the 5% was when buried. The ruble could easily be the exploded, devastated pieces of other buildings and ancient advanced stone machines or buildings. My kingdom for a quantum computer to scan all the dust and ruble and piece them all together again. Humpty Dumpty : (

GOBEKLI TEPE

From Forbidden Archaeology by Michael Cremo and Richard L. Thompson...

> *"...Coles's proposal adds nicely to our collection of examples demonstrating how scientists adhering to the particular view of human evolution now in vogue must often engage in speculative mental exercises in order to bring anomalous evidence within the bounds of an acceptable time frame."*

This is exactly how alternative and traditional archaeologists have applied their views on Gobekli Tepe. About 56 years ago, there was a bump on a hill That was noted by Chicago and Istanbul archaeologists for pottery shards. They wrote a note about it. A German archaeologist takes an interest in the site after seeing the original notes. Klaus Schmidt, of the German Archaeological Institute goes from kinda curios in 1994 to furiously digging up less than 5 percent of the site over 21 years. Gobekli Tepe, or in English, Pot bellied hill, seemed like a good site to find a new archaeological site. Schmidt was previously working at a site called Nevali Cori. He had seen the brief mention of site in the 1963 researchers notes, at the time they had thought the large

47

megalithic pillars that appeared to be grave markers to them. They made note of it, that had been all that had happened. Schmidt thought it might be more interesting having been in the area already and thought maybe there would be more results than luck by actually digging.

Another view of the site. Not exactly the Reichstag. These large ancient columns were quarried close to the site. At least that is what appears at the time of abandonment. It doesn't indicate if a simpler people, mimicked the building technique and produced their own pillars. The wood, metals, cloths, anything of a more advanced ancient technology would have turned to dust or repurposed 12,000 or more years ago. It would be easy to have stacked ruble and build thatched roofs and reclaim the site for a newer less advanced human group. Messi tribe anyone? Senegal island natives?

Gobekli Tepe is the new mile marker for ancient timelines. Despite many ancient sites in Ukraine, Siberia, South America, America, and first and always most important, UNDERWATER SITES! Currently this is the site that is finally being given a blessing by mainstream academia as a legitimate site. a site that is approximately 9-12,000 years old. This is a made up date again. This date is still older than they want. This is important because there is a belief that man didn't build like this at this now hypothetical window. We were all hunter gatherers and even though hypothetical, mainstream sciences is saying 9-12,000 years. This significantly pushes back standard academic models. The most advanced society per standard dogma was the Sumerians, that the modern man originated in Africa and moved out from there. This site straight up changes the timeline. If we could build Gobekli Tepe, then wouldn't we have already been farming and settling down in like locations? Nope, they are calling it a ceremonial site. It sounds like a joke, nope. How and why would they conclude this. Easy, they have been digging for over 30 years. They must of dug it all up and this is why everyone is writing on it now.

There have been surface surveys using ground penetrating radar showing that only 5% of the site itself has been dug up. There are other Tepe in the vicinity, Hamzan Tepe, Karahan, Tepe, Harbetsuvan Tepesi, Sefer Tepe, and Tasli Tepe. None have had extensive research at this point or excavation. They all appear to have "T" shaped pillars. Little is known. They do know that there are at least 20 circles, more than 200 pillars, through geophysical surveys. Pillars are approximately 20 ft. tall and weigh up to 10 tons.

Interesting side note, as it has been excavated to the point it is at now some observations about the cut stone pillars have been made. The most recent uses of the site before it was buried in ancient times indicate the pillars get smaller in construction. At first cut from bedrock and always over time done with a corner cut. When you see pictures of Gobekli Tepe you see these large pillars with carved down animal and symbol reliefs which are very complex to accomplish from a single piece of stone. Along the sides of these large complex pillars are stacks of stone rubble. Sophisticated has nothing to do with the added stone, it's like a car was coming off the most advanced assembly line and someone finished off the car with barn wood and rusted square nails.

SOIL, AGAIN

Terra Preta and Chernozem! Seems like a digression, Gobekli Tepe is in the vicinity of Karaca Dag. Karaca Dag happens to be ground zero for the suspected original source of our cultivated grains. Let's keep a running dialog about the fact that we are talking post flood, Darwinian out of Africa story. The DNA of modern wheat with wild wheat has shown it is currently closely related to the wild wheat on Karaca Dag. This is only a theory and through the narrow lens of modern academia, the stamp on this has been sealed as the location of the first domesticated wheat. FYI, unknown for the make up of the soil, is it an engineered chernozem or Terra Preta? Also, an assumption of where our wheat started, is based on the find. If there are only so many grains to test, then eventually if the oldest grain is in a certain area, couldn't the assumption also be that there is a wheat as old or older in other locations? Just because other wheats trace to this source why the assumption that it is the first location? Remember our map of the world and the lost societies on it is vastly different if we just use Doggerland as an example.

MEANWHILE BACK AT THE TEPE

A common theme running through the mainstream academia world and now unfortunately coming from the alternative history crowd is vast assumptions of the purpose of a site they didn't even know was there. Yes, every time something comes you should revise your theories. The issue over all is that building off the old template is officially pointless. There is more than enough evidence as we are discussing to show that we have missed a massive chapter in human history and the templater should be allotting for that. What instead is happening, is that some of the most famous researchers are parroting the same blurring of facts. Fact one, this is the first ever built anywhere, everybody was coming from Africa, no farming and all nomads. Fact two being perpetuated, it was a ceremonial site. Fact three, it's all about the stars you can see in the sky. Models are being built using known post flood star systems like the entire zodiac.

IT'S NOT ALIENS, WORSE, IT'S US: Discovering Our Lost History

What is the problem again? Approximately only 5 % dug up. Guess where a lot of those groups are at about conclusions on 5% of a dig, if you guess 100% you're close. It's older than Stonehenge, they are all in agreement, alternative and modern academia together. The first thing done to this find is the standard template, artist drawings of sticks leaning on the tall megalithic pillars at the site and my fav, people in loincloths doing all the work. Always gotta have loincloths. Ancient people can always work out how to finish really without more than 5 % dug up of a site we didn't know was there, by a people we didn't know existed, there is already massive conclusions about the builders and their lifestyle!?! Every single symbol was important on the pillars and with no thought to big pillars, in loincloths. They never figured out paint, plasters, wood construction or how to make a cool sweater. Wires or metal doors or windows are definitely out. When I first heard about the site in 2017, they talked about how organics were found and carbon testing to over 34,000 year. That ended, I can find nothing about the German Archaeologist having had organic testing to approximately 34,000 years. Just like the Sphinx was dated to at least 34,000 years ago and now, along with Gobekli, it's labeled to at least 12,000 years. Now we hear dates of about 12-14,000 years For Gobekli. Discovery Channel, History Channel, BBC everyone comes running and the agreement is to label the site to approximately 10-12000 years old. It has been repeated and repeated over and over in the last year. 34,000 year old and other carbon testing has evaporated. As Michael Cremo put it, agreement by theories make the facts or anomalous facts must fit the theory. The results even these results, still make a little sense if you crunch it into 10-12,000 years. By ignoring the original findings, or only quoting it to 12,000 years, facts that don't fit the spoken theory will be thrown out! All this serves to do is push us further from our own truth of our past. The site is a mystery.

Humans weren't supposed to be building massive megalithic pillars and anything like this site, they were supposed to be pushing bison over cliffs and picking out new loin cloths. The site represents an in your face to victorian theory of history and there for Darwinism dates. It pushes them back at a MINIMUM. Yet the template of night sky watching loin clothed people weaving baskets is still being pushed. At the first site of its kind, this temple site.

Common standard path...astronomy. Yes. Many ancient sites line up to astrological maps of star groupings. However, we only got 5 % ish of Gobekli site dug. With animal carvings on the large megalithic pillars, they wasted no time creating theories immediately that these are star constellations as known by the Greeks or Egyptians. Because the other simple thing about ancient people is that they looked up and liked stars. A bunch. They didn't have technology to see star systems past the night sky, they worshipped the stars, followed stars they could see. This is something we have to build to and cover in depth in a coming chapter of astronomical awesomeness. For now you don't need to be an anthropologist or archaeologist or alternative alien hunter to know that this must have been a religious site. That is always what is assumed, it was a site of gathering for important things, no one ever finds the ten minute oil change building of its ancient day. We never find the local American keeping up with the jones culdesac set of houses or the strip mall of the day. Neolithic hunter gatherers built it so it must have been important. Maybe, but we have scientists going, we have grossly underestimated the population and constructions in other locations as we speak. Maybe dig it all up before we even begin to assume it fits into our prior picture of our development as hunter gatherers. We never would have dreamed of a device like the antikythera device was even possible. Here we are at Gobekli Tepe and it is stretched to the time that there were not supposed to be these structures anywhere according to the Victorian theory. This past paradigm is constantly screwing with identifying our true highly advanced past so this old Victorian theory just needs to die. Was that my outside voice?

Without more than 5 % dug up of a site we didn't know was there, by a people we didn't know existed, there is already massive conclusions about the builders and their lifestyle!?! Every single symbol was important on the pillars and with no thought to rotting wood and the desert just reclaiming organics, they are looking through the pinhole. There could have been re-purposing at the site, additions and or subtractions to the subtractions. It may not be the original builders that used it before it was allegedly intentionally buried. All of this needs to be considered before you begin to have a group of people nailed after 5%. As we consider the overwhelming evidence that we have been here longer than we have currently believed then we can easily look at a site like this and consider an alternative. First, that there are massive megalithic work. It's so old that there is small rubble mound being stacked at Gobekli Tepe between the pillars. It's clearly a rebuild, but how many years has it been used like that?

Cap stoning the whole endeavor, making assumptions early is the mother of Emperor's new clothes archaeological statements....

"It's the first site ever, EVER of it's kind."

It has to be beat like a dead horse, every time your watching a TV show, at the grocery store or bookstore or see an article online and the title is the FIRST:....Fill in the blank, it keeps the paradigm in the general conversation that we are the most advanced that we have ever been. That no one has made it on earth before further than the iPhone or the laptop. They fell and we rose again and maybe again. That the site found is a site that is unique, isolated to itself or that it's a regional culture center and that might be true, however it should never be assumed that we have found the first.

The gloves are off on our standard history just accepting Gobekli Tepe as the first ever. We haven't learned from what we have found already in Guatemala? There are two sisters sites near Gobekli Tepe. Also there is already obvious signs the site has been use by more than one culture. Why? Look at the crummy rock and pebbles filled in between the large pillars. The monoliths themselves have been mimicked by lesser and later people. That is why based on the pillars found, that the later pillars are smaller. It's not that they ran out of stone, the later cultures couldn't work with the prior advanced cultures tools or skill sets. The site may have gone through an initial abandoning and then occupied much later by a squatter culture that found this advanced site in ruins. This later group may have re-erected and repaired the site and additionally added what they had the technology to add. This may help us understand the rate of technology loss. Just sizing the later pillers and the stone may help us at least point to our ancient more advanced ancestors. Gobekli Tepe was above ground before it was buried. The pillars may have been supporting wooden or metal beams. There could have been plaster, plastic, metals, other building materials. Those building materials are gone, the site could have fallen into nomadic people that adapted what was left for them to use.

In looking at the pillars themselves, the rock pebbled rebuild around the monoliths are additions. An ancient culture had the technology to carve and place these massive T shaped pillars, then they gave up and stacked rubble between them. Just like all over S. America, Egypt and the earth, the site was reoccupied by more primitive constructions and social constructs. New archaeology list one: does the surrounding stone look similar, have similar carving and surfaces, or is it dramatically different? Is it possible that the site was hit and part of a cataclysmic event and left in ruins. If so, does the pebble rock rebuild between the pillars look more like remnants of other structures. 3-D image all rubble for future spintronic quantum computers to put back together. Also, fire all loincloth sketchers.

It's a mystery or is it grossly underestimated. A vernacular that would be more valuable would be to say, "this is the first of many sites we hope to re-evaluate and locate. We are discussing a plan right now to get the digs done, in a reasonable time to point us to these other sites. At this point to assume we know are history would be a gross understatement." Wouldn't that be refreshing? Paradigm shifting with extreme excretion.

After 21 years, the idea that waiting for a better time is ludicrous. Digging up Gobekli Tepe site fully and get the information to everyone in an open source way is critical. Here we are with artist drawings of Gobekli Tepe with only 5% dug up and 100% speculation on its purpose. Applying all sciences for a better read on a site is imperative. If you have 10-15 million people in a few new radar scans in 800 sq miles of the Guatemalan jungle, perhaps clearing the sand and exploring the site would be imperative to an assessment that reflects truth and accuracy. This is about our present as much as our past. There are a number of zealots that would love to continue to hurt, kill and hate people based on their post flood beliefs and traditions. It would be really hard to do that if everyone knew our true and more complex history for one.

Absolute relevant side note: The estimate of the amount of Egypt still under the sand, 90 percent.

EASTER ISLAND. HEADS...

First thing everyone will tell you is about the Heads. They are Heads. They are actually full bodied on the side of Rano Raraku. This is the volcano depression on the Island. Many people do not know this. Approximately 150 of the 1000 Moai (the big Heads) are buried in sand, mud and other material that slid down from the volcano. Prof. Robert Schoch suggests that it is sedimentary build up over time. That maybe it wasn't a mass deluge of ocean sand but a slow build up of soil falling down from the erosion of the volcano slopes. This doesn't exclude that there was cataclysm tidal wave or multiple combos and that it ended up contributing to burying the heads. If it was a slow build up that would likely push the time frame back even further than a massive cataclysm.

In 2009 archaeologist Jo Ann Van Tilburg, methodically started excavations that were to be the most extensive on the island. Digging up two of the buried Moai methodically. Big Easter island heads works for tiki parties if you can't remember Moai. Mrs. Tilburg is an associate researcher the UCLA Cotsen Institute of Archaeology and the directors of its Rock Art Archive. She is the Director of the Easter Island Statue Project. This is a collaborative work with the government of Chile.

The mysterious Easter Island Moai

Of the 149ish statues buried to the head, about 90 have been excavated. Some of the most interesting points of digging these two up was that the same sedimentary/erosions having been found around the Moai, was found in the quarry near by where they came from. Indicating that they were buried around the same time at the same rate. They found a burial at the base and a lot of red pigment To possibly paint the statue. Wouldn't it be interesting to genetically test the human burial that was found at that Moai? There was writing on the back of the Moai. The written language of the island, rongo rongo is to this day undeciphered. The two Moai that were completely scientifically researched were treated with chemicals and re-buried. The issue with this is what about the surrounding soil at the base of the Moai? Terra Preta? Anyone, a culture that was there at that beginning, when the first statutes were built, who were they and what is that known and unknown soil level? This entire area, laminated in naturally eroded ground, layered possibly in other cataclysm information or just cultural information. Now this information is no longer accessible, instead of planning it to be a longer, more extensive area dig, they snuck out and the team left.

As a reminder, we are discussing the fact that humans have occupied the earth much longer then we thought. There is evidence we advanced to a highly technical state. Easter Island relates to this part of the story because it has megaliths and megalithic blocks on some of it's foundational structures. The island itself is on the lay line grid of the earth. It is a natural energy grid encompassing the whole earth. There is a sweet spot for the last advanced society, it appears to be pre 12-13000 year ago. The flood and all indications based on what we find around the earth is that it was thriving at least 50,000 years ago. They knew how to build big, accurately and they frequently used the hardest stones on earth. On Easter Island, there are only 20 known statues to the EISP that are carved of basalt. Basalt is approximately 6 on the Mohs scale. The British museum has 2. One of them was re-carved on its dorsal side. It has base relief and incised petroglyphs. The re-carving is unique in style, detail and quality. Around the island there are 30 more statues with similar carvings. The similar etchings seem to be related to a reocurring theme of later peoples adapting and placing new meaning on old sites, a trend starts, and disappears as the re-occupationists change over time so do the stories. The oldest statues on the island are basalt, focusing on the soil and subsoil starting at the base of those oldest statues would seem to be the best place to start if you're looking for an older unidentified civilization.

Here is a recurring song and dance, a place we know of in popular culture and in the last 250 years yet is massively un-dug and current measuring and instrument research has not been done. LIDAR, geomagnetic and soil samples could be taken. Much is written on the general history of finding the island, a few statues removed to the British Museum and other locations. Of the research done, nothing complete, conclusive or chemically complete. An unknown language and a lot of agreed upon assessments of guess work and recent history after the island was rediscovered. There is no conclusive evidence on which direction the original inhabitants came. The assumption is post flood and in primitive boats. There are gaps in the deep ground to below "original" Basalt Moai and they didn't even start until 2009 to study. Where does this fall in reference to a lost highly advanced society we are trying to resurrect? Because there are signs of cymatic polygonal construction on the island, along with Basalt megalithic Moai that weigh tons in Basalt. Cymatic Polygonal masonry is chapters ahead, we will get there, for now an island that remains at least a compass toward understanding our past waits for more detailed scrutiny.

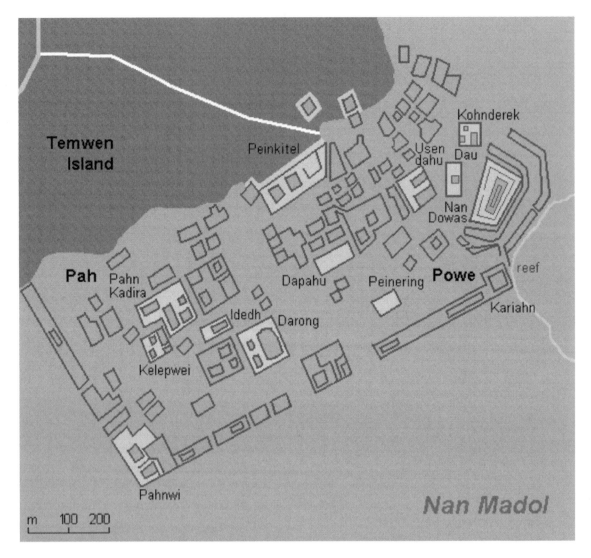

Sites like Nan Madol are labeled "mysteries" and frequently the recent, post flood, histories are so poor and spotted it is an overwhelming task to piece it together. This is another city like many in Egypt that show a repurposing of stone. It appears primitive in much of the construction. Is this another example of high tech metamaterial being restacked into a city by a less advanced human element?

NAN MADOL

This is a site that is made of megalithic basalt. Located in Micronesia off the eastern shore of the island of Pohnpei. This is located in the western Pacific. This is an artificial island made of basalt and was connected by a series of canals. There are 100 islets or more, stone and coral fill platforms and approximately 1.5 by .5 kilometers in size. The basalt blocks are 5 to 50 tons each. Brought and built on coral foundations. Guesstimates on the amount of basalt: 750 million metric tons. To this day they don't know where the stone is from. The pieces appear to be natural formations from volcanic plugs. There is no definitive explanation of where the Basalt has come from but at lease a couple of educated guesses like this quarry 25 kilometers away. However, this could be a later society finding similar stone and building on top of this older structure.

The city, considered "sacred", has no fancy statues or carved walls. There is no known writing or graffiti. They can not find indicators of the source of fresh water or food other than obviously seafood. There is a theory that it was once part of an older continent. Like Mu or Lemuria. Maybe Greek sailors built it.

Chisel marks, saw marks, weights, dimensions, and the quarry location itself remain a mystery. Like many truly ancient sites this one is labeled as cursed and sacred and to be left alone and as is.

Like many megalithic sites, the oldest portions are the most interesting. The older portions of the structures are facing the sea but closer to shore. They are more elaborate. Is this another case of people adapting an ancient site by mimicking what was found? Having found similar material and out of reverence for the "Gods" they tried to rebuild what they found, adding new buildings and repairing the older ones. The site line to the original builders is blurred by this work and later traditions. If a portion of the original structure is now underwater, the newer societies had rebuilt outward from the original more complex structures but the original structure may have been larger, unrepairable and the newer cultures built over it. The site is under UNESCO (the United Nations Educational, Scientific, and Cultural Organization).

> *"One cornerstone is estimated to weigh 50 tons... Eight columns form the basis of a roof that lets in shards of sunlight... The bodies of kings were placed here and later buried elsewhere."* - The Smithsonian Institute

This represents the stone only, what about finish materials like plaster, finishing bricks, metals? Again all gone. Could these stones be from a meta structure that was once above water? Priority abandoned, a lesser advanced crowd moved the material into the format it is in now? What was the shore line 8 or 15,000 or even 50,000 years ago? The repurposes of this site could easily be in that time period. Modern people today abandon sites, there are ghost towns in the American West that boomed and fell never to be used again. A site like this could have been abandoned multiple times or once over thousands of years.

The interesting stand out about the existing site is archaeologists estimate the population at about 30,000. Archaeologists point out that there was a greater effort to move the stone there than it was to move the stone for the great pyramid. Maybe the Gobekli Tepe crowd moved around a lot like a global contractor getting things done.

But there's more:

> "Rufino Mauricio, Pohnpei's only archaeologist, has dedicated his life to studying and preserving the ruins, which are built of 750,000 tons of black basaltic rock.
> We don't know how they brought the columns here and we don't know how they lifted them up to build the walls. Most Pohnpeians are content to believe they used magic to fly them," Mauricio told Smithsonian.
>
> For now, the ruins remain isolated from the rest of the island, avoided by the locals who fear that disturbing the site will bring bad luck,
> says Archaeology magazine."

....Sound familiar with all ancient sites? "...disturbing the site will bring bad luck?" What in the hell in the Wu Wu magic what the f????? It's the mystification of sciences.

We have one guy, one digging and attempting to discern the site. This is like having one archaeologist in all of Egypt or Tellinger in South Africa, or Osmanagic in Bosnia.

GUNUNG PADANG: "THE MOUNTAIN OF LIGHT" ..... AND CUICUILCO SHHHHHH

Not very far away in the same region is a 23,000 year old megalithic site by the village of Karyamukti. This is in the West Java Province of Indonesia. Of coarse the site is considered sacred and the local legends go... a king tried to build a temple in one night. Modern academics willing to give it a go say it was built for worship. Various methods put the site as a contemporary of the Sumerians.

Built of andesite blocks, there are at least 8 stone terraces on the south side, the east side has over 100, the west side from surveys has terraces that are covered in soil and plants. the north side has a 6 ft wide staircase and more terraces. There are indications of multiple chambers or rooms from geo-surveys. What is extremely interesting is it shows wall construction similar to Machu Picchu in Peru with more cymatic polygonal masonry.

There are estimates putting construction on the site back over 20,000 years, then there are artifacts that have been pulled from the site showing occupations through 9, 7 and 3,000 years ago. This easily making this pre and post flood and contemporary with Gobekli Tepe. How does anyone use the words. "First" ever in reference to our infancy in archaeology?

Approximately 3000 years ago the site was intentionally covered in soil. Just like Gobekli Tepe was allegedly buried intentionally. Based on back fill to being of a consistent nature, as if it was a dump truck and excavator buried the sites. Here is an ancient mystery. What ancient advanced society didn't want the past uncovered? Why bury a whole pyramid? Teotihuacan was buried? Drifting soil or intentional? Who didn't want the simple tribes to catch back up?

2010 geologist Dr Danny Hilman Natawidjaja (who earned his doctorate at Cal Tech) recognized this "hill" as a possible man-made pyramid and began to explore it using ground penetrating radar, seismic tomography, resistivity survey and other remote sensing techniques, as well as some direct excavations and deep core drilling.

On October 1, 2014, surveyors halted excavation because indications showed a large structure below the surface and a core anomaly was confirmed. Here we go crushing another 100 years of slow go no revelations and a quick halt and stop at a major archaeological site. This is a pyramid structure, it is extremely old, made of andesite, a volcanic stone in the family with Basalt and rhyolite. A typical characteristic of Nan Mahdol, the earliest Easter island heads, basalt. Not moving forward with entering subterranean spaces in this structure is incredibly ridiculous. To this day, it has not been done. If there could be future flash mobs, they should be turned into flash archaeological teams. We are paused and it is a structure that requires an immediate acknowledgment that our historical cycle is wrong.

One of the brush offs to explain Gunung Padang, is that it is a volcano. That it was never a pyramid. There are many unexplored pyramids and sites buried still in China, Russia, Italy, France, South America and Egypt that are not excavated. Gunung Padang shows a clear man made archaeological structure.

This is Cuicuilco, it's a massive nail in the standard academic timeline of, well, everything. This site should not be here. The problem with the Guatemalan LIDAR scans is that it shows miles and miles of modern construction not long after this pyramid site. Only 800 square miles has been done in Guatemala of 5000 sq miles.

CUICUILCO: BIG UP YOURS TO ACADEMIA, BIG GEOLOGIST WIN

Speaking of volcanic rock, lower on the rock formed by volcanoes are just lava. The best part about that is lava creates layers that geologists and standard academia types have gotten down really well for judging ages. Rocks just don't lie. They is what it is. A volcanic buried pyramid in Mexico that throws established history another home run to oblivion. Cuicuilco is a pyramid excavated for the first time by Mexican archaeologist Manual Gamio in 1917. It was covered by a lava flow that would put the structure to 8000 years or older. Quick reminders, because it is old it doesn't mean that it is an advanced culture. There are tribes all over the earth still eating people, living in loin cloths, and doing some crazy stuff. There are also Quakers and groups that just use some of the current technology and shun the rest for one reason or another. Just because this structure dates to an age helping us prove that there is more to the past than we know, doesn't mean the site is able to corroborate the existence of a more advanced society. It appears the structure has a core of rubble, small stones and is circular in shape. It is unmegalithic, it contains some basalt stones however and it shows it may be more of a mimic culture. This is a society that sees the more advanced society and builds similarly.

This pyramid predates Teotihuacan and would be by all accounts the oldest pyramid in the world, in a country and on a continent that as described early, as a place cultures go to die. Interesting, is that Teotihuacan show cymatic polygonal work and couldn't predate Cuicuilco but as a primitive site near more megalithic sites, Cuicuilco could be another representation of a side human tribe.

National Geographic discussed Cuicuilco in 1923 (no. 44). In the 1922, Byron Cummings of the University of Arizona became interested in the structure when he learned that a geologist named George E. Hyde had estimated the age of the flow, the Pedregal lava flow, as being 7000 years old.

In 1923 National Geographic published extensive photos of the site and an article written by Professor of Archaeology, Byron Cummings of the University of Arizona. In 1922 Cummings dated this structure to approximately 8,500 years based on the lava and the accumulation of soil on the structure. Cummings identified the lava flow to be 15 miles long, 5 miles wide and 5 to 30 ft thick. What is also an interesting point is that the Aztec and other contemporary surviving peoples have no traditional stories of an eruption of this type. If there were, the gleeful and terrifying sacrifices to the gods would not have gone unrecorded. This means that this structure is so old, the Aztecs and later cultures just didn't know about it. The structure was buried 25ft below the existing soil level. Here is an incredible point, if you're thinking in your minds eye that there was a big round multi tiered pyramid with lava rolling over it, wrong, the place was buried 15-17 ft. first in clay, sand, and rock. As the article in 1923 put it, it shows human occupation for 1000's of years prior to the lava flow. The lava being the last layer. 8500 years before it was covered, occupied prior to that. For thousands of years. Cummings states in his article, "Cuicuilco presents to us today positively and forcefully a chapter in human history on the American continent that many have supposed never existed."

Geologist Goerge E. Hyde from New Zealand was in the Mexican valley from 1921 to 22 and estimated the Pedregal lava flow at 7000 years. They found many female figures that correspond to figures in Paleolithic Europe. Gotta ignore these details if your degree is based on Victorian dogma, the oldest pyramid in South America is said to be 2000 years old. Anything in South America isn't advanced as what you'd find in Egypt nor would it share similar Paleolithic statues. This is the logic. It's straight scientific biased of a western society adhering to a theory and not facts on the ground.

Both Gunung Padang and Cuicuilco represent terrifying contradictions for the current "theory" of human civilization. These discoveries are after and before Gobekli Tepe, yet they weren't the "first temples" or special places on earth? To discern our true past whether simpler people or the missing super advanced society of our past, learning to see the biased on both sides of the research is imperative. Either alternative history investigations or National Geographic peeps, the envogue times determines whether a site has a spotlight. In Gobekli Tepe case, it is a site, in "western" research, getting labeled the "first" while Gunung, with hidden chambers, and Cuicuilco got the shaft, again. There are many moving parts of our past, the fog of our history swirls stopping at any moment means taking into consideration all sites at that age, not with the theory that it all gravy trained from one place like the Oregon trail from Africa. A picture with Cuicuilco and Gunung makes new truth with Gobekli.

NAZCA AND PENGUINS

Nazca Lines Of Nazca, Peru and associated geoglyphs are...say it with me - a mystery, an enigma, anyone have an actual clue? Nope. There was a German researcher that had looked at the lines for many years, German born teacher Maria Reiche. Maria made the first survey of Nazca lines after WWII. She stayed involved with them and their conservation for almost 50 years. Erik von Daniken made Nazca famous from all of his research and books. Starting with Chariots of the Gods and shows like Ancient Aliens. The lines are huge, some being in the shape of animals, spiders, birds, apparently one looking like an astronaut. Other lines are lines. They seem older, they are straight, some going over 25 kilometers. Lines carved in the ground and continuing straight for kilometers. These creature drawings and lines are the size of stadiums you can mostly only see them from the air or atop another mountain. You could walk right over them which happened before they were protected in the past and not see them. They are geometric and look very circuit like. Most people like to look at the animal geoglyphs.

There is a flat one on a mountain top that appears to have been shaved down to make room for it. Von Daniken has called it an airstrip. He points out he never actually said it was one, just that it looked like one.

Despite being in the spotlight since the end of WWII, direct research by passionate people like Maria Reiche, an uncountable number of flights of tourists to see the lines from the air, 50 more glyphs were just found in 2017. They were not hidden in jungle, they were just not accounted for. Either not noticed or bothered with. Don't find this surprising, there was also a turn in Antarctica, a place you can count the number of researchers. PENGUINS, love to hook up there. They breed in the Antarctic and we have all seen the movie with the penguin dads holding the eggs, hatching them in 60 below. It's adorable. People love penguins and we think we use a lot of science to figure Antarctica out and explore it. Well there is the Piri Reis map thing...so you wouldn't think that they would miss 1.5 million Adelia penguins on the Danger Islands? Ever seen someone covered in bees, just imagine that many penguins. After a recent satellite mapping apparently all those penguins finally waved for a camera. We apparently didn't notice millions of penguins that show up every year to a well known area in Antarctica. The most recently found geoglyphs in Nazca that are the size of stadiums, no one noticed. Our reality is that this world is still here to discover and on the broad side of a barn still.

Nazca, like the Paracus people of Peru, have been preserved because like Antarctica, it's dry. Really really dry. Slightly different, it is dryer. So dry, that if you wipe a boot across the desert it will stay there. Forever. The lines are made by wiping away the volcanic surface so the lines are not very deep. There is no wind, no rain, and the marks stay. This is a standard academia point. The oldest lines are straight for kilometers and have a strange chemical profile.

There are layers to the lines. The lowest are the lines, the graffiti is the creature shapes. The lines are straight. Very straight, like the Giza pyramid, like other ancient megalithic structures. That straight. Little known fact about the lines, there is plumbing. Plumbing from the Andes mountain range and drains. That is not a comfortable subject. For the very small amount of precipitation in the Nazca area, who thought to put drains in the glyph areas? Something that is going to be coming up more, if you don't have geologists, physicists, and anthropologists and archaeologists open to what is there, they will only find pottery, and loin cloth worshipers...oh, aliens too. We always find aliens helping simple people get one more bean planted.

People like the animals. They make sense. A primitive people in loincloths came along and put their graffiti on top of some very advanced Earth Circuitry. Academia theorize cultures having big ceremonies of coming to age or sacrifices to the Gods. Lot of time spent on it. A lot of books on it. They walk the lines of the glyphs of animals praying, ascending or taking ayahuasca tripping balls and walking away. This is like any hobby studying recent cultures. You can spend a lifetime studying graffiti on the outside of a shed that houses a space shuttle, or a Tesla or an electrical box of advanced circuits. Here is the issue. Let's assume the majority of the electrical box has disintegrated and the only thing left is the circuit board. Along comes a new society, all they see is lines.

Who cares about these long lines, let's put something meaningful on it, lets throw on a monkey, a tall guy, That is a geo-glyph Graffiti for squatters.

What about those mysterious lines? One of them goes over 25 Kilometers. Straight. Doesn't deviate. Doesn't deviate for 25 kilometers. There is arsenic in the soil found from testing. If it rains there is drainage under the lines, this is not talked about. There are actual pipes found under the lines in places water might pool. Arsenic keeps plants and vegetation from growing, maybe they were just thoroughly eliminating weeds? However, there is an idea that this is like a giant earth circuit. So how far do the lines go?

Where is the map that shows the lines directions? This is very important if the Pyramid of Giza is looking more and more like a power plant then let's follow the lines of Nazca, see where they start and stop. There are similar lines in Bolivia. How many more places they were just tilled over or buried?

If you had a multi ton spaceship or a F-15 type of plane it would easily blow the dry sand off the Nazca lines to a blur. There was a couple truck drivers in late 2018 that accidentally ran over the lines. Of course there are the locals, old tribes, free ways, trains, that have all destroyed the lines to a point also.

These lines are a good example of something that could be studied more scientifically with machines and their electrical qualities determined to see if Earth Circuitry was the actual purpose of these straight lines. Soil test is the chant of the day.

Great, there are big animals on the hills and you can stand as an ancient society on one hill and see some of the Nazca creatures. Where to find a book that explains and maps the Nazca lines layer by layer. There is none. There is a plumbing system running into the mountains and at different points in the Nazca lines and there are drain points. Plumbed drain points. One of the tests I heard Von Daniken himself did is that they put electrical current through two points in the Nazca lines to show that they could have been part of a giant earth circuit. If we have known archaeological sites that we have not put the latest technology to experiment to reverse engineer technology of ancient advanced machines, then we are coming up short. I have been unable to come up with a complete view of the Nazca lines from any researcher. Reiche was one of the first to study the lines and sadly she missed a massive amount of geoglyphs despite 50 years of research.

Everyone else missed a large number of geoglyphs found also! What about the straight ancient high tech lines? What about the electrical research and soil testing to explain these long straight circuits? Do they connect to trees, flow through the jungle through natural circuits like roots, mold and moss, were there metal structures or plastics, stone spheres jumping waves of energy?

Chapter 4

HOW OLD ARE WE vs. THE RELIGION OF ARCHAEOLOGY

We didn't start the fire! First comes Archean, then came Paleozoic, then Mesozoic and Cenozoic sittin in a tree, then came modern academia's fairy tail of morphology. Morphology is when they stare at a bone, frequently a piece, and by academic agreement, not by scientific investigation they place human bones on this chart to fit their theory of evolution. Not the facts of where Virgina Steen-Mcintyre dated her site in Mexico or Hans Reck's 1.5 million year old anatomically correct skeleton. Evidence, irrelevant to professional and academic rivalry or victorian sooth saying techniques of starring at bones and giving them a completely unscientific magic date doesn't change the fact that anatomically correct humans have been found in the Pleistocene, Pliocene and Miocene. Then there was Gobekli Tepe and the cities of the deep.

CHAPTER HOW OLD ARE WE ?

".....actual human skeletal remains in Pliocene and Miocene strata. These discoveries are practically never mentioned in modern textbooks. It bears repeating that the existence of human beings of the modern type in the Pliocene period would completely demolish the presently accepted evolutionary picture of human origins."

Forbidden Archaeology, Michael Cremo

There is much in the form of genetic evidence that will discuss in later chapters. We have been here as modern anatomically correct man likely forever and the physical evidences and suppression of it we will discuss now. We will go over a bit of the history of archaeology and how standard academia resists evidence and science to simply stick with popular theories, essentially making facts heresy. Theories that are given a place as science, while evidences and facts are consistently thrown out. There is the long parasitic marriage between religions and academia and filtering to fit their theories & dogma vs the reality of what is found. Another cancer of academia is of hoarding and withholding our history from the world, details of which we will describe. The truth of us, is so shocking, so intolerable to standard academia theories, that for everyone to read and to comprehend the facts will force necessary change so that tonight we might see.

We still have so many pieces to pick up in our big puzzle to put it all together and build an ancient lost society, which we will in the chapter: LETS REBUILD A SUPER ADVANCED ANCIENT SOCIETY. We will for now keep peeling away layers of blindness preached, produced and recited from schools to TV shows that continue to distract from the facts of our true human history. Getting a bearing on our antiquity means getting into knowledge filtration, which is rampant in academia and becoming a problem in alternative research. The only way to not accept the lies is to see the emperor's new clothes for what they are and go back over our whole history, again.

How do we miss millions of years of our history? As upright, modern humans? We have gone on a bit about Victorian age, western archaeologists and researchers some outstanding, found the factual evidence in the dirt, but just like high school, it wasn't the cool kids stuff and those findings were buried. If the Victorian founders of modern religion of academia had open minds, we'd have an IPhone by 1920. That is the shortest explanation, that standard education only leads so far in imagination. Dogma created blinders. There is the thinnest sheet of lies now between all of us seeing that there is no "pre-history" there is no mystery, just a large advanced unknown human history that we had been trying really hard to ignore.

Klerksdorp Spheres are machined. They represent some of the oldest objects on earth ever found that show the hand of modern, advanced humans working with material in ways we have yet to imagine.

WE ARE OLD 3.5 BILLION? MILLIONS?

We need to touch on them so do we start with the oldest thing known on the planet, that has been found, yes. The Klerksdorp Spheres. Our Earth is carbon dated to be approximately 4.5 billion years old. The Klerksdorp Spheres are dated to be approximately 3.5 billion years old. They were found while mining pyrophyllite near the town of Ottosdal in the Western Transvaal, South Africa. There is a debate if they are naturally formed concretions, which is Mother Nature making a snowball basically from Volcanic activity. The other option is they are machined. They are very hard and if you google them, you'll find that they are said to be harder than steel on the Mohs scale. Great. They have fibrous centers, and little to nothing is published or studied about them. They have clear, straight lines on them, impossible almost to explain without machining the lines. The hardness thing is irrelevant, the reason they were found was because the saw being used to cut the blocks of pyrophyllite kept hitting them. The pyrophyllite has a hardness of 2 and the age of this material is a few billion years old. No matter what, these balls have straight line designs on them, are multi layered like a gulf ball, stop steel saws and are about 3.5 billion years old. There is also a formation of stone balls in Utah called Moqui (Mo-Key). They were found by the Moqui Indians and are also called Shaman Stones or Thunderballs. They are mainly sandstone. Believed to be natural concretions, they are very different then the Klerksdorp Spheres.

We have talked about 2300 ft. deep cities off Cuba and India, millions living in Guatemala that weren't supposed to have that number in all of South America, theological conversations that Plato and Herodotus had with Egyptians about their ages of civilizations and all of it pointing to that big 12-13000 year old disaster. There are kings lists from Egypt, the Bible lists their patriarchs and of coarse the Sumerian Kings list we will be talking about in later chapters and all of them showing rulers and "gods" living for 1000's of years. There are too many histories in the last 6000 years that include histories beyond the physical finds as of yet. Anything found to contradict the established timeline are called out of place out of time artifacts. Apparently we can have out of place artifacts and not have any of them weigh in and effect the established timeline.

These are natural concretions. Allegedly. We have no examples of this happening in our eyewitness accounts.

The machined Klerksdorp spheres are real, they are old, one could speculate that we, the human race stopped off on this planet, crashed or made it home intentionally. We could have been visited by another race, that put the "human" on the path of evolution to evolve to where we are now. That part, the part where tribal or "simple" people by modern standards have always been around confuse older archaeological sites maybe apart of a later history. It is possible we started genetic experiments as we expanded from our infancy billions of years ago. We could have easily risen and fallen on the "great year".

IT'S NOT ALIENS, WORSE, IT'S US: Discovering Our Lost History

Before we talk about the history of Archaeology, I wanted to discuss a lecture I attended in Dec of 2018 at Macalester College in St. Paul, Mn. The featured professor was Prof. Melissa Sellew. She holds a BA in Classics and History from Mcalester College, M.Div in religious studies from Harvard, and a Th.D in the New Testament and Christian Origins also from Harvard. She specializes in early Christianity, Greek and Roman religions, the New Testament and Coptic language and literature. In short, she is pretty bad ass about ancient texts, falling under the entire history of the Western religion of archaeology.

The subject of her lecture was ethics in archaeology and tomb robbing and a history of it throughout the last 150 years or so. One of the examples was of a Professor of the British Museum who cut up an ancient document in about 1910, hid the manuscript in his over coat and distracted the custom officials with 200 lbs. of oranges. There was another case of the Israelis sending high resolution back ups of the Dead Sea scrolls to the U.S. for safe keeping. They were stored in a Californian data storage facility and thanks to the bravery of one professor who lost their job after releasing the images to the general public, we all have them. So we are clear, the Dead Sea scrolls, in their entirety, were not released to the world intentionally or even if you believed they were ours, the worlds, that was not how the governments saw it. The Dead Sea scrolls belonged not to humanity, but to a government. In America's or England's agreement, complacency, whatever you want to call it, the Dead Sea Scrolls and many other histories are not ours, the public's. These data hoards are happening all over. Governments, fund and have university's that find things around the world and that data is not shared, if it is called out then they'd have to call out themselves. The Dead Sea scrolls being released caused a wave of research to be done, by having many eyes on it right away. Keeping it, the pieces of history from the greater populations, denies an acceleration of knowledge. If you are a conspiracy type of person, which government, banking system, religious system wants the general population to get a real grip on who and what we are? Let alone the degree you got for a quarter of million let you know loin cloth was the only way 50,000 years ago. Alternatively with a little help from our alien friends and the ship, Pepe.

Prof. Sellew, didn't name names, but a recently deceased colleague, kept an original Dead Sea manuscript in his personal desk hoarding it to himself for approximately 40 years. Prof Sellew pointed out that great research was done after the Dead Sea scrolls were released to the public. She raised the question does hoarding even one document in one professor's drawer unethical, immoral, is it illegal? Unfortunately, no, it is not illegal. She continued pointing out more progress was made by it being kept in open academic hands. Think about how terrifying all this is to general academia, their prestige their "knowledge" being first the top down decimation of information, all of it threatened. Control issues anyone? She did point out that there is a release required now after 5 years. If you have or haven't figured out the piece of the past in your possession, then it is to be open for others to have and handle. Personally I wonder if the 1000's of years in the ground was enough non release time? Prof. Sellew spent the lecture with a very insightful and provocative points. To what ends do we allow "standard" academia, from the British museum to the Smithsonian or the countries at the heart of our beloved western origin story like Israel, keep any find from the public's eye? There are so many issues to

68

overcome to understand our past and the history of archaeology stands to completely confuse us. Then, there is this very group, stealing, hoarding and outright lying about history to reaffirm theories not facts. Representatives from the British museum taking a document that should have never have left Egypt, including statues and other finds. A professor holding a Dead Sea scroll in his personal desk drawer for 40 years, sums up the click clacks of academic morality. On this alone, when you hear this group and their supporters talking about "pseudo-archaeologists, or pseudo-researchers" to invalidate the research going on at this very moment, is arrest worthy. The work that has been accelerating and accelerating to seek the truth of the human origin, are many and by much bolder citizens of the world. Standard academia uses many methods to discredit alternative researchers. "Standard" academia has the longest record for stealing, taking or removing items as they see fit without permission and with varied "scientific" methods themselves. On Easter Island, Rapa Nui, the oldest of the Statutes are Basalt, three were taken to the British Museum. This was not with the islanders approval, this is just an expeditionary team that grab the giant heads and left. In Egypt, there is a long history of not just parchments being smuggled but many items leaving since the day it became popular to dig it up or repurpose stone off the great pyramid. This isn't the tomb raiders of Indiana jones, this isn't your average grave robber, this the Smithsonian, British and many other academic institutions, taking property of sovereign nations for their collections. Anywhere you see an Egyptian stone obelisk that is in Rome, the Vatican, these items were taken. Uncountable Egyptian artifacts left Egypt not through illegal, grave robbing, through the ordained western academic stations. A different standard is applied to ordained institutions. Institutions that go hand in hand with religion and governments. There were gatherings all over Europe and America to have mummy unwrappings. It was popular to have a few friends over and all participants got to unwrap a mummy. This is not scientific, a desecration of these ancient bodies was an early 1900's phenomenon. Yet, not illegal, endorsed as entertainment of the wealthy. The amount of unknown loss of information by these completely unscientific activities is sickening. Genetic information, some of these mummies may have had drugs in them from South America, the ink on their tattoos, elongated skulls and all the information now gone.

In the infancy of archaeology, they dug for art, not bones. Sites in Greece had temples with bones in it thought to be of dead Gods. It was later theorized by an author that the Greeks were the first archaeologists. There were many dinosaur bones exposed in Greece along mountains and hills. The theory goes that an ancient Greek would see a bone sticking out of the earth and they would dig it out. Ancient Greeks knew of Titans and here were bones that seemed to be bones of titans. Likely, a mastodon or other dinosaurs femur, the Greeks took the bones back to the temples as relics of a god. Just like the Catholic Church having relics of Saints in some churches, they hoisted up the mastodon bone as a bone of the gods or some fallen titan. If you are unfamiliar with relics, in the Catholic Church, pieces of a sainted humans were cut up and encased in gilded and bejeweled containers. Like a hand, or a head, a leg, you name it and they have cut it up and put it in a jeweled case, and displayed it in the church. In the Middle Ages it would be quite a thing to make it to a church with sickness, concerns, a desire to be with something reported to be pure and holy or what have you could save you 42 percent more. Instead of praying to or meeting god, you could walk right up and or sit right down and now that you are in the proximity of a "relic" all sorts of miracles could happen because you can rely on that part of a Saint to talk to god for you. Maybe you're cured, maybe you are just feeling 32 percent better. Here you are by a piece of a Saint. The church may receive a larger donation, having been in the presents of a saint, it might mean more to the pilgrims coming to see it. There is a lot to unpack with relics, the same thing would be true if you're in Greece, at the temple of Athena, and there is a big thigh bone of a titan. Here is the problem, in the early days of archaeology, the bones and other scraps of material would be tossed into the debris pile. There are no apologies for this, academia has no track record for apologies to destroying the human record. They are on record for out right stating if the evidence don't fit the theory, throw the evidence out.

Before we can get the the more recent religion of Archeology, developed over the last few 100 years, we need to look at an organization that is almost the complete source for the first loss of information,. Well, let's back up one more step and speak about the Great Library of Alexandria. One could argue that there are other post flood knowledge wells. We are building up a case about a pre 12-13000 year old highly advanced society. The Piri Reis map is one example of that pre-flood knowledge. The idea that library's were able to retain various scraps of this information and the existence of some of this knowledge in cuneiform tablets and Hindu texts is well established. The library of Alexandria is the flagship for the story of all libraries of antiquity, they were burned, pillaged, and destroyed. This leaves the histories of our past even more confused. There were great libraries of the Greeks, Romans, Ottomans, Egyptians, Assyrians, and all are gone. It has varied in estimates but the great library of Alexandria held over 800,000 scrolls of the histories of the world and sciences, philosophers, you name it. It was the Hogwarts school of magic. There is a couple of theories on how and why it burned. Burned by Julius Caesar, other Romans, maybe others and the bits of knowledge that survived was placed in private collections as long as there have been wealthy powerful people collecting and hoard things. The Piri Reis map represents valuable cartographic information needed to sail. Even if your a fervent religious empire, you need to know spreading your way around the world that you can get there. Maps survived because the need to navigate out weighed the need to suppress that information. It is a problem if you have been systematically burning and destroying histories that disconnect us from our true past. Here you have a map showing science and math that you personally are too ignorant to understand, that in context to a later society, ours, namely, that the complexity would easily show use that there was a more complex science and society at one point. If you are going down the conspiracies road, you'd want to consider what other fail safes could you use to throw up a smoke screen to the truth. Well religion and academia to the rescue.

One more thing before we crash through a short history of archaeology and to wet the conspiracies agendas, there is this one giant global organization that is and has outlasted all corporations, expanded and expanded to all continents. Here is one example of one library we all want to go on uninterrupted. A library belonging to a religion that has assuredly collected and or destroyed any competing religion or history that has come in it's path. This is not meant to be an attack on one single religion or another, but in the western world, it is at the center of the matter, The Vatican Library.

Here is the 50,000 ft. view of the Catholic Church. We talk about paying reparations for slavery, if anyone ever owed reparations to all of humanity it's got to be the Catholic Church. Think Spanish Inquisition, Galileo, told that he better recant that the earth is not at the center of the universe, if we don't agree, literally burn objectors at the stake. The Catholic Church built an empire beyond the capacity of this book. Guns, Steel Germs covers the expanse of the modern rediscovery of the Americas by Columbus/western Europe with the Church. They brought disease that wiped out millions and left Native American populations either wiped out completely or to estimate of 90 percent dead. Burned or destroyed any "pagan" histories and almost no Mayan writings survive to this day because of it.

Side note: mutations of the viruses and bacteria to get to the diseases of the conquistadors could be reversed to see what a contact date would have been with the native Americans via a similar bacteria or viral level.

The Catholic Church built on many ancient and native holy places. Literally on the foundations of the local holy and sacred places the church placed buildings in order to eliminate the memory, belief structures, and traditions of local populations. This practice is not limited to South America it is used throughout the world and in Europe to burn the history of the past and rewrite it for religions and for governments. The "faith" of Christianity has other titles, liking it or not, Catholicism got franchised out and re-branded.

This brings us back to the fall of Rome, the rise of the Catholic Church and the dark ages. Gregorian monks and monks in many places begin to collect, store and copy every piece of ancient writing that they could find. Collecting them in every state, every province of every kingdom along side as royal "advisors" bring land to the church, money to the church, and for the common sheeple, a focus on faith, not on history, but faith. There is no need of facts when you have faith.

50,000 ft view again, ancient works kept and copied by monks for 100's and 1000's of years weren't just copy, they decided that they were in need of a rewrite. They made copies of great works, think Plato to the Bible, noting as they were copying from older copiers in the manuscript sides, that they "corrected" an error in translation or passage. As the accepted story changed, the monks took the socially agreed story of the current day and "corrected" our story at the time of correction to match. In turn the original manuscripts were put to the torch. When you study at a college an ancient history, you have to look really hard, are you reading a book written by a professor and peer reviewed by another, or are you reading a copy of a manuscript that is truly within the time of the fall of the Roman Empire? Is what you are learning from straight source material, or material from a direct translation by inspired monks making their own edits?

CHINA DID IT TOOO MOM!!!

This is not limited to the Church, lets turn to a perfect government example. The first Emperor of a unified China, Qin Shi Huang, buried 460 scholars alive in 212 BC and followed up with a burning of histories prior to his rule The very next year. Executions we're for any scholar, family members, people who reported on people that were remembering or preaching about the past, they too were executed. after having the great book burning they rewrote the history of China.

This is as bad as you could imagine, the stories, your favorite Greek myths, Homer, the histories of Rome, what is the source material? This is another book or a 100, there is this assumption as I personally had, that in the British Museum or somewhere in Rome, there has always been benevolent, kind historians that carefully kept the very scrolls Plato, Julius Caesar, Herodotus, well, all of them safe. I thought the histories and documents of the world were saved and sacred. Wrong. Every so many years, the older copies were destroyed, "lost" or if a durable parchment, were erased and written over with a new history. There is new MRI and X-ray scanning techniques showing that older, even some of the original works are there. That is amazing and good news, it will rewrite or should we say un-write some of the monks edits.

It is the same in biblical studies as it is for all the classics, we are not studying off the source material. It is not given to us in school, it is not readily available outside of a "degree" program in a collegiate program. In the case of the Bible, millions believe in the Bible, but walk into any church and say, I would like to see a copy of Mark, they will open a bible. No no, I would like to see original letters or writings, pick John, Paul, and you are going to get a blank stare, you will never be able to go into a church and see the source material, they don't have it. No church has the originals for your study.

You can pick up many different versions of the Bible, and go to a church bible study, they will discuss, what your King James say on that verse, what does your ESV or American Standard say on that verse, isn't that interesting? No one, no one, in the coarse of their faith journey, ever questions, who, who wrote these texts, where is the originals in pdf for me to review? No one asks, it's all worked out and just a faith issue, Agrapha, the Yahwist source(J source), the Priestly source (P source), the Deuteronomist source (D source), the Elohist source (E source) this is your actual "bible". There were not millions of identical writings, there are pieces, the book you call the Bible, is a collection of writings that are not equivalent, not written by the same authors as you have been convinced to believe. There are multiple writers for every book. This study is called biblical theological study. It's the reality of the faith, anyone that has studied the source material has to make a choice that it just doesn't matter that there is not one written record that shows the Bible written the way you see it. Every Biblical scholar knows this, yet somehow no atheist or intellectual seems to be able to communicate it. The original writings are by mostly unknown people conveying very different ideas. Take this with the gnostic writings of the Bible and you have a broader belief system if you accept any of it, all of it is in. These are just facts. As Rick would say, "think for yourselves".

Believing that our histories, from caveman through the Greeks to today has all been preserved and is all worked out, having been cared for by honest and benevolent keepers of knowledge is so far from the truth. There is a desire to believe without personal research. The Bible as the end user sees it, is nothing close to what is actually known and available to scholars. The scraps, multiple writings of the above source material, sound and look nothing like what is read in a church.

As for these theological sources for the "bible" on your own, find it, look at it, this is not to reduce or change your faith, it's to wake you up, to see the foundations of some of our deepest core values and what that means to you, what do you know? Self experimentation for your life should always be first. Keep asking: Why do you know what you know, why aren't you reading the source material and whom are the authors? Are we not still looking for the meaning of life or just settled on being sheeple?

For example, In theological studies it is believed by researching the writings that there was no john and that there were at least 3-4 authors for mark. This is uncomfortable to your average tithing christian, the author is Mark if you just read the Bible that you buy at the store. Let your pastor or priest explain away your questions when doubting or questioning faith. To a theologian it is interesting to read, speculate, to an organization collecting billions in a monetized corporate system, it is lethal. If the oldest texts of the

Bible are written by a few people under the 4 "gospels" or any of the doctrine "bible" texts is looked at directly, you will not be comfortable as an average faith driven Christian. The truth is of what is surviving in the oldest source material, many people maybe wrote it, that is squirm worthy. Terrifying for the average person just trying to 9-5 it and get through a life, a death and marriage etc. Keyword, "surviving" it's always assumed that somewhere the meeting notes from the twelve apostles are going to be found. The writings don't point to a common point, they point to a common era of people developing a new faith franchise.

There are really big things in our life we have propped up on faith despite what is actually available to read. The revisions are indoctrinated as truth. Just like history, the theories are dictating the facts, as if religion set the template for academics to follow in their own way. The documents that came from the Middle Ages, are not the originals, yet we are told Plato wrote it while all along we are reading rewrites of monks. The cuneiform tablets, ancient Hindu texts, some of the Chinese texts that survived the purges, individual documents that have survived the great burning of the library of Alexandria and other libraries like it, these documents are all potentially originals. The Sumerian cuneiform tablets have not all been translated, can you believe that despite being considered the first and oldest civilization. We assume that the important ones have been translated. That the remaining tablets are basic inventories quick notes, administrators accounts of livestock...etc. People just haven't gotten to it how the hell do they know?!

Emperor Qin was one example outside of the Catholic Church that showed a government can destroy a history, another is the United States vs the First Nations. The amazing and under appreciated Native Americans. I bet I could just say Pocahontas, Lewis and Clark, Custards Last Stand, the Sioux, Cherokee, Camanche, The last Mohican and I am sure you'd think of Walt Disney. Picture a cute little Indian woman with a single feather and long black braided hair in a canoe helping Lewis and Clark through wilderness of America or John Wayne killing Indians from a horse. America at it's start, being christian and all, couldn't take America from an existing culture, it had to justify it. Manifest destiny is an educational k-12 term you will learn growing up in America. It means that there was a belief, to escape religious persecution, immigrants from England and Europe came to America and this land was god given to western pilgrims to take. "Manifest Destiny" god created and made America for christians from europe. Savages, I.E. indians were not good god fearing people. But, what if there were pyramids in Illinois, the largest known earth mound, Serpents mound in Pennsylvania, ancient canal systems in Florida, New Mexico, carvings and out of place artifacts including Jewish writings in Indian burials showing Canaanite writing? Well christian Americans would have been pretty shitty to take, well, the whole country from savages if they weren't savages. To take it from people that actually have been here well before western academics decided cavemen came across an ice bridge from Alaska was impossible by doctrine. Well we did take it. Hand in hand with the church. You can chalk it up that the conqueror writes the history, 'tis true, 'tis pity tis pity tis true'.

Governments in the Americas needed to maintain that they were the first "modern" non savage people. Looking through the finds of larger skeletons, newspapers of the 1800-early 1900's you can find many examples of the Smithsonian blocking information that doesn't align with manifest destiny. Don't need to go to conspiracies for this either, the curator of the Smithsonian himself published to paraphrase, "we will not accept any history that doesn't support manifest destiny. People who are not Western European are savage".

John Westly Powell, 1882-83 Smithsonian annual report. Director of Ethnology, stated,

> *"artifacts found prior to the discovery of Christopher Columbus arrival would be deemed illegitimate, only finds of the savage Indian culture would be considered"*

Government, sciences, religion is married together. Sacred Fire, a book by Dr. Peter Lillback. George Washington, Sacred Fire, book by Dr. Peter Lillback, is worth the read of this rabbit hole.

BRAZIL WANTS TO GET IN ON FAKING HISTORY

Since we are on a role with x file government cover ups. What would the government of Brazil do if there were Roman vessels sunk off the coast of Brazil? That means a big rewrite for a lot of history books, and the Portuguese aren't the first to be settling brazil. This just isn't very patriotic and we know exactly what the Smithsonian and Parent, the British Museum would say.

In an article from the New York Times, Oct. 10, 1982 "Rio Artifacts May Indicate Roman Visit" by Walter Sullivan

> *"A large accumulation of amphoras, or tall jars, of the type carried by Roman ships in the second century B.C., has been found in Guanabara Bay, 15 miles from Rio de Janeiro, according to the archeologist, Robert Marx, who is a well-known hunter of sunken treasure.*
>
> *The Portuguese navigator Pedro Alvares Cabral is generally credited as having been the first European to reach Brazil, in the year 1500. Mr. Marx said yesterday that the Portuguese authorities were trying to block Brazil from issuing him a permit to excavate the wreck he thinks is buried there. Like the 5-Gallon Jerry Can. Amphoras are tall jars tapering to the bottom and usually fitted with twin handles. As described by Mr. Marx, they were to the ancient Greeks, Romans and Phoenicians what the five-gallon jerry can was to mobile units in World War II.*
>
> *They were used to carry wine, oil, water or grain on long voyages.*
>
> *Mr. Marx, the author of many books and articles on early exploration and underwater archaeology, believes the amphoras were carried to Brazil on a*

Roman ship that was blown off course. It may have anchored off Rio, then been driven by a storm onto the reef near where the amphoras now lie.

According to Dr. Harold E. Edgerton of the Massachusetts Institute of Technology, a pioneer in underwater photography who has worked extensively with Mr. Marx, the amphoras are definitive, both as to the age in which they were used and the identify of the users. Reached by telephone, Dr. Edgerton said of Mr. Marx's qualifications, "For my money he is as reliable as they come."

Mr. Marx, interviewed by telephone at his hotel in Rio, said he suspected a hoax when he first heard of the amphoras, but was convinced a few days ago when he dived at the site and saw an area comparable to three tennis courts strewn with jars, most of them broken. He brought some to the surface and plans to have their age and origin authenticated by specialists.

The amphoras could not have been planted there, he said. Four intact amphoras and parts of at least 50 more are on the surface. Digging with his hands into the mud he encountered some as much as five feet down. The jars are barnacle-encrusted and some long ago became enclosed in coral."

We are going to get to the Elephant in the Room, but wait for it…wait for it. Have you ever heard anything about this ? Three years later, here is an excerpt of the follow up article by the New York Times, dated June 25, 1985

"UNDERWATER EXPLORING IS BANNED IN BRAZIL" by Marlise Simons.

A DISPUTE between the Brazilian Navy and an American marine archeologist has led Brazil to bar the diver from entering the country and to place a ban on all underwater exploration.

The dispute involves Robert Marx, a Florida author and treasure hunter, who asserts that the Brazilian Navy dumped a thick layer of silt on the remains of a Roman vessel that he discovered inside Rio de Janeiro's bay.

The reason he gave for the Navy's action was that proof of a Roman presence would require Brazil to rewrite its recorded history, which has the Portuguese navigator Pedro Alvares Cabral discovering the country in 1500.

The Brazilian Navy has denied that it covered up the site and has in turn charged Mr. Marx with "contraband" of objects recovered from other wrecks in this country. Because of this, Navy officials said, the Government had issued an order "to prohibit him from entering Brazil."

…All other permits for underwater exploration and digging, a prolific field in Brazil, have been canceled as a result of the Marx controversy and none will be issued until Congress passes new legislation, Navy officials said. Although the

decision was taken a year ago, it was not publicized and only became known as a result of new inquiries into the Marx case.

The ban has affected a number of projects in Brazil's harbors and along its 4,600-mile coastline. Mainly foreign diving teams have discovered a panoply of gold and silver objects, but most of the sites, though known, remain unexplored. In Guanabara Bay of Rio de Janeiro, more than 100 English, French and Portuguese shipwrecks lie unexplored like the pages of an unread, underwater history book.

But few spots seem to have aroused as much interest and intrigue here as the remains of a ship that struck a reef some 15 miles inside Rio de Janeiro's bay. The story goes back to 1976 when lobster divers first found potsherds studded with barnacles just off Governor's Island in the bay. Then a Brazilian diver brought up two complete jars with twin handles, tapering at the bottom, the kind that ancient Mediterranean peoples widely used for storage and are known as amphoras. Brazilian experts disagree over the age of the jars, which have been turned over to the Navy and stored them in a warehouse.

...According to Elizabeth Will, a professor of classics and specialist in ancient Roman amphoras at the University of Massachusetts at Amherst, the jars are very similar to the ones produced at Kouass, a Roman Empire colony that was a center for amphora-making on the Atlantic coast of Morocco.

Reached by telephone, Professor Will said of the fragments she had studied:

> *"They look to be ancient and because of the profile, the thin-walled fabric and the shape of the rims I suggested they belong to the third century A.D."*

After Mr. Marx and Dr. Harold Edgerton of the Massachusetts Institute of Technology had explored the site with acoustical echoes and long metal rods, Mr. Marx said he became convinced that, below the potsherds, they had found the remains of a wooden wreck. A Roman vessel, he argued, had been blown off its course and reached Brazil.

Mr. Marx's expeditions received wide press coverage in Brazil, with some reports asserting that he was perpetrating a hoax and was defaming the name of the Portuguese discoverers of Brazil.

...In January 1983, when Mr. Marx returned to Brazil to start salvaging the wooden wreck, he said, the tides had turned. "The Navy people I worked with told me the Navy had covered up the site to keep it from being plundered," he said. "They also said this thing is causing so much controversy, it's better if you leave." Mr. Marx said he nonetheless went diving and found that the spot where objects had been close to the mud surface was now covered by a large mound. He added

that other Government officials then told him: "Brazilians don't care about the past. And they don't want to replace Cabral as the discoverer."

Brazilians don't care about the past, all permits canceled to dig. Do you need to "dig" for conspiracies or a cover-up. Why? Because of the Elephant...

THE ACADEMIC ELEPHANT IN THE ROOM WESTERN STYLE

By making Africa as the center of the origin of people, it marries The Garden of Eden story with evolution/Out of Africa theory. Sciences and Christians could play nice moving forward. As long as it is out of Africa first...dam those facts...Christians are happy, schools with a lot of churches on the campus could be pleasant to one another. Facts that don't support this must go away. It makes prehistory, no longer relevant history, it makes our true history harder to discern, people don't like hard. Make pre history a mystery makes degree programs that already work, continue the social status as wanted, keep praying and writing checks for degrees and student loans.

The filtration of knowledge in the church doesn't mean the church didn't collect information, there is that Vatican Library we likely all deserve access too. This is the big elephant in the room of Christianity, western manifest destiny, and the reoccupation of the Americas by Europe in the Middle Ages and the very source of why it is necessary for the religion of archaeology to have fallen into its pattern of education. The marriage of christianity and early arrogance of what they did find. Throughout the whole of Western European education, there it is, hubris. If you are a university and supposed to be the smartest, best place to learn, then this miss is beyond epic, especially for a $200,000 plus art/history/archaeology degree. Bill Gates, drop out, Facebook guy, drop out, Michael Dell, drop out, name a musician you truly love that learned to write music in a university...Sure, I want my surgery done by someone that got practice and my lawyer the same. To say that the bubble is long burst on academia having the "cutting" edge is an understatement. When all the dark ages had was dark, learning to read, write, do math, epically important. The conscious mind is not developed in this setting. Statistical fact, your job and your degree have little in common. This is a black hole more than a rabbit hole, moving on...The issue isn't that mainstream universities don't know, they do, and they act exactly like the inquisition in complete hubris on a mountain of stupidity and at this point to quote LetterKenny, "It's Fucking Embarrassing!" (Watch that show)(Period)

HOW THIS MARRIAGE WORKS UNIVERSITIES & CHRISTIANITY

The Bible says, Adam and Eve are real, the garden of Eden is in the Fertile Crescent Therefore all life started there whether christian believer or atheist. The atheist can call the garden of eden, the "fertile Crescent" and now for academics, western academics, or an atheist can accept Adam and Eve as a story about the origin of humanity in the Bible had a kernel of truth. The idea that we were monkeys in africa, evolved and moved on is plausible. Peace on earth. Science and the beliefs in the Bible and the modern western world moves on. As long as that is the story.

If man shows up millions of years earlier, and everywhere as we will clearly show, then christian faith, and christian like religions will not play nice with non believers and academia. There is a long standing zero win, mutually assured nuclear destruction between christianity and Western Academia. Western academia has a check mate if it wasn't for personal careers being built on a fable of a historical record. They could just admit it and start building a new paradigm with the truth. For some christians, finding humans all the way back shows that the Bible is still true and validates Adam and Eve. Some believers like to come up with a 10,000-year-old number. Seriously, they believe the whole earth is 10,000 years old. This is not a rabbit hole you should put at the top of the Breyer pile. There are some believes that see the science of god, including millions of years and the example of the garden of eden is not 10,000 years old but as old as the earth and seems to prove in a non christian scientific way Biblical truth. It's billions of years old and therefor Adam and Eve still happened and they are open to the idea that it wasn't 10,000 years ago but millions or billions. The key point for christians is that god made the earth, god made Adam and Eve in the beginning. The belief being that we were not evolved from bacteria and simple cell creatures.

Without the out of Africa theory, it falls apart for academia and this ever silent agreement with christianity. They would have to discuss their failure to see epic amounts of history. The cost of the degrees, the syllabus changes and the plaques will cost a lot to change in the museums too. Not to mention a number of bad grades given to students not listening when we explained the land bridge to North America. A lot of re-education of teachers and a lot of arm chair academics that have to learn new things. This is another rabbit hole and one that is not a new conversation, nor one we can burn new pages on. This is the elephant standard academia has pushed all facts that don't fit because that is where the Garden of eden was as validated through christian based, Western European archaeology. Proving that the cities of the Bible are real, it validates that the biblical stories are true. It helps validate the religion, which is a good reason to dig up the Egypt that Moses sets his people free in. Facts however, are not free to be free. Apparently the juice is not worth the squeeze for academia

ONCE UPON A TIME, ARCHAEOLOGY:

To the history of archaeology, as South America becomes a spotlight, lets look at a history of archaeology by Father of South American Archaeology, German Archaeologist Max Uhle, born March 25, 1856 - May 11, 1944. He was born in Dresden, Germany. His first trip to research was in Argentina and Bolivia he worked for Konigliches Museum of Volkerkunde in Berlin. He published "The Ruins of Tiahuanaco in the Highlands of Ancient Peru" in the same year, 1892. Uhle's work is considered the first in depth scientific work on Tiwanaku, Bolivia. Sponsored later by Mrs. Phoebe Hearst, Randolph Hearst's mother (think, Rose Bud!) he excavated at Pachacamac off the coast of Peru, Mochica, Chimu. His work is still a 101 for studying South America. He also worked in paleontological excavations finding a complete mastodon and obsidian and bone tools with pottery shards. He excavated the Emeryville shell mound in San Francisco Bay. They named the school in Arequipa, Peru after Max.

At the turn of the century he did a lecture about the origins of Archaeology which in turn gives us all a crash course. This lecture does sum up our zero to in the know of how archaeology evolved, helping us further in how we are where we are missing the broad side of the barn and ancient high technology.

TRANSLATOR'S NoTB.-In 1923 Uhle delivered a series of four general lectures on archaeological theory and method at the Universidad Central del Ecuador in Quito. They were delivered in Spanish, apparently from notes, for the published text (1924b, c, 1925b) is based on a stenographic record rather than on the author's manuscript. ...

History of Archaeology by Uhle lecture excerpt...LECTURE 1, MAY 9, 1923

..." *archaios, "primitive," and with the derived meaning "ancient."*

It was Winckelmann, the founder of Classical archaeology, who, about the middle of the eighteenth century, invented the term "archaeology" to designate the study of ancient Greek and Roman art. In its classical sense, archaeology still means the study of Greek and Roman antiquities,such as the legal system, state organization and administration, customs, and rites, and is based primarily on the evidence relating to these subjects found in the works of Greek and Roman writers. One of its branches is the study of monuments and artistic objects, facilitated by excavations of various kinds of remains, such as buildings or buried cities like Pompeii.

The purpose of these studies is exclusively that of making clearer to us the character of ancient civilization and the beauty of ancient art, but generally without any preoccupation with explaining the origin of civilization itself. It was for this reason that the excavations of Schliemann at Troy and Mycenae caused so much surprise when they showed that Classical civilization could be explained by the development of others.

There is now also a "Christian archaeology" for the purpose of finding the sources of the art style which now dominates the religion. Its purpose is strictly limited, like that of the science previously discussed; and neither of these can properly be compared for breadth of aims with "prehistoric archaeology," a branch of learning which studies all lost civilizations and which concentrates on the whole history of man is also called.

The difference between the aims of this last science and those of the ones previously mentioned is most clearly seen if we examine its origin and note the difference of time which was necessary to its establishment.

Modern archaeology matured about a hundred years after the origin of the archaeology concerned with Greek art. All branches of modern archaeology were products of the development of modern science, which, as is well known, stimulated almost simultaneously the most diverse branches of learning. However, in 1828 the first remains of fossil man were discovered; and the first essay on "The origin of primitive society," written in 1829, was published in France a few years later. Interest in a general empirical concept of the world had meanwhile been growing stronger daily in other fields with historical interests.

In 1804 Alexander von Humboldt returned from his American journeys, and his researches had a very broad influence on the development of science. The German scholar Grotefend had already deciphered the first cuneiform inscription in 1802. The French scholar Champollion followed him in 1822 with the reading of the famous "Rosetta stone" in Egypt. These discoveries indicate that a curiosity with respect to the ancient civilizations of Babylonia and Egypt had already been aroused.

Soon thereafter, Humboldt began the series of great scientific travels in America.

The first to follow his example were Prince Maximilian of Wied and Spix and Martius in Brazil between 1815 and 1820. In 1831 Lord Kingsborough published his costly work containing reproductions of Mexican art. Alcides d'Orbigny was at the ruins of Tiahuanaco in Bolivia in 1843 and made notes there which were later published in his great book of South American travel.

In 1841 John L. Stephens' work entitled "Incidents of Travel in Central America, Chiapas and Yucatan" produced a well-known revolution in people's ideas about the importance of the ancient monuments of Mexico. J.J.von Tschudi published his work on Peruvian antiquities in Vienna in 1851. About the same time, Lewis Morgan, Squier, Davis, and Schoolcraft started the study of the antiquities of the United States.

In 1858 Desjardins published valuable information about ancient Peruvian ruins, and even before this there had appeared the great travel work of Castelnau with many illustrations of ruins and of Peruvian artifacts. In 1866 [sic] E. G. Squier began his exploration of the monuments of Peru, the results of which, published some eleven years later, even today give the impression of a completely modern study.

Thereafter, through the excavations of Wilhelm Reiss and Alphons Stübel in the Necropolis of Ancon, whole Peruvian civilizations were brought out into the light of day, ensuring a continued interest in ancient varieties of culture which was no longer in any danger of declining.

Long before, systematic excavations had already begun in the Tigris and Euphrates region and in Egypt. Botta, and after him Layard, undertook large-scale excavations in Babylonia and Assyrian 1842.

Meanwhile, the study of prehistoric European man had also developed in a surprising fashion. In 1836 Thomsen, in Denmark, published his classification of primitive history into stone, bronze, and iron ages. The Swedes and the Swiss followed with their relative chronology. The French undertook another line of study, working into history from geology, the so-called "palaeo-ethnology" form- ing the link which joined these two fields closely together.

It was Boucher de Perthes, the famous antiquarian of Abbeville, who discovered the first evidence of the existence of man during the Diluvium, or Quaternary period of the earth, in 1836 in the Somme Valley near Amiens. He was derided at first by the Paris geologists, but finally secured full recognition of his extraordinary observations in 1859, with the aid of the respected English geologist Charles Lyell.

On the occasion of a fall in the level of the lake of Zurich In 1853, as the result of a drought, the whole civilization of a primitive people appeared for the first time in the lake bottom; and excavations near the salt pans of Hallstadt, Austria, begun as early as 1846, revealed the full range of a civilization of the bronze and iron ages.

The theories of Darwin on the development of species and the transformation of types gave a notable stimulus to interest in the evolution of the human race from the more primitive forms to the historic ones of our time, beginning in the 1860's. Then, in 1866, a Palaeo-ethnological Congress convening in Neufchatel gave shape to the new science. The following year, at a new congress meeting in Paris, it appeared with the name of "prehistoric archaeology," its definitive title hence forward.

Museums were also being built everywhere, following the urging of the Dutchman von Siebold, who had recommended the installation of "collections of archaeology and ethnology" as early as 1843.

The only undesirable feature of the situation was that at that period ethnology was still considered the more important branch of knowledge, with archaeology as its Assistant, charged with the task of illustrating the character of lost civilizations by means of works of art.

Consequently, the excavations in Babylonia and Egypt had, at first, no other purpose than that of bringing to life again the civilizations of those regions. It was more curiosity than scholarly interest which dictated the nature of the expeditions of that time.

Similarly, the first American archaeological collections deposited in the museums of ethnology served only the purpose of giving an idea of the greatness of the civilizations represented and contributed nothing to their study. As a consequence, the museums acquired chiefly collections assembled with the assistance of huaqueros (pot hunters), consisting of mixed specimens without indications provenience and selected to eliminate the less attractive objects. Cultural differences were not indicated in these collections, and consequently their formation implied the destruction of the cemeteries from which they were made rather than a contribution to our knowledge of the civilizations they represented.

No one thought, at that time, of the possibility of reconstructing the types of the civilizations involved, much less their application to the reconstruction of history.

A scholar of the caliber of Adolf Bastian, who traveled through the chief

American countries of ancient civilization and took back with him extensive new materials for the exhibits on ancient civilizations in the Berlin Museum, sadly summarizes the scientific result of the observations he made during his travels by saying that wherever one looks on this continent there appear the remains of great civilizations of the past, but for lack of writing it will never be possible in the whole of future time to reconstruct their history from the tiny crumbs that have remained."

Isn't it interesting, opposite almost? The tiny crumbs are going to make it impossible to reconstruct their history, and when has that stopped unqualified builders and structural engineers like archaeologists from pasting whole monuments together in Mexico, to Puma Punko. They moved original blocks, didn't document, just set things were they thought they should go. This was done from Stonehenge to Egypt. My fav, every statue found, a fertility goddess. Anyway, continuing with Max's Lecture with geology...

> ''....*Geology and paleontology give constant aid to our science, determining the age of strata which contain valuable human remains, either by the succession of geological layers alone or by the age of the fossil animals or plants which they contain. We have already noted that in France the science of most ancient man took geology as its point of departure.*
>
> *...the beginning what his goal is, and his goal can only be one of a historical nature. The well-known Egyptologist Flinders Petrie states the postulates in this way: "The old saying that a man finds what he is looking for in a subject, is too true; or if he has not enough insight to ensure finding what he looks for, it is at least sadly true that he does not find anything that he does not look for" [Petrie,p.1].*"

....on history of the age of humans Max Uhle continues...

> "*Florentino Ameghino, for example, was the author of a theory that the human race originated in the preglacial period in Argentina. This theory has already been rejected by North American geologists and anthropologists, who proved that the geological levels which contain these human remains are of more modern origin, that the types of skulls found correspond to those of modern Indians, and that the artificial deformations of the skulls assigned to the Tertiary and Diluvial epochs are comparable to those used in the period of civilization. The study of the types of deformations and the determination of the period when their use began in a particular part of the world is, of course, also a matter of great interest to archaeology.*
>
> *In the soil of the Argentine pampas, fragments of pottery have been found beside the bones of extinct animals such as the glyptodon, an association which appears to indicate that men of advanced culture were contemporary with such fossils. But archaeology must show that this pottery certainly originated long after the Quaternary, and hence suggests that the animals in question survived much*

nearer to our own time rather than that men of advanced culture lived in the Diluvial epoch contemporary with these animals.

Similarly, it was claimed that some finely made stone mortars were found with a human skull in the Tertiary or preglacial layers of a California gold mine; but they could not have belonged to that period because man only began to manufacture such objects late and in relatively modern times.""

This is something Michael Cremo and Forbidden archaeology tackle, and we are going to look at it. Here in the middle of this lecture he is flat out denying the existence of these finds because it just can't be true. It just can't be accepted that the skull was of the Tertiary layers. Not the facts, just can't be true, so... "it wasn't me!"

Lecture continues...

"Flinders Petrie, the famous Egyptologist, has attempted to set up certain rules dealing with this subject. The twelfth chapter of his useful book Methods and Aims in Archaeology deals with archaeological evidence and begins as follows:

The nature of proof is more complex than it seems to be at first sight. True enough, all proof is merely a matter of common sense; it does not appeal to any different faculty. And though a proof may follow as simply as possible from the facts, yet it cannot be understood by one who is not familiar with the facts to begin with. Trigonometry is the most obvious common sense to any one familiar with the formulae; and the formulae themselves are only common sense to any one who takes the trouble to argue them through. Yet, for all that, trigonometry is not obvious to the ignorant. In the same way the evidences about the past of man are simple and clear when the facts and methods from which they are deduced are already known. Yet it requires a good familiarity with the material before the conclusions can be felt to be self-evident results "

Despite denying the existence of finds that he made himself and the knowledge of things being found all the way back to the quaternary he then talks about Flinders opinion of the COMMON SENSE of it and if you don't know, you wouldn't understand. Michael Cremo's point about what archaeologists say to facts, if you don't know, we will tell you how old it is, is not common sense yet prevalent in the culture. It is by this Egyptologist, Petrie that common sense goes out the window and so with Max Uhle, he had heard of the great ages of the finds in South America, America, and Europe. He on one hand substantiates findings of ancient man himself By Boucher de Perthes in Diluvium, or Quaternary period of the earth, in 1836 in the Somme Valley near Amiens.

At the same time acknowledges the obvious Chinese connections to South America also. Max Uhle sums up the history of archaeology and the awareness of the histories of people and not just the art of an ancient society can be found or reverse engineered. Touching on the focuses of the christian faith to search archaeology for faith finds.

In court, if you are going to have a biased, for any reason, lawyers, judges, jurors, they are removed, if they are to be suspected in a case of having a bias. How is it not done with Tells? On digs, when you have known published academics claiming something cannot be something when the proof is there, how are they allowed to fund or manage digs? If their agenda is religious, again can their motives be trusted for finding everything? Not just the truth they want to find?

Max Uhle, at the XXIII International Congress Of Americanists in New York, Sept. 1928, gives three papers. He reports on his general theories on American cultural development, on the Temple of the Sun at Cuzco in 1905 and on a very curious discovery he had made at Alangasi east of Quito. On the mastodon again, the idea of Pleistocene being the date of reference struck him as ridiculous. There was painted pottery, there were many details and notes. Uhle explains in the papers that the mastodon must have survived till more recently in the Ecuadorian highlands rather then the find represents modern man in the Pleistocene. Uhle is happy with the idea that the Pre Peruvian civilizations arrived from China fyi. This is not discussed today, despite many towns having Chinese influence in their names and words being similar in some tribes vocabulary. This is another western academic elephant.

"There is thus nothing in the types of civilizations which is not capable of throwing light on the character and ancestry of civilizations, and it should be the duty of the archaeologist to omit no observation on any object he finds, so that his results will contribute to the history of civilizations."

Max is acknowledging the idea of Chinese migrations to South America. This is not an archaeological thread that is documented on the history channel is it? Yet here we are with straight sideways talk about nothing should be omitted. Yet he is.

MORE SOIL VERIFICATION

Max Uhle during one of his lectures points out, "These shell mounds, of which there are some also in the region of Santa Elena on the coast of Ecuador, are important to the archaeologist because they are among the most ancient remains of man, giving evidence frequently of periods different from those represented elsewhere. So, for example, the lowest levels of a shell mound at Taltal contained stone implements of the earliest known European types, some fifty thousand years old; hand axes and daggers hitherto not found in other sites in America and belonging in consequence to a period which in America also was one of the earliest in relative age. The explanation is that fishing is the most natural way of life for primitive man, and fishermen cluster in small settlements at certain places on the coast and leave us evidence of their earlier presence in the shell mounds.

Shell mounds have another unusual interest because they developed slowly through different periods and reveal to us in their stratification the way in which cultures lowly developed."

"The visible remains of cultivated fields representing an advanced agriculture form another subject for study. There are enormous quantities of terraces built for this purpose in the whole Andean region between Ecuador and Argentina, especially in Peru. These terraces are made by modifying the slopes of hills, which are too steep in their natural state to be used for agriculture, in to a series of steps rising one above another, with or without the constructions of walls, and with corresponding leveling of the soil. Along the Oroya railroad the traveler can count sometimes as many as 170 or 200 steps or terraces rising directly one from another on hillsides rising 500 meters and more above the river. They give excellent evidence of the millennial antiquity of human agricultural industry in these regions. Terraces representing the work of ancient man can also be observed in various ravines in the province of Loja."

Max's point on the size of the agriculture lends more proof to the LIDAR Scans from Guatemala point to things we are currently overwhelmed in comprehending. Millions would need food, and in the inherited lands of a high tech ancient past society these agricultural lands have been repurposed and used. Michael Tellinger points to similar terracing in Southern Africa going on 400,000 sq. kilometers.

One intriguing report surfaced in an American journal called *The Geologist* dated December 1862:

"In Macoupin County, Illinois, the bones of a man were recently found on a coalbed capped with two feet of slate rock, ninety feet below the surface of the earth. . . The bones, when found, were covered with a crust or coating of hard glossy matter, as black as coal itself, but when scraped away left the bones white and natural."

The coal in which the remains were found have been dated at between 320 and 286 million years old, which, despite a lack of supporting evidence and little information on the discovery, is certainly worthy of inclusion here."

What do you do with these finds? It's an anomaly, it's a mystery, it's pre-history. Isn't that lazy, it's not education, it's pre-education? Isn't that preschool? Cremo/Thompson have many finds like Uhle. Uhle is seeing the immensity of the soil finds, the cultivation, the mastodon find, and there is a mental melt down to grasp the overwhelming evidence of finds that great societies beyond the written record and or studied are here.

HOW OLD ARE WE AGAIN?

"....One very good reason is that no one is looking for it. Evidence for intentional human work on bone might easily escape the attention of a scientist not actively searching for it. If a paleoanthropologist is convinced that toolmaking human beings did not exist in the Middle Pliocene, he is not likely to give much thought to the exact nature of markings on fossil bones from that period." -Forbidden Archaeology

86

Which brings us to Michael Cremo and Richard L. Thompson authors of Forbidden Archeology. After 10 years of research, thinking it would be originally a 9 month book project, revisiting the actual dig sites of many of the researchers they write about, looking at the finds of past archaeologists, they document over 700 examples of finds of human record established by standard academia. They show established finds of anatomically correct humans dating back millions of years. Their book should be on everyone's shelves and basic introduction to our human history. Imagine the greatest baseball player of all time for hitting home runs of truth, Michael Cremo and Richard L. Thompson are it.

Michael Cremo and Thompson investigations into finds that put man easily back to the Tertiary epoch like Boucher de Perthes in Diluvium. The Quaternary period of the earth, in 1836 Max Uhle acknowledges de Perthes yet rejects the finds that Cremo/Thompson verify themselves by simply stating that it is not possible to find those works in that period. This is a common thing, just don't go to the site, don't look at the physical evidence so you rely on peer agreement. The individuals that have found these evidence range from geologists to anthropologists, each should be named on a public monument of truth while the detractors should be listed with the worst of humanity. One of the most credible researchers studied by Cremo and Thompson in this body slamming fight hitting into the timeline of a out of africa story comes Virgina Steen-McIntyre. Cremo has long championed this female Geologist's case that deserves a marble statue for many reasons. As a reminder of the shame of academia and to the perseverance and Testament to the truth of our great human antiquity and prior advanced status.

A site found in Hueyatlaco, Mexico in the 1960's southeast of Mexico City, had stratigraphic geological evidence dating the tools in that layer to at least 250,000 years. A U.S. Geological team was brought in to date the site. Virgina Steen-McIntyre of Washington State University. They used multiple methods and the date was 250,000 years. These tools that were found were not simple tools, they were not eoliths, these tools, in that layer, with that date, would mean in North America, the complete change of everything the anthropological world tells everyone what they know about humanity. It is a total house of cards. These tools are found, in africa, for the first time, approximately 100,000 years ago according to esteemed academia.

This seems like a random middle point in proof of our human antiquity but this example embodies the scope and breadth of the problem with standard academia. If you only got one thing, one Lynch pin, one keystone to the history of humanity not adding up, this is a stab to the face of persistent victorian western theories. This one example if you are not a sheeple should make you go, well if this site is real, if these tools are what they are, then do what Flinders Petrie and Max Uhle said to do. Do what your moral center should be telling you to do, question, look and seek our true human history. This one example burns the established history. Despite the Piri Reis map, the math of the past, the examples coming up, this one piece destroys the out of africa series AS IT IS CURRENTLY DESCRIBED. Our true past is buried and we all ask who are we, why do we have amnesia, we can feel it even in the most logical people, that everything doesn't add up.

The Hueyatlaco site and the near by site of El Horns all had initial estimates of 245,000 years. Just like Cuicuilco, our earlier volcanic covered temple dating to 8000 years, there was a volcanic layer on Hueyatlaco. Using Fission tracks found in crystals of the volcanic deposit, the minimum for the layer above the tools was 260,000 years old to 960,000 years old. There was a mud layer called Tetela dated to 170,000 to 570,000 years. Cremo sites, Malde and Steen-McIntyre 1981, p. 419 in chapter 5.4.4.2 of Forbidden Archaeology. The artifacts were found under 10 meters of sediment fyi. 33 ft. This for any geologist as Steen-McIntyre and her team saw, as any geologist would, that it would have taken at least 150,000 years to get to that point.

Remember way back we started with a quote about ancient Mayan populations and development in South America as being "grossly underestimated"? Same Cremo chapter 5.4.4.2, Roald Fryxell said in an article on November 13, 1973, "We have no reason to suppose that over decades, actually hundreds of years, of research in archaeology in the Old and New World our understanding of human prehistory is so inaccurate that we suddenly discover that our past understanding is all wrong...On the other hand, the more geological information we've accumulated, the more difficult it is to explain how multiple methods of dating which are independent of each other might be in error by the same magnitude"

How bad could Virginia Steen-McIntyre be treated for daring to give facts? Remember the inquisition? Thought we were past that in our neat, modern iPad driven classrooms? Attack her character, accuse her of incompetence, just don't publish it or have it bounce from publisher to publisher and just don't publish. Stone wall the findings. It will make anyone sick to read the extensive fact burning by the academic system on her find. Our purpose is to point this out, if you want to travel that rabbit hole do it. There is nothing like a good internet rant, just one worth having. This is a site and it is delayed into the 1980's for publication. It gets more medieval. Despite example after example of Pliocene, Miocene, and earlier periods from Cremo and Thompson, and Max Uhle the father of South American archaeology, Roy Schlemon, so many researchers from Canada to Southern California showing ancient man way back outside of desirable theoretical degree programs, here we sit and your reading, pondering is there some truth in it? There are tools of neolithic nature found in Australia!

There are many places and examples you can go and find documented evidences of ancient humanity. In another example Cremo sites the Foxhall Jaw discovery. This is a human jaw found at Foxhall, England in 1855 at least 16 ft deep. This layer dates to 2.5 million years. The disbelievers just didn't believe it, a jaw that earlier should be more "primitive."

A complete human skull in Buenos Aire, Argentina was found in a Pliocene layer. This puts humans at 1-1.5 million years in South America, sorry land bridge theory people. In a quarry on the Avenue de Clichy, Paris, parts of a skull, tibia, foot bones and femur were discovered by Eugene Bertrand in 1868. Go Victorian researchers! This layer would make the skeleton approximately 330,000 years old. The theory at the time was that Neanderthals were not believed to be in the Pleistocene till 300,000 to 150,000 years ago....so the Clichy remains dating to over 300,000 is a epic swing and miss to creating a new dialog if you aren't willing to admit that your straight up wrong. No beuno. Hard nooo.

Here we go again, 1911, another modern human skeleton was found beneath a glacial boulder clay layer near Ipswich, England by J. Reid Moir. This would put it at 400,000 years old. The layer that the skeleton was found in was recorded by the British Geological Survey as an intact layer of glacial clay. Everyone is using science not as a foundation for truth but as a highlighter to their preferred theories.

The discovery of anomalous skeletons suggests humanity may be older than we think. Source: CC0
*This article was taken from the chapter 'Bones and Stones' in **The Myth of Man** by J.P. Robinson.*
y **J.P. Robinson**
HideReferences
Robinson, J.P. 2018. *The Myth of Man, CreateSpace Independent Publishing Platform*
Keith, Arthur, 1928. *The Antiquity of Man, Vol. 1, Williams and Norgate Ltd., London*
Ragazzoni, Giuseppe 1880   *La collina di Castenedolo, solto il rapporto antropologico, geologico ed agronomico*
Sergi, Giuseppe, 1884. L'uomo terziario in Lombardia *Archivio per L'Antropologia e la Etnologia*

Forbidden archaeology:

> *"De Mortillet (1883, p. 86) said that the layers of clay in which the flints were found were of Early Miocene or even Oligocene age. This would push back the presence of human beings in France to around 20–25 million years before the present. If this sounds impossible, one should ask oneself why. If the answer is that modern science's ideas about human evolution prevent one from seriously considering such a thing, one should honestly admit that one is allowing preconceived notions to unduly influence one's perception of facts and that this is unscientific. One with faith in the scientific method should maintain a willingness to change one's notions, even the most dearly held, in the face of facts that contradict them."*

Hear no evil, see no evil, speak no evil. There is no need to look for these facts as you dig if your education of origin is a christian judeo evolutionary 19th century school. All the supporting literature you have been graded on is based on supporting theories not the facts on the ground. Remember life is out of africa, garden of eden. Beat that horse.

Professor Giuseppe Ragazzoni was gathering fossil shells in the Pliocene strata in a pit of Colle de Vento in the alps near Brescia. He also starts finding pieces of cranium, filled with coral cemented with the layer of clay. He found other bones, the thorax and limbs that he identified as human. Of course this is treated by geologists and scientists, as heresy. No Pliocene age could be accepted so it must have been from a burial. So Ragazzzoni was pissed, and was able to note further finds in the clay including more jaw fragments, teeth, ribs, legs, arms, feet, backbones, all in a layer modern geologists place at 3-4 million years. All of these bones showed penetrated layers of clay, small shells and coral were attached to the bones, this was no way a recent burial.

In February 1880 Ragazzoni is informed of a complete human female skeleton is found. In 1883 they were confirmed to be bones of a person living during the Pliocene period of the Tertiary. Confirming the find was the anatomist Professor Giuseppe Sergi of the University of Rome. He studied the remains at the Technical Institute of Brescia. Commenting on the find, Sergi wrote,

"The tendency to reject, by reason of theoretical preconceptions, any discoveries that can demonstrate a human presence in the Tertiary is, I believe, a kind of scientific prejudice. Natural science should be stripped of this prejudice."

'By means of a despotic scientific prejudice, call it what you will, every discovery of human remains in the Pliocene has been discredited.'

Michael Cremo goes looking for research and information on some of these finds and the researchers that do the work, it is a needle in the haystack.

"...we searched libraries, but turned up no works under Ribeiro's name and found ourselves at a dead end. Sometime later, Ribeiro's name turned up again, this time in the 1957 English edition of Fossil Men by Boule and Vallois, who rather curtly dismissed the work of the nineteenth-century Portuguese geologist. We were, however, led by Boule and Vallois to the 1883 edition of Le Préhistorique, by de Mortillet, who gave a favorable report of Ribeiro's discoveries, in French. By tracing out the references mentioned in de Mortillet's footnotes, we gradually uncovered a wealth of remarkably convincing original reports in French journals of archeology and anthropology from the latter part of the nineteenth century. The search for this buried evidence was very illuminating, demonstrating how the scientific establishment treats reports of facts that no longer conform to accepted views. Keep in mind that for most current students of paleoanthropology, Ribeiro and his discoveries simply do not exist. You have to go back to textbooks printed over 30 years ago to find even a mention of him. Did Ribeiro's work really deserve to be buried and forgotten? We shall present the facts and allow readers to form their own conclusions.

Carlos Ribeiro was not an amateur. In 1857, he was named to head the Geological Survey of Portugal, and he would also be elected to the Portuguese Academy of Sciences. During the years 1860–63, he conducted studies of stone..."

Look at the effort Cremo has to put in to find evidence. Look at what Virginia had to do to just try to stay on her find. Then there is a language barrier, in French, they had to look for translations, footnotes. Uhle's lectures were translated from Spanish, and Uhle was German! The barrier is the language this time, others the omission in "learned" institutions just deleting information that contradicts the established story. There were stone pestles found in California gods mines, there are finds in Canada equally ancient.

It is important that we revise and include the archaeologist that we have found and who have been lost or buried strictly due to the religion of archaeology. This act by academia is no less then the murder of our history for personal and institutional condoned human historical genocide. Drastically told right?

There is an assumption in the English speaking world that Egypt and Stonehenge are very important. The western world is well traveled. Whether due to communism and the Cold War or other world conflicts, there are sites in Russia, formally eastern bloc countries that have large stone circle ruins, buried cities, glyphs like Nazca, and pyramids yet less known to us in the west. There are also western sites that fall out of desired research. Let's take the Roman Empire, there are huge megalithic ruins that all sit under more recent ruins they call roman or greek. The above example that Cremo points out is common, the left hand doesn't even care what the right or the left is doing if academia doesn't speak the language or have a successful English speaking tv shows talking about how important the site is. We just have a massive barrier to knowledge in the east.

Angry birds, you know the game, the placebo, the endorphins from thousands of hours of knocking down walls and objects. There is no point to this game then to get through one more day of working at a crappy job. There are a zillion other games that people play. What's the point of angry birds and Egyptology? It's really fun to find things that are easy to find. The draw to Egypt is from romanticized modern western history of the pharaohs, king tut, movies, Indiana jones, etc,... why go to a site that is nothing but a pile of blocks, dust or soil. In Egypt you can fall on a find and likely a mummy. Even in Peru, Bolivia, all of South America shows advanced constructions. Yet all the research goes into rebuilding a pot, a thatched roof town. Going to Russia if you aren't Russian and researching the large megalithic under ground structures, or buried ruins isn't easy if you don't speak Russian. Russian ain't easy FYI.

Burning or delaying Steen-McIntyre, revoking all permits by the Brazilian Government, the Smithsonian not accepting any history outside of manifest destiny, it is endless on the obvious inquisition of it. There is just straight up war against any history not inline with this absurd story we have been graded on.

When the data set doesn't work, the bringers of truth are fired, defunded and called lunatics. Cremo and Thompson tried to get permission to photograph and publish the tools found from Hueyatlaco and were told as long as they were willing to cite it as "Lunatic Fringe date". (Forbidden Archaeology Chp. 5.4.4.3). The lunacy and hubris is with the academic religion.

There are sites at Calico, with bones of animals and a date of at least 180,000 years, again met with silence and opposition. Why aren't current anthropologists learning this, why don't know? There is a general lack of knowledge according to Cremo with new anthropologists and archaeologists about these finds. They don't have books that list the finds, the study books for their 250,000 degrees don't have them in it. If they want to pass a class and pay for that degree, stick with what you are taught.

Finding ancient technology is a couple steps past just acknowledging that you aren't staring at a large tomb that no body has been found in the Great Pyramid system is likely a power and communication plant. Possibly other things but let's not blow the excitement of the genetics chapter.

"We live in an insane asylum" - John Anthony West

Along comes John Anthony West, recently passed but a great researcher, adventurer, writer, journalist, and lover of Egypt. He has this idea that the water weathering around the sphinx was much older than the current theories. West contacted a respected geologist Robert Schoch. Schoch confirmed the weathering on the sphinx indicates ancient wear and tear way older than dynastic Egypt. I saw West in a YouTube clip discuss the first time Schoch sees the Sphinx and West says about Shoch's first comments, "don't quote me but this could be 200,000 years old or maybe over 350,000 years." This is West in a video, talking about the very first look at the aging of the Sphinx with Schoch on site. Schoch and West end up in an academic inquisition. West has no credentials so the only person allowed on the panel to be roasted was Schoch. The debate of Egyptologist telling Schoch he doesn't know what he is saying has led many researchers over the years to ultimately verify that the weathering on the sphinx maybe 10,000 to 30,000 years old.

It can not be stressed enough that the weather needed for this would have to have been at the end of the last ice age and when the area was tropical. This puts the sphinx at 30-40000 years old. Then you have Schoch's initial comments, they can be explained away but he isn't someone that exaggerates. West and Schoch change a paradigm, the sphinx is acknowledged to be old, however it's a mystery. It's an enigma. The age of the Sphinx is mysteriously hovering around the age of 10,000 - 12,000 years in the vernacular now. No reason but I guess that 38,000 year is just to out there for now.

Standard archaeologist (traditionalists) that say it's not that old, that it's about 4500 years old. This fight is still ongoing. Here is some indisputable issues, the head on the Sphinx is incredibly disproportionate to the body, indicating a re-carve. The head has been theorized as being maybe Anubis originally.

Side note, if you look at a map there is a second sphinx that should match this one in an area on the Giza plateau that apparently the Egyptian authority will not issue a permit to excavate. If there is a matching one why not find it ?

There is this uncomfortable issue that keeps coming up, we don't know our past. Early Victorian researchers couldn't fathom a cell phone, they could images iron plated panels on a wood ship, they could imagine digging up things that are in the Bible. There is a mystical quality to connecting Constantinople, roman, the Middle Ages, the pre-Greek Middle Ages and the Bible. That is comfortable and manageable. The idea that history is more complicated than what they can just see outside of dinosaur bones is obvious. Deny, disclaim, ignore, it upsets the situation and degree program.

Ancient-Origins Reported in an article dated sept 3, 2017 "Skeleton Stalagmite Reveals Human Inhabitants in Mexico At Least 13,000 Years ago"

> *"A prehistoric human skeleton found on the Yucatán Peninsula is at least 13,000 years old and most likely dates from a glacial period at the end of the most recent ice age, the late Pleistocene. A German-Mexican team of researchers led by Prof. Dr Wolfgang Stinnesbeck and Arturo González González has now dated the fossil skeleton based on a stalagmite that grew on the hip bone.*

> *"The bones from the Chan Hol Cave near the city of Tulúm discovered five years ago represent one of the oldest finds of human bones on the American continent and are evidence of an unexpectedly early settlement in Southern Mexico," says Prof. Stinnesbeck, who is an earth scientist at Heidelberg University. The research findings have now been published in PLOS ONE." ..."In recent years, however, this theory is being increasingly called into question by new finds from North and South America. They indicate that people arrived there earlier, explains Prof. Stinnesbeck." ..."The water-filled caves near Tulúm on Yucatán -- a peninsula separating the Gulf of Mexico from the Caribbean Sea -- offer a rich area for finds. Seven prehistoric human skeletons have already been documented in the intricate cave system near the coast in the eastern part of the peninsula, some of them previously dated by other researchers. The caves along Yucatán's Caribbean coast were not flooded until the worldwide rise in sea level after the ice age. They contain archaeological, palaeontological and climatic information hidden there from the time before the flooding, which is extremely well preserved, according to Wolfgang Stinnesbeck."*

Oh here is a point to review, it wasn't flooded till the worldwide revise in sea level. Again Pre flood society. For your conspiracies pleasure the article continues to some more hair pulling points...

> *"It was, however, difficult to exactly determine the age of the human skeletal material using conventional radiocarbon dating, because the collagen in the bones had been completely washed out due to the long period spent in water. Prof. Stinnesbeck and his German-Mexican team of earth scientists and archaeologists therefore chose another method. By dating a stalagmite that had grown on the hip bone, they were able to narrow down the age of the human bones from the Chan Hol Cave.*

> *The analysis of the uranium-thorium isotopes gave the skeleton a minimum age of 11,300 years. However, the climatic and precipitation data stored in the stalagmite showed a clearly higher age. It is measurable in terms of oxygen and carbon isotope ratios and was compared to "environmental archive" data from other parts of the earth. Aged at least 13,000, the Chan Hol Cave inhabitant presumably dates from the Younger Dryas. "It represents one of the oldest human skeletons from America. Our data underline the great importance of the Tulúm cave finds for the debate about the settling of the continent," says Prof. Stinnesbeck.*

According to the Heidelberg earth scientist, the enormous urbanisation and growth of tourism in this region threaten the palaeontological and archaeological archives preserved in the caves. Shortly after the discovery of the human skeleton in February 2012 the site of the find was looted; unknown divers stole all the bones lying around on the ground of the cave. Only a few photos and small fragments of bones bear witness today to the original find situation. The hip bone investigated by the German-Mexican researcher team only escaped being stolen through the protection provided by the rock-hard lime-sinter of the stalagmite."

To Professor Sellew's point stealing antiquity disallows our ability to discern our past. Shortly after discovery, the site is looted. The question now is whether its basic tomb robbers or a more organized boogeyman named higher academia and government or religious institutions.

Top image: Prehistoric human skeleton in the Chan Hol Cave near Tulúm on the Yucatán peninsula prior to looting by unknown cave divers. Source: **Tom Poole/Liquid Jungle Lab**
The article, originally titled ' Human bones in south Mexico: Stalagmite reveals their age as 13,000 years old' was originally published on **Science Daily** *.*
Source: Wolfgang Stinnesbeck, Julia Becker, Fabio Hering, Eberhard Frey, Arturo González González, Jens Fohlmeister, Sarah Stinnesbeck, Norbert Frank, Alejandro Terrazas Mata, Martha Elena Benavente, Jerónimo Avilés Olguín, Eugenio Aceves Núñez, Patrick Zell, Michael Deininger. **The earliest settlers of Mesoamerica date back to the late Pleistocene.** *PLOS ONE , 2017; 12 (8): e0183345*

Our ancient past is a search and rescue, not just a 20 year journey to put pieces of pottery back together. Now enrolling more people to do more work and discover who we are is good. There is so much evidence across the planet of similar Neolithic tools, bones and human skeletal remains. The idea of the out of Africa is just a popular theory and looking ever dumber. Remember that the evidence for most of Egypt is still 90 percent buried in the desert. This is a statement made by Egyptologists.

The difficulties of digging are not just technological or finances. Here is a war example, The Eye of Africa is not traveled to due to unstable warring local governments. Locations and places around the earth that were remote and intangible to Victorian man are still inaccessible due to conflicts of people, governments, financing. To the credit of Victorian researchers, they were too stupid or just that badass tougher that they didn't have the sense not to go to some of these remote places (i.e. Col. Percy Fawcett).

There is an amazing book on human sexuality called "Sex at Dawn", credited as being the most important book on human sexuality since Sex and the Human Male was written by Kinsey.

Sex at Dawn talks about anthropologists only recently were able to study bonobos. A gentle and wonderful monkey that lives mainly deep in the war torn conflict ridden Congo. This monkey is much more closely related to humans than the savage, murderous chimpanzee. However chimps were studied first and psychologists and researchers use the relationship of chimps to explain human monogamy, our interpersonal relations and advice is given based on this research. One of the points of the book is that relying on what we have studied historically doesn't make it fit human evolution or behavior.

Simply basing human behavior on what was available to study is a start. The true relationship to humanity, sexual relationships, and how we are truly designed to relate to each other is different then explained. If we haven't researched something there has always been a trend to take what we have researched and squeeze our ideas into facts however unrelated. Round hole, square pegging and putting theories before facts.

WHY IS HISTORY SO CAMOUFLAGED?

If an advanced society fell, the people that would take over and repopulate a site. Half destroyed or have built? A tuff tribe likely having survived by not being in these population centers at the time of Great War or disaster, could easily come in and pick up the rubble. Just like at Machu Picchu.

There is know going around a simple assumption that has been out there about tribal and remote people, that they are stupid. Consistently they have the hands on ability survive if a first world nuked itself. They know how to grow food, treat wounds, live and build shelter from what we smartphone users would have no clue. They are better equipped throughout history tribes have lived with a more "modern society" simultaneously.

Imagine a huge high tech billion-dollar cruise ship of today, with sonar, radar, satellite and TVs, wifi, espresso makers, kitchens, bars, a city on the water with an engine system and workshops, wood shops, tech shops, welding torches, plasma cutters, Cnc machines. There is an incredible amount of technology specific to the ship and then there is all the technology of what the passengers bring on board. iPhones, androids, laptops, iPad, even retro tape decks, recording devices and bikes, games, shuffleboard, slides and pools and chemicals to maintain them, medical and surgical units on board. Safes, banks, money, stores with jewelry pots, gifts.

The ship is beached, the world as it is known ends. Along comes another culture and they find one of the emergency escape dinghies. They piecemeal it into useful items. There is a flashlight with a battery. It still has a charge and there is someone just smart enough in this group to re-engineer the battery and they create new batteries. Now look at the Baghdad battery and what can you tell now knowing that it came from a higher advanced society. Well the Baghdad battery had to be a reengineering as there was no more metal batteries but the applications to simpler metal plating would only have needed a smaller charge. The more advanced flashlight knowledge is lost. The concept of current is still available and the application technology is to plate gold on per say tin. A battery in a pot is possible. The technology of a metal battery culture is added to obscurity and we find one Baghdad battery, sorry, like 5 that we know of. Is it likely there was only one, no?

This is one example where the technology of the past is repurposed and the society that created it reduced to mystic feelings and essentially ignorant rubble. The applications of directional maps important so how did the maps like the Piri Ries map come about except from a higher society? Theories now imagine the dumbest non high tech way to understand longitude and latitude and move big blocks.

Again we have a ship, the emergency maps were found and applied, re-written the ancient geo satellites are unknown. The cultures re-emerging would re-learn eventually what an ancient advanced culture did before but would they be smart enough to look for ancient satellites?

Let's delete the academia created stories about every object they find in the earth. I was in my first year of college and every statue I saw I was told it was a fertility goddess according to my first Art history class. I immediately thought this is ridiculous, what if it was some ancient kids 8th grade pottery class and he made a statue with big boobs because it was funny or sexy? To the point of pinholes, there is this assumption that if all your finding is rock tools and simple stuff that there was nothing advanced. Focus on finding a pestle and look for a loin cloth.

Leaving this to standard academia or waiting for them to get it, is a waste of time.

We are standing on the precipice of knowledge that is so obviously available to the common man that we can step in and finish. Academia is not even scratching at the deep pool of truth we are at now. There is clear evidence that there was more to know even then but in retrospect it is obvious, childly obvious that we are trying to fit an earth history to our christian western beliefs.

Becoming aware of the disagreements amongst academics and their personal, what should be criminal hoarding of findings of our past should be a nightly news story. The hoarding of knowledge, the dropping or filtration of knowledge is clouding our past.

It is easy to just start grabbing at the slivers of truth and knowledge left in myths, legends, religions of all the post flood cultures. People have had the same questions, where are we from, what's our story? Post flood is a scramble of all the human races and ideologies.

When everyone has a video camera and in many ways is smarter or more worldly than a Victorian researcher, you are going to get real evidence that has accomplished the obvious. We got our story wrong. We should be discerning of we are told in the current dogma of our past story and what has actually been found. We need to know that the things found might fit in a larger historical picture then what is being shown. To know that the closer we come to understanding our longer unknown past, the better we can be preparing for our future.

ABOUT EVOLUTION AND HUMANS AND ANIMALS A LITTLE....AND SOME MORE INTELLIGENT ARCHAEOLOGY

The number of species of animal is unknown. There are, very few bodies found of any type of ancient animal, insect, fish, human, or human type like denisovan,

Neanderthal other humanoid related evolutionary ancestors. Not because evolution isn't possible but because the pointers to say this is our ancestor is still unknown. Evolution is a theory. This is Beethoven's 9th symphony torn up and redistributed in pieces. So you just have to pull all the pieces tape it all together and you have the music again. In genetic technology, there is not a strand of DNA where you can say this is the human symphony and these are our ancestors and here is the music to prove it. There are almost no genetic differences between us being a pig or a pig being human. Genetics is interesting in that there are only a "few" differences between any species. We are similar to worms sharing some genetic similarities.

What's the point? So remember the pinhole view? This is not a case of well because we don't know, the theory I am putting forth must be the answer. There are scientific means just currently out of reach that can help us with finds from the past and future. For instance, bone fragments from humans to animals laying in site, that are ancient can crumble to dust as they are exposed. This has been noted by any Archaeologist at any time point in the field. Our general ability to analyze this is limited. The dusted pieces are brushed aside and whole pieces are kept. Unfortunately, it isn't a priority to photo a site as it is dug or video it. This has led to an uncountable loss of information by not doing in situ photos and visual documentation. Just like the dusted genetic material, it's lost from neglect. The archaeologist isn't considering a pending technology that could clarify from dust.

You know it should be noted that all these finds that show an extreme age of antiquity of man, didn't happen once, or twice, it happened immediately after we started digging up our past and it happened to appear in almost every layer of soil.

If there was a highly advanced society living at the simultaneous time of these early finds. If anything is clear from these simple stone implements, then it's their existence near more advanced cultures throughout history. Some or all of these implements may be invasive after the higher culture fell. Or it could be that they moved in as the more advanced culture moved or was reduced. Or a new semi more advanced culture came or evolved from the remnants of a more advanced culture that had fallen. The ancient more advanced society also may have observed these less advanced humans and left them alone.

Bearing in mind a better reconstruction of our ancient past shows very different shore and coast lines. Sites not taken in context to a coastline that has vanished looks more and more like describing the play from the background to the back of the stage then it does the play. If we were to redraw our coastlines and how they may have looked, the ancient locations of the simple flint tools would be more akin to giving us a bearing to where the advanced societies were not. As an example, if we have an advanced society living on a coastline that is now sunk and we can correspond the less advanced societies to the layers found to the coast line that was originally there, wouldn't we know better where to look for the most advanced ruins? It's not that our former advanced society wouldn't have maybe mined, carved, or used the places this less advanced group would have moved into.

Then there was living in harmony....

It has to be beaten into us that in the archaeological conversation or alternative history world that the idea that there have always been sites around the world where a lesser advanced society may have lived. Lived at peace near or far from a much more advanced society that left them alone. Even if it was incredibly backward, including the suppression Of women, science, and the worship of whatever. We constantly take a stone fire pit, stone tools, and continuously stamp them into the current paradigm of evolution and history. In our modern world, there couldn't possibly be a billion-dollar Apple Computer Headquarters with a group of people somewhere else living in grass huts, genitally mutilating women, belief in witchcraft and sorcery?

Dead horse, need to keep beating.

There are to many silver bullets, you have to stand in the face of facts and just say, "it wasn't me." Taken on their own, each instance would be explained away. The Smithsonian, straight up stating, no evidence will be accepted that contradicts Columbus finding America. Fighting the finds, rather than putting out the layers and specifically pushing the paleoanthropological search for the older flints, tools, and bones would put us on coarse for our true past. There are so many instances that are not "mysteries" not enigmas, out of place out of time artifacts, they is real evidence that our history is much more complex. There is enough evidence on every continent. Evidence that we will be exploring further that indicate that our shores are further out, that our coastlines were centers of activity. The academic system has, throughout time deleted information that was not congruent to their ideas and theories, governments have colluded for national patriotism and power. The Catholic Church has walked hand in hand with the entire system, even now holding information that belongs to world history that is not available to the world. Bigger questions are how and who should make world historical records available to everyone? What are the distinctions of theories and facts in the treatment of finds? Could there be a new subject introduced to all levels of education that begins a discussion in having a grossly underestimated understanding of our history? To be able to recognize new and established theories against the reality of what we are finding. There is no such thing as out of place out time artifacts, they are where they are.

Chapter 5

ANCIENT ASTRONOMY AND THE PROCESSIONS STARS

Depending on where you live the night sky can be like nothing you have ever seen. The stars can cluster so close you think its a sea of clouds. Stars, you look up, no skyscrapers, no street lights, you can see a lot. Pre-satellite, pre-telescope, here are the Egyptians and Greeks, and Chinese and Indus Valley peoples and the entirety of humanity making a big deal out of stars they can see. Sailors find their way across the seas with stars, they are assigned deity status, there are stories about them and lets not forget we all came from mars. Not likely, but it is where you go with the tin hat. Seriously it looks like we may have colonized it already.

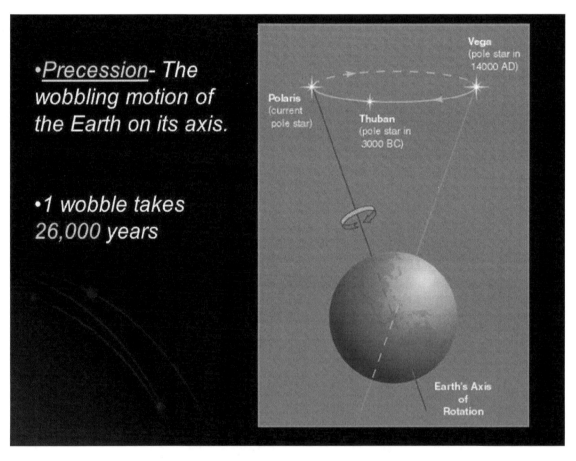

In order to observe this wobble, you would have to tell your loin cloth lovin' descendants to keep workin away on the pyramids while tracking stars for approximately 26,000 to 27,000 years. That's if you thought you saw one cycle! The only way to know for sure would for it to perfectly repeat itself? Maybe 52 or 54,000 years for making sure?

Stars were used for aligning buildings, earthworks, and geoglyphs like Serpent's Mound in Peebles, Ohio. 1348 ft. long and considered the largest serpent earth work in the world. Various dating methods puts it at approximately 321 BC. There is a reference that the oval head of the serpent is aligned to the summer solstice sunset. There are lunar alignments to two solstice and equinox events annually. It isn't a small thing to have a single monument containing the winter solstice sunrise and the equinox sunrise.

Isn't it always interesting that ancient people are always concerned about an equinox, or lunar eclipse? Apparently the only thing besides hunting and not dying was to make the earth into a giant celestial pocket watch. The random exactness of ancient people is insanity unless there was more advanced knowledge and it digressed into this. The pieces you could grasp because for the most part, the details were visible. For example, if the only thing left of a grandfather clock was the face. If that face took on significance to a later people after the painted numbers and or letters faded. Coupled with a later society's traditions, the face of the clocks importance may now be the back side not even the face. The importance of alignments for launching craft, navigations, and sailing are incredibly important. Alignments for radio waves, frequencies for TV and cell phone technology as we know it may have been completely different in the ancient past. A mound or a flat pyramid as seen in South America and the southern Pacific are easy targets for a rebuild with high tech equipment accurately lined up to send or receive waves and frequencies.

There has been brilliant work on alignments of Stonehenge, Adams' calendar in South Africa, many pyramids being aligned to the cardinal points. Most, if not all truly ancient sites are under some kind of star alignments. Gobekli Tepe and as Mary tried to prove, the Nazca Lines maybe star aligned. Of course we have already covered Erik Von Daniken's observations of the Golden Ratio and the alignments of everything truly ancient Greek. All the major sites are aligned in some fashion. The demonstration for Erik Von Daniken and the Colonel Of the Greek Air Force was for fuel efficiency. If a more advanced society was on the planet, they would and could have been just as concerned about fuel efficiency or communications. The technology of the past would for various reasons dictate the placement of sites.

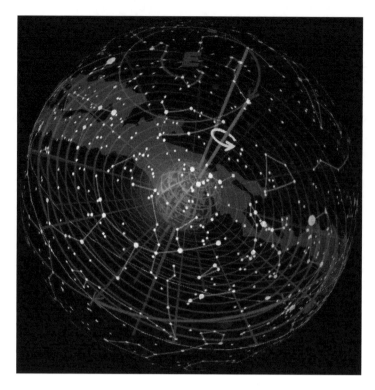

Observable star systems to the average tribe would not be the observable star systems to a more advanced society. Particularly to one understanding the vibrational, frequency, magnetic and dielectric universe. Perhaps in an ancient advanced high technology society they too had observed in a more simple time the observable sky, records of their ideas of the night sky may be for extinct animals millions of years ago.

In what is a great example, over 30 years ago Robert Bauval had a theory that the great pyramid complex was a mirror of the Orion's belt. This sent Egyptologists up the banana tree again. They threw objections as fast as you could shake a pointed stick. Now after books, articles, TV shows, public debates, there is a general assessment and agreement that the Great Pyramid complex is a mirror image of Orion. Graham Hancock and many others have gone on about the alignments in accurate, insightful and inspiring ideas.

However, This is our horse rising from the dead to be beat. Again.

The observable universe at the time of this book's writing includes the theory that magnetism, gravity, and electricity are all part of one thing. They are not separate sciences. The observable effects of magnetism are seen in a macro universe down to the smallest particle in more than one effect than "magnetism" which is a description and the theories around it would take you to where KenWheeler has brilliantly gone.

The observations, that Orion is significant to the post flood cultures around the earth, is a fact. It is interesting that Giza does align with Orion as a "mirror" however not exactly. Detractors will say that a mirror of it is not Orion, it's close but it isn't exactly dead on so it is a coincidence. Either way you are talking about a very hard coincidence. There is a driving assumption about the sky and post flood people were of one kind, a group of people or isolated tribes that made it through a disaster and independently looked to the sky and came up with some cool stories and shapes to represent those stories in the sky. The myths, the associations of the equinox and solstices, the religious and traditions generated over time create familiarity, after 1,2,10,000 years, those traditions have valid roots to living people. We've mystified it, write some books on it, and have societies for these traditions and it is real. Can't fight it, just recognize it.

This treatment of the past by filtering it through our feelings and experiences change our DNA expression. Our recent traditions seem to bury our true genetic society memory to our deep unconscious. Joseph Campbell spent a lifetime studying tribal cultures, myths and traditions. There are many common threads throughout the earth. The Hero with a Thousand Faces and The Hero's Journey are worth checking out. Try interrupting the Luciferian group or some cult that has been worshiping a skull from Larry the Ladder guy that used to work on thatch roofs. Larry's skull is now a venerated artifact used in sacrifices to someone's whims. No buddy cares it was Larry the Ladder guy, there are so many sacrifices over so many special blood moons or summer solstices.

We are building the case that there was at least one large advanced society on planet earth. The technology we will continue to look at in later chapters clearly indicates a unified planetary advanced ancient society. From the ability to line up these ancient structures to earthquake protection via wave cloaking and canceling technology. This ancient society would be looking beyond the night sky. The technology we are continuously pointing out from Egypt to South America in stone, can't be an isolated technology advancement in other fields would be simulations. At Contract in the Desert, 2018, Erik Von Daniken brought up six satellites that are orbiting the earth that may not be human or may be ancient. The frustration that we should have over the idea that this is exactly the kind of knowledge that will not be shared with the general public? This doesn't seem to benefit governments other than to shield the potential panic of the sheeple. The higher the technological achievements of a society living for thousands of years across many disasters would account for celestial disasters. You can see that there is development to see beyond the night sky in order to watch for incoming objects. We are aware of many star systems, black holes, galaxies, and our general observations of the universe are increasing daily. An ancient societies multigenerational survival would be on knowing what was going to hit us, looking into deep space would be as important as cutting and moving a 3000-ton stone. Side note, there is an uncountable list of idiots that think they are the "chosen people". Show me one set of people that got us to the technology we are at now? There isn't one set of genetically separate humans that are responsible for where we are now. It would do us a world of good to start recognizing that.

If you look at history, ignore the technology of the structures remaining, you can make many romantic assumptions about how the stars align. This is in no way to look at Bauval's observations other than to help us clarify that standard academia and modern alternative researchers are still anchored in a perspective of our past that we were once not as advanced. We align the Great Pyramid of Giza in the past and it is now approximately 3/60th of a second off true north for funzies, and we once were pretty mystified about the night sky. Ancient people aligned the building to Orion for religious purposes. This makes sense when you look at dynastic Egyptians stories of faith. What they believed, the alignments ad up for simple post flood people. Simple compared to highly conscious cymatic polygonal Never Ending story people that were once completely connected to each other and the planet.

The best example I can think of to explain the absurdity of our current observations of these alignments of the Pyramid for religious purposes and being built so accurately to true north would be for you to make a call on your Android phone and still be driving to work in a horse and buggy. Because we haven't invented the combustion engine. That is the extreme we'd have to deal with.

There is a constant disconnect in everyone staring at the obvious, "say, there is an ancient lost high technology here. No way we built or drilled this rose granite and andesite without higher tech. This math is really advanced. This structure is built to an accuracy that lasers couldn't accomplish."

Isn't the very next point that it isn't that there were sharp, accurate tools but satellites in ancient times? Archeoastronomy is generally looking at how ancient structures and peoples related to stars, equinoxes, solstices, etc. They also cross over into Archaeoacoustics. What about ancient satellites? Corresponding technology that was in all fields of science left on the ground would look different if they had been repurposed wouldn't it? Re-adapted ancient Earth satellite technology would still have antenna? Maybe an obelisk? Wiring, metal, external sheeting remember dusted away. Satellites could burn up and fall to the earth. Panels of an orbiting satellite could be pounded into shiny plates, with stories of sun gods.

Is it more likely that the pyramids were aligned for the sake of obsessive accuracy or for scalar waves, vibrational energy and frequency technology. This is another side of the puzzle. Communication, energy receiving and sending, reflective surfaces, etc. We have vampired away years of precious research time trying to figure out what the survivors of the great flood are doing with pottery. They painted a lot of stories and gods on them, while not continuing on our search and rescue of our highly advanced past.

If you are going to look into the night sky, take the next big boy step reframing the ancient past space technology. The alignments are not as elementary as what is seen by loin cloth Dave and Eve. We really nailed down directions, ohhh, look up, that star system is neat, we got a story, lets build this for a endless human mind fuck in the future. We don't have enough going on with the killing of big beasts and survival, lets send the future residence of this world "messages" in stone....

F you, seriously? Are you thinking one day your going to make a flower wreath hat and dance around a fire on the summer solstice and you should carve something up for your great great great grandkids to ponder over? The technology to put the Great Pyramid and other megalithic structures like it where they put them and build with what they built with would include satellite technology. There is a structure in orbit approximately 12,000 miles above the earth, the Black Knight Satellite. This object is believed to be space junk, a blanket, or to some, an ancient satellite of unknown technology. Possibly an internet hodgepodge of bullshit. What about other possible satellites that we think are just floating rocks? If it is of a crystal vibrational technology of a more advanced society, the remaining satellite could just be a rock in orbit to us. It could be cloaked still. An ancient high technology satellite could still be in use. We see an orbiting rock.

We really aren't covering conspiracies beyond the focus of the book but imaging the governments with orbital tech, getting a reading on what is in orbit and a reading of an unknown origin proves itself to be an ancient satellite. When did we re-reach the technology to even identify that there was something in orbit? The Black Knight or other ancient satellites may not be at a height we put things in orbit. It isn't orbiting in an explainable direction, and it's huge. If the black knight satellite is real, the implications of the technology behind it, the fact that it is old, and it is in orbit can leave you wondering, is it alien, is it ancient human?

NASA identified the "black knight" as a space blanket, it could also have been from a Cold War era satellite that burned up and this is a piece. The imagination of the internet has created associations with Tesla, radio waves, that this satellite is communicating or watching us. The overarching issues with it are just that, there is only one credible public accounting agency for space objects and NASA says its a blanket. Here is the birth of conspiracy. The issue isn't whether the black knight is real, the issue is whether or not an advanced ancient people would have been using satellites and therefore the only people we can look to for answers are the governments we literally don't trusts to tell us the truth. That is more than a frustrating conundrum. We are in the dark enough about our true history. If the Catholic Church and or all religions post flood, have shaped belief through the skewing or hiding of our true past, we are in the dark if we can't find the ancient technology and put many eyes on it. There is a lot to unpack here. We look back and seeing ancient people left very advanced pieces on the ground. We are not creating an open dialogue about looking for advanced ancient tech in the sky. Only aliens are in space. There is a lot of research pointing telescopes toward far away objects in the galaxy, solar system, universe and no one that we publicly know is admitting or looking at the orbit of objects in our sky asking if it is new, or if it is old. Not alien, it could be ancient advanced human technology. This is our first direct dialogue to ask ourselves, if we have so many in the ground pieces of a highly advanced past, wouldn't there be these ancient advanced celestial objects?

PLAN NINE FROM OUTER SPACE

If you want to vampire away a couple of hours try this movie. Johnny Depp was in a movie about the director. There is a theory about a missing planet in our solar system. This is not what the movie is about, the title along with the movie is wack. This idea about another planet is not far fetched. The planet is identified by the Sumerians. There is mounting evidence for it now. Frequently there are "super Earths" found around our galaxy. These are large planets and we could have a ninth planet circling our solar system like others in our galaxy. It is also common in other galaxies to have dual stars. Livable

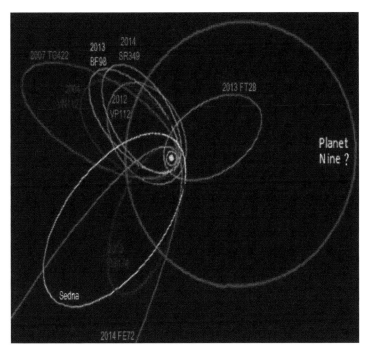

Earth is seen here with planet nine. Despite our most powerful telescopes pointing to the sky, we are unsure and unable to confirm the existence yet. We are unsure of all the planetary impact threats, many are tracked, some must be classified, either way your graduating high school senior should be able to site known planetary threats.

planets accompanying two habitable planets and two suns.

Evidence for this planet was given by Caltech scientists Konstantin Batygin and Mike Brown. They have mapped out the hypothetical orbit. There is a strange orbit to six Kuiper Belt objects. This helped them create the possible orbit for planet nine. The Kuiper Belt is a band of icy objects. The strange orbit is due to a pull in gravity by an unknown planet that is orbiting our sun out of alignment of the planets we know.

There is an Outer Solar System Origins Survey that is tracking objects in our solar system. They have found over 800 objects so far that are "trans-Neptunian". The team is running the project at the University of Victoria. It would be a 15,000 year orbit for planet nine to make it around the sun. This planet explains the weird orbit of these objects on the far side of the sun.

One reason this is important, it shows we don't know what is in our own solar system. This is another reason for situational awareness. Where are we in the universe, what objects are potential threats to our planet? We have been hit, we will be hit again, Capitalist, Communist, Christian, Muslim, or Hindu all gonna get hit. The information as of 2018 has revealed a massive 19 mile diameter crater has been found in Greenland. Apparently unknown to our current sciences till now. The possibility of this crater being the impact site that is responsible for the 12-13,000 year ago disaster is decent.

Forget about it. Forget the Black knight, focus on the results. The physical structure that is most looked at in the western world, the Great Pyramid. To coordinate the placement of this structure, the likelihood that the same society would have a satellite is evident. The inability for us to be able to put some observatories on it, to be able to have access to UFO satellite objects that military satellites have seen, in short, sucks. Not being able to digitize and reference the Vatican libraries, sucks sucks. This is some of the missions we have before us, we have a battle, to access our own histories, illegally enslaved to colleges, governments and religions dictating accessibility and knowledge filtration. Not to mention academic quackery and simple evil hubris.

MAYBE THE ANCIENT SITES ARE ALIGNED TO UNKNOWN OUT OF THE VISIBLE SKY

Observing star systems beyond the ones we are looking at from the ground becomes important if you are an ancient advanced society. If the ancient monuments we have been studying were aligned with out of solar system star systems? Communications open to another star system might require focused scalar wave communications equipment that may now appear to align to constellations we see in the sky but simply rack up to coincidences. Instead, is it a star system beyond? Any combinations of stars may create new theories. This is a rabbit hole. Are we looking at a repurposed Nazca lines with simpleton graffiti on the great high technology of the earth grid it represents? Is it the giant bird we should keep looking at or the hyper straight lines that are beneath this graffiti? We have to test the soil and hook up current devices that can test and measure electromagnetic anomalies. The possibility of an ancient advanced satellite is more than possible, it helps with the placement of buildings. Ancient societies may have been searching for other universal life, that may have been a goal thousands or millions of years ago. Ancient humans could have been searching for habitable worlds to expand too. Could we have left this planet, colonized mars, destroyed ourselves through war or intergalactic miss hap? The assumption that we rose to where we are with only high tech development of stone placement is unlikely. There could be remnants or pieces of the tech that would still be in orbit floating and looking no more than rocks. Orbital astroarchaeology to the rescue! Talking about a needle in the haystack. Would you like to look for deep galactic line ups for the Pyramid complex at Giza? No more Orion's Belt. The idea of a post anti-diluvian line up of the pyramids for religious reasons is romantic. Fits safely in our Victorian flying saucer 50's romance with our history. Our badass ancient ancestors could cloak a building with cymatic polygonal construction against earthquakes and build to withstand million year floods.

Terrorism, now is a good time to bring terrorism up. How naive is it to assume that in the infinity of the universe, all higher advanced societies would not be religiously zealous, sociopaths, or just murderous monsters on a galactic level? We are busy sending out blinking messages and SOS and maps on satellites that NASA has sent on the Voyager missions to say, here we are, come enslave us galactic cabal aliens!

It is daunting to have to re-evaluate the possibility that the alignments of the ancients structures were based on higher technical purposes that appear or have become in devolved times or post flood times religious, holy sites, mystical and I am not sorry but simple. Blurred by thousands of years of repurposed use and repair. The idea that ancient people aligned every major megalithic structure or worked only in the sky they can see from the ground or rudimentary telescopes only makes sense if we were never more advanced. The Math in the ancient sites, the polygonal masonry, the complex and beautiful objects found that are just not chip away products of rudimentary work, there are too many pieces to not point to a more complex advanced past. I hear the zombie dead horse rising to beat again.

ANCIENT ASTRONOMY AND THE PROCESSIONS THE EARTH IS WOBBLY

The age of Aquarius, it's the age of Aquarius! Great song. The processions of the equinoxes takes approximately 25,772 years. The Mayan calendar is based on about 30,000 years with a working theory that it is based on the processions. Stars hypothetically don't lie. There is a procession of the stars. Gobekli Tepe being the big star studded focus, has animals and other glyphs all over the monolith T shaped pillars. Here we go again. The structure shows advanced work, with rubble as discussed between the pillars and now we have the immediate assumption that the animal reliefs at Gobekli are processional and night sky related. Probably and maybes. Perhaps, since it's only 5% dug up we should stick with why is this structure here and look for more that are similar in age around the planet? That whole sunken city thing again off Cuba? Anyone? Would the real researcher please stand up, please stand up?

The processions is about how the earth spins not only in a circle, yes it also circles the sun, but it also has an axis point on the poles like when a top is spun. When you spin a top it eventually starts to wobble before it falls, that is the earth, it's spinning, it's wobbling and it made for a great song.

The Age of Aquarius, for our example is the forthcoming astrological age, depending on how you look at it. Astronomer/astrologer potato/potato. The astrologer looks at it as the earth's processional rotation lasting 2160 years averaging about 26,000 years equals 12 zodiac signs. The interesting thing about being western is we give credit to figuring this out to Hipparchus. Approximately 350 years earlier, Vedanga Jyotisha documents the same thing in 700 B.C. In Indian texts. Boom goes the East, bitch. The more you dig, the more you will see just how biased a western perspective is.

About the procession, there are astrophysicists, astronomers, and astrologers that argue about when the procession changes and how, so the current agreement is that we may have entered it around 1400 A.D. or we have yet to enter the Age of Aquarius and maybe will enter it around 3500, this is quite a swing. There is again, a rabbit hole for you to figure out and vampire away your time. The signs in order are Aries, Taurus, Gemini, Cancer, Leo, Virgo, Libra, Scorpio, Sagittarius, Capricorn, Aquarius, and Pisces....aaaand repeat. However, do it in reverse. First comes Pisces, then comes Aquarius, then goes Capricorn and so on. That is how they proceed at approximately 2160 years a pop. This is calculated of the Earth's gyroscopic precession of 25,800 years by 12.

Plato was aware of the Egyptians and Babylonians having the knowledge of the processions. There is constant reminders by Herodotus that there was a much more ancient time, the Egyptian priests of the day said the same, that they were living in an age of decline, that the time had long past for the greatness of the ages and darkness was upon them. China again, they all had their references for the equinoxes. The Mayans, the Sumerians both had references of the equinox. Either you measure the equinox with machines, like telescopes, satellites and other electronic and faithful PI based math or you watch them go by, you tell your kids to tell your kids, that there is a not so random pattern in the sky and we will figure it out as we develop math and measure, the sky, over 26,000 years. What do you think, the Mayans to the Sumerians already had access to information that was from a prior society, or they were really observant over an unexplainable period of time for standard Victorian academia? Taken separately it's a "mystery" not if you want to call an apple an apple instead of supporting theories of human development rather than the evidences right before you. Piri Reis Map, the Antarctic coastline, Black Knight fiction or another ancient satellite? The 26,000 years to figure out the equinox destroys the human fairytale still being embraced like a huggy blanket for mainstream science. Either they had the equipment at one point to establish the 26,000 year cycle or the Sumerians observed it. Here is another F up for academia, the Sumerians were not around for 26,000 years to observe the cycles, they also didn't have electronic equipment. The Sumerians say they have been around, ruling Sumar for about 280,000 years. That would be enough time. Unless they were not being truthful or accurate about the length of time the Sumerian kings ruled.

TED TALK!

Sarah Parcak, seen here, is responsible for finding a presently uncontested amount of unknown archaeological sites while simultaneously expanding our knowledge of existing sites. Many well known sites where no digging is done, or little digging is done beyond a certain depth due to standard academia believing there is nothing deeper can finally be put to bed. Specifically sites like Tiwanaku, where the H blocks are.

If you haven't seen a TED talk, google google google away and enjoy an introduction to a wide range of sciences and ideas. TED Prize winner of 2016, Archaeologist Sarah Parcak developed a satellite imagery system to locate and find buried archaeological sites. In 2007 she founded the Laboratory of Global Observations at University of Alabama at Birmingham. She wins the Smithsonian Magazine's American Ingenuity Award in history and has been featured on the BBC showing how she uses infrared satellite imaging. With the help of NASA satellites she has made discoveries of unknown pyramids, 1000's of tombs, 1000's of ancient settlements near el-Hagar, Egypt, several finds in Romania, Tunisia, Italy, and Nabataea.

What happened to Sarah Parcak since 2016? She wins the TED PRIZE and does it with satellite imaging of buried sites. Why not take her work with the new global explorer site, and the LIDAR work and start with the big questions, how big was the ancient worlds? Let's do a map for us to see.

Her research showed vast unknown details of the Giza Plateau, unknown pyramids, buildings etc. How it works is that there is a temperature difference between the stone, mud brick and sand of the desert, she was able to image this using satellites and showed extensive unknown underground networks of former buildings.

Ted Talk awards her the TED prize and now global explorer is using citizen archaeologists to look at satellite maps of the world and find new archaeological sites and unfortunately sites already found by grave robbers, thieves, and not the ones from national museums. Well maybe national museums. People are given map sections of satellite imaging and are asked to locate potential archaeological finds, potential grave robbing etc..

This is pretty amazing. Sarah and her group have identified many finds. My question is why can't we track, map, see the finds? This is just a question that is not answerable in this book but has to be part of your mind and dialogue about to whom does the right to know belong? We are going to go into genetic memory, isn't it all our history? Isn't the possibility within a context that there is a memory that could be jogged, that a citizen of the world may recognize more about a find than the person whom has rediscovered it? As we explore all the different levels that we could be connected, all of us have access to a consciousness and stored genetic memory that may help us remember who we are.

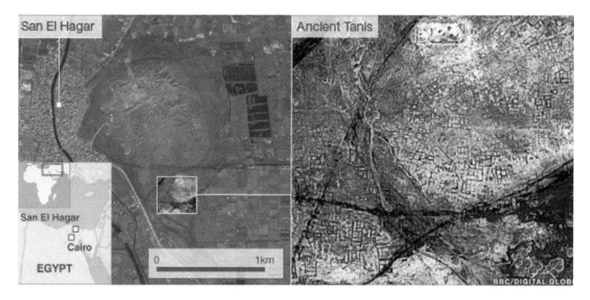

This is a perfect example of of site clarity of recently ancient and extreme antiquity. Better plans can be put in place with LIDAR and satellite imaging. It is important to put the pieces of our history together, starting with the water vessel and painstakingly putting it together is needed, just not before we establish holistic dig plans to the lowest layers of all sites to get to the heart of the ultimate human question, who are we?

Here is a stand out question that is just one example how we could digress endlessly: there is a theory that the Great Sphinx has a twin. If you look at the plateau of Giza, it appears that there would be a matching sphinx and we would just have to dig to possibly identify the foundation. There would be a couple assumptions, one, since the great sphinx is known to be greatly older than the dynastic Egyptians, the second sphinx having been as old, may have suffered a demolition in the contemporary past of the great sphinx and the site maybe a rebuild in ancient times. To continue the conspiracies, the government of Egypt receives billions in tourism dollars and has a good thing going as is. As for modern governments else where trying to maintain a story of our past, it doesn't fly to have the sites dug up that extend the Egyptian timeline, contradict the religion of archaeology and undermined modern control of the general population, all from having another sphinx. Extending a permit, to dig and find a second sphinx does threaten that. Worse almost, is that if they admit they missed a second sphinx well why are you giving them money for a degree? It just invalidates that. Simply out of embarrassment they don't want to admit they missed something so big and popular as a downed sphinx. Meow.

SO ABOUT THAT MOST RECENT CATASTROPHIC EVENT FOUND....

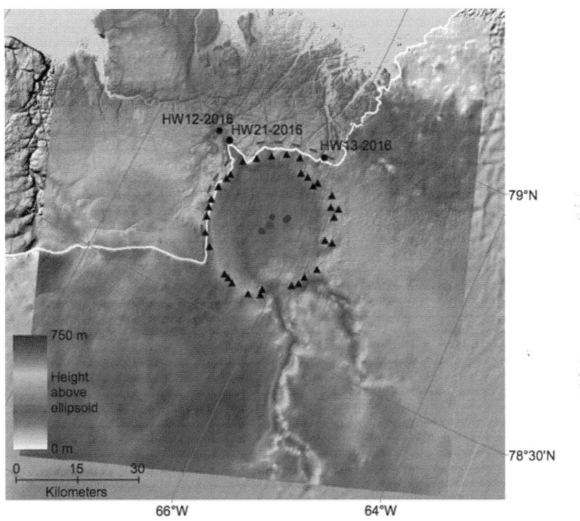

Although recently found, this is the new ground zero for our 12-13,000 year old world wide flood. The impact site is massive. It is frequently theorized that an impact like this or a solar flare caused the various extinction events on earth, there is a more terrifying possibility, that during a massive ancient unrest, a long gone advanced human society wiped themselves out with much more advanced weapons causing the deserts and climate we live in now.

While writing this book, a 19 mile wide diameter impact site in Greenland on a partially completed ice age hit the earth with the force of at least 45 million Hiroshima bombs. There was a huge hit to the earth in the Yucatán Peninsula and that has been a well known.

Just recently there was a crater found that indicates that a meteor hit Greenland with the force and equivalent power of a 700 megaton bomb creating a 19 mile wide crater. No one noticed because it is in Greenland under a mile of ice. A piece of iron at 700 megatons is significant. In 1908 there was another meteor impact with a 10 megaton bomb equivalent in Siberia and it had a 1000 mile sq mile epicenter that flattened trees for 800 sq. miles.

Thanks to Bright Insight on YouTube for the following leg work... Did you know, (according standard academia) the camel originated in North America. 75 percent of animals in North America, a lot of animals found 12-13000 years ago all disappeared at the same time. Antelopes, ground sloths, giant short faced bear that was double the size of a big modern grizzly, lions were in North America, the American cheetah, all disappeared 12-13000 years ago.

The journal of geology recently speculated that the there was a massive fire approximately 12,800 years ago at least 10 percent of the earths trees burned. This matches the cosmic impact that nailed the dinosaurs 64 million years ago. This is also about when the Clovis people which occupied most of Alaska to Mexico on the west coast of the Americas were wiped out about 12,000 years ago. Clovis is the name given to the people that standard academia wanted to identify as the culture that developed out of the group that crossed the land bridge. The land bride theory that is. It is not fact. It is a theory. There is no information on the Clovis that would make them a coherent race or the only group in the Americas at that time.

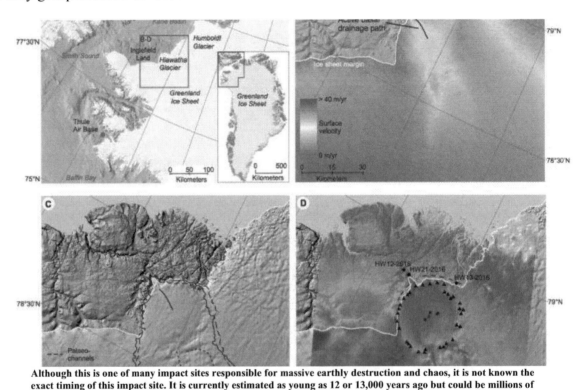

Although this is one of many impact sites responsible for massive earthly destruction and chaos, it is not known the exact timing of this impact site. It is currently estimated as young as 12 or 13,000 years ago but could be millions of years old. Notable is that it was not public knowledge until 2019, there are many possibly classified sites that could in size, or collective quantity tell us about our past here and in our solar system.

Would it behoove us to really track the objects in space, including the junk in uber orbits and create video games that the citizen could play that gave them access to data and could help identify and track solar, galactic, and universal threats that have and will hit us again. Think about the billions of hours wasted playing video games? We all need to relax, imagine if level two of a video game is because you helped identify an orbital comet or meteor and an impact date or location. Maybe helped the math on how to move it causing it to eliminate another interstellar orbiter, using one to destroy another rendering them away from our planet. How about some money for that person vs a sports star?

If there is a ninth planet as the computer and questionable orbital objects indicate, was or is this planet occupied? This planet is identified by the Sumerians. Is it a planet that is a sister to earth? Does it have remnants of an ancient society still on it? Could the aliens we see just be our ancestors checking in on Mother Earth from this Super Earth? Are we situationally aware of our place in the universe? Do we need a giant alien space fortress to crash for us to stop fighting each other and start working to get off this planet and expand beyond it?

Pointedly in our past are night sky alignments, build sites, construction that seems to make the most sense when explained with complimentary satellite technology for either communication, viewing the Earth and outer worlds. We would not be looking for it if we didn't think it a possibility, we say aliens and what we might need to start saying is our ancestors left pieces of technology that may still be in use by them. One of the questions is is this technology being used from another planet or station in space and or is this technology in use on the planet by ancient advanced selves? Aliens or us? Not some space traveling race from somewhere else, a race of humans, being here already and advanced way beyond where we are today, continuing to call earth home while interacting with us intentionally or by accident.

Chapter 6

TECHNOLOGY VIBRATIONAL, FREQUENCIES, VORTEXES, QUANTUM MECHANICS!

Pascual Jordan, who worked with quantum guru Niels Bohr in Copenhagen in the 1920s, put it like this: "observations not only disturb what has to be measured, they produce it… We compel [a quantum particle] to assume a definite position." In other words, Jordan said, "we ourselves produce the results of measurements."

Hungarian physicist Eugene Wigner. "It follows that the quantum description of objects is influenced by impressions entering my consciousness," he wrote. "Solipsism may be logically consistent with present quantum mechanics."

Adrian Kent, a quantum philosopher, University of Cambridge, UK and one of the most respected "quantum philosophers", speculated that consciousness might alter the behavior of quantum systems in detectable ways. The reality that our very consciousness is quantum, makes quantum physicists uncomfortable, puts the alternative fairy and magic gnome loving people who don't think it's relevant to their dream weaver and woo to sleep too. It definitely makes a certain cable TV watching crowd and social media group turn the channel. It is fascinating, that we have observed in sciences, that observing the quantum universe changes it. You could call it god like. The science of god...maybe consider it a bit before changing the channel. The level of technology from our soil to our genes shows signs of being engineered in a logical way. In a high tech ancient human society, the consciousness of the mind, fully engaged, would be amazing. The indications of that are all over, in stone, in our genes and now in observable "new" science. We allegedly only use 15ish percent of our brain, either evolution gave us extra up front, or we once had a fully plugged in brain and body to a giant earth grid from Nazca to Jordan. Many rabbit holes in the either. Call it quantum or either. The focus here is to bring to light the very likely hood you are a sleeping Merlin. A walking Harry Potter with amnesia.

Old and new sciences are mixing with an awakening of human consciousness and abilities are being tested and observed. While quantum sciences are accelerating, we are still in the infancy of that understanding. Rediscovering our ancient ancestors most advanced technology in stone is literally a foundation and gateway to the other technology that would be present in the ancient past. We are going to look now at the higher quantum/either, and wave technology that would be related to the past that we are now rediscovering. With a fully connected mind to an ancient earth grid and antennas reaching to the heavens, what could we personally perceive on a galactic wired network at some great epoch of our past?

If a tree falls in the forest does it make a sound if no one is there to hear it? Quantum theory has been around about 100 years, research has been it's most serious and applicable sciences in the last 40 years in our time. More recent quantum sciences like spintronics to the observations of cymatics is a realm that applies to the ancient past as well as our present. We are going to take a look at the ancient past and how cymatics, quantum science were applied in the ancient past and the remnants of those sciences are present in ruins while also exploring the amazing technology that is just starting to re-emerge in today's technology.

We are going to go over some individuals that are reconnecting to their personal super powers like Wim Hof and Stig Severinson. We are going to talk water, which is displaying unknown quantum properties never before observed in "modern times". Connecting the observations or language of quantum science with the "natural world" will help us start to see that it is by ancient advanced design or grooming. If mainstream academia continues to perpetuate 10,000 years ago we were in loincloths, then Wim Hof and Stig and the lot are super human and it's all witchcraft. The awareness, the application of these bio-abilities to control your immune system, breathing, strength, it has a mental component on the quantum level. There actually seems to be a human consciousness that connects us. This is where I jump into Obi Wan Kenobi mode and continue and say, it binds us, flows through us...like the Force. For the actual many of you whom have not seen Star Wars, the energy, nature, Mother Earth, God or Gods, Spirit, etc. The very real examples of experiences where people are connecting through Synesthesia. We will discuss Synesthesia. We have to look at practical science we know of today to connect it back to how we fit into our past, possibly why we fit on the planet and to look holistically how everything does connect. Somewhere between what is our actual spiritual selves and science is a fuller more natural explanation for all the connections by design. Looking at quantum mechanics and our "technology" will reveal more about how all of it connects.

MODERN CHEMISTRY AND PHYSICS FOUGHT FOR POPULARITY

In the last 100 years a brilliant mathematician came along and gave us a cat in a box. There is still an uncomfortable relationship with classic Newtonian physics and quantum mechanics. Why? First came the Middle Ages, then let's fast forward to the industrial revolution, here we stop and visit chemistry. Forever people have been into alchemy, the idea that if you get some sort of metallurgical soup together in the right way, you could make gold, or silver or Harry Potter potions. Chemistry is the bases for mixing for meds, baking a cake, creating steel, in the high school of sciences, chemistry was captain of the football team and prom king. Then came physics. Not only did chemistry loose top spot, it was pretty obvious that chemistry was more like marching band. Personally I love marching band, however it was clear fast that physics is how those kilonewtons work, weight works, gravity works. Einstein's theory of relativity is nifty, if it was actually his and a fluffy distraction. There is an avalanche of proof that a lot of his work may have been borrowed from some French, English and other scientists. Another big rabbit hole, Einstein was considered by Tesla, an idiot. The proof of his theft is annoying. Annoying that Einstein was awarded credit for others work. For your conspiracies books, for all accounts Einstein is a fraud propped up by people that do not want you looking toward the reality of our universe. Back to Chemistry, as we grew up in the dark ages, we had a lot of time to boil and toil, chemistry appeared to be the top sciences till physics was better understood. Our perspective and understanding of the universe grew as we learn and apply our new sciences. Chemistry is important, it's just part of the either.

Which brings us to Schrödinger, the father of cat quantum theory. We will get to his poor cat soon. The current model of the atom is wrong. The world of subatomic particles of what was soon called Quantum theory is the way the universe actually works. The scary thing about the either/quantum, is that it explains the physical universe and it tackles things like human consciousness, which makes no one happy in science, religion or woo woo feelings and fairies. Quantum mechanics and the observations already made are unnerving when your very conscious thought toward a particle, or test or observable wave, is literally changed by human consciousness. There is the very likelihood that we once understood this ability in our ancient past. That is was well designed into ancient high technology. We have to continue to explain some of the higher concepts of quantum theory while also looking at some of the very real mainstream explanations for pyramids on every continent and the absurdness of it too.

This might be a good time to explain the 100th monkey theory. One of the craziest jumps to explain pyramids and similar building techniques and flood myths around the world. The 100th monkeys say that the reason monkeys on Madagascar and the mainland of Africa can use tools the same way despite being separated for tens of thousand of years is that one monkey taught one monkey how to use a stick to get ants out of the large African ant mounds. The way to do it is to stick a stick into the ant colony hole. The ants crawl on the stick, then the monkeys pull out the stick and eat the ants. How this applied to consciousness theory goes: one monkey kinda figures out sticks are useful, then one kinda gets the idea, then the next one starts to figure it out before anyone told him, and so on till the 100th monkey just knows how to use the stick from birth. Hence the theory of a greater community consciousness transferred the memory of how to use the stick to the monkeys either on Madagascar or in Africa. The how too of stick ant eating technology had been used by enough monkeys that it transferred to a group intelligence on the quantum/either level and now they all know how to do it.

That was one of the ideas on how every culture on earth decided they should build pyramids at the same time. It was the age of the pyramids. You can't make this up, that was an easier idea to believe because it was already set in stone that no continent connected. They all have to have come up with it on their own. We know from engineered soils alone, this is untrue. The game of Clue, it was Col. Mustard, in the Library with the soil! The idea of a connected human consciousness was tested by an MIT researcher before spintronics and nano technology were an actual application. There was a measure of a quantum particle that had a reaction every time the crowds reacted to a play during the World Cup. The World Cup is thee most watched event in the world. It was a crude and early look at a mass human control of quantum things. Imagine having a mind that was in touch with all living things and the buildings and roads you walked on.

Basically think of the wizard Merlin. It's easier to imagine Harry Potter magic and Merlin stuff being a way to connect, then the idea that there's an understandable science to nature. What we call nature, the animals to plants and us, like our soil, may have been intentionally shaped by man, millions or hundreds of thousands of years ago. The idea that a computer may one day be nanobots in the blood fabricating your dreams into reality and repairing your cells. There is a real possibility that the very planet we live on is a giant computer that is in safe mode. We are trying to get some quantum history in for those that have no experience in this world, while tying in old and current mainstream theories. There is a lot here, bare down...

Max Planck, creator of Quantum Mechanics and Schrödinger, somehow becoming the father of quantum mechanics and says everything works even smaller than the atom. REMINDER: the model of the atom is an established theory. It is not fact in fact and changing quickly. Schrödinger has to explain quantum with a cat. The idea is that there relationship to conciseness and all the laws of the universe and it works like this down to the smallest particle:

If you took Schrödinger's cat, stuck it in a box with a lethal dose of poison and close the lid. Is the cat dead or not when the poison is released? The relationship of particles of the universe is that they all have personalities that act literally as observed. Does a tree make a sound when it falls in the forest? That feeling that your alone in the universe that if you didn't go outside there is no one there. Quantum mechanics covers everything from the cat in the box to why the automatic doors work at the grocery store. This is part of the entanglement questions of quantum theory. The implications and complexities of the quantum world led Schrodinger to say,

"I don't like it and I am sorry I had anything to do with it."

Circling back to the pinhole and Nagasaki and Hiroshima. Boom. "Now I am become death, the destroyer of worlds" Oppenheimer knew the Hindu Vedas. Upon testing the first nuclear weapon in modern times, he quoted the Bhagavad-Gita. Many years have passed the atom bomb is a huge deal, however, there is material sciences, graphene conductors, and quantum machines made of 60-187 atoms. By 2008 we made nano sized machines that could build other nanomachines that are only atoms in size. This is all pointing to the really big megalithic buildings high in quartz and other minerals perfect for communicating and energy machines.

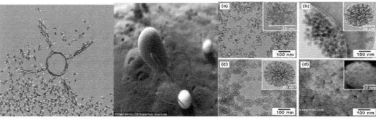

These examples of nano bots range in examples and sizes that could appear mechanical as on the example to the left to viral or bacterial on the far right. The idea of moving from putting pots together to sifting sand and collecting particles for archeo-nanobots is mind numbing and necessary in the near future.

118

IT'S NOT ALIENS, WORSE, IT'S US: Discovering Our Lost History

Ray Kurzwell, modern day renaissance man, holder of over 200 patterns, cofounder of Google University, and theorist, writes one of the most important books in the 20th century called "The Singularity is Near". Like Michael Cremo and Forbidden Archaeology, this is a required reading. He goes from economic models that justify the future leaps in technology to actual quantum applications of technology by 2008 when it was published, to discussing theoretical quantum applications as to when and how the convergence of man and machine will happen and why. It covers the deeply troubling and exciting world that is coming with quantum technology. Being able to create nano machines that are already able to be Wi-Fi controlled that are so small, they can be placed in a single cell and manipulate single points of DNA within the helix. Is this witchcraft in another age? It's magic to another deifying modern science? No, it's part of our rediscovery of our already known abilities. It is in our ruins, myths, sounds and music. It's in the patterns of our cloths.

To assume that man was advanced in placing 3000 ton stones and setting buildings within nano seconds of perfect north by south and unable to figure out the human body or advancing in other technology is idiocracy. The constant paradigm we need to shatter is that some external alien race came and gave us a leg up, rather than we just advanced there on our own. It is the same 100th monkey jump to explain pyramids. The idea that we fell is impossible for some to accept. All the alternatives are considered and mixed with post flood myths. We humans were already here, modified to suite "gods" or we were engineered by an advanced race from scratch, it's too hard for most to start, we advanced to a superior place than where we are now, fell, rose and wrote ourselves a new history.

This is one of our first alien points. There is some theorization around the Anunnaki of Sumer or the Sumerians, that their gods, the Anunaki enslaved humankind and had them dig up gold. Gold is important to the gods according to the people of Sumer. According to their religion. Here is the short on the Anunnaki:

1. They are from our missing solar system planet Nibiru and came to earth for gold.
2. They needed precious elements like gold for their atmosphere and longevity
3. They made man kind to mine gold for them and be slaves.
4. They created the basics for "modern human society"
5. They gave individual humans knowledge of ORME, StarFire to create human managers through kings and queens or Aristocracy.

This is a brief on Sumer's own cuneiform history. The missing planet Nibiru that may be in our solar orbit that may have a 3500 year orbit or a 15,000 year orbit, planet nine, it comes to legend that this planet nine may contain life, perhaps the life that came here first. Perhaps the life that is on this mysterious world is life we sent there from this planet?

THE ABSOLUTE TRUTH ON ALIENS NEEDING GOLD/MATERIAL FROM EARTH, HARD NO.

First thing, we are 50,000 ft. on understanding the details of the either or quantum world. In it you can make anything you can dream up. We are looking at all these post flood stories and theories about aliens, gods, whomever, fill in the blank, coming to earth, mars, the moon on a Star Trek deep space nine universe of nations coming to earth to get anything from the planet as.....wrong. The paradigm derives from us holding on to this idea that we started as cavemen. That we are as advanced as we ever were, now. That the only humans in the past advanced were helped by aliens to achieve anything other than loincloth life. Again, post flood stories may have slivers of truth, they don't account for millions of years of human history that Cremo and many scientific researchers are just revealing almost daily now.

Back to clarifying that there is a crowd that is propagating an idea that aliens are here, currently and in need of gold and or minerals on Mars. That there are aliens here hiding on earth on the dark side of the moon, well pretty much anywhere you can hide, the aliens are hiding because they are studying us and they need minerals. One more time, they are here for gold, other minerals and to experiment on humans. The stories include experiences of individuals that are abducted and experimented on and others that are shown things. Brought up by "friendly" aliens that want us to join the galactic federation of aliens. "We are almost ready" they say, allegedly. This conversation attracts a crowd that is looking for hope and understanding of their place in the universe. there are people who have had similar experiences of abduction. We can't possibly address peoples individual true experiences of being taken. There are too many to not be true, the issue is are they alien? Not secret military groups of different governments or shadow governments, but another group that maybe here on the planet and may have been here for a very long time or always.

If you control either, the quantum particles that make up the universe, to travel or make flash drives or a million other things we have now, you don't need gold. Everything in the universe can be made essentially from thin air, well quantum particles in thin air. You don't need to leave your planet except to explore. This is far from the 50's flying saucer movies. In that world you have to mine and melt things to make stuff. In the quantum, you let nano bots build.

We are going to handle one thing here. The quantum truth, genetics are around the corner.

QUANTUM TECHNOLOGY...

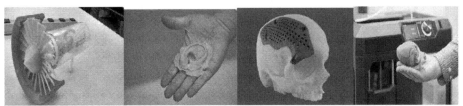

In our infancy of nano technology and 3-D printing we have gone from mechanical devices to printing biological parts. How soon before it's whole people, animal, or vegetable? What does that say about our engineered soil all over the earth?

Anyone with the technology to travel efficiently through interstellar space in an organic form. Has control of the quantum universe, their genes, and can create whatever they want out of atoms, electrons, subatomic particles ETC... It will look like witchcraft and magic AND if you've never seen one, any touchpad device today to anyone uncontacted in the jungles. Ok, maybe they can't do everything, however putting bits of atoms together and making gold would not be a problem. Intergalactic and or inter-dimensional space traveling aliens who have control of quantum science, do not need minerals, human spirits, souls, energy, no one needs that kind of shenanigans. You make it out of any two particles you want to build something with. If an ancient high technology human race fell in ancient times, a remnant group may have had access to surviving technology.

These surviving people may have presented themselves as aliens and may have needed mining to sustain their declining technology. These survivors may not have had enough knowledge of their past technology to sustain it after a major catastrophe.

The story about Sumerian gods the Anunaki goes they wanted or needed gold. The Anunaki came and need gold for their planet Nibiru, our famous planet nine. The story of the Anunaki is that they get lazy about mining and call on one of their elites, Enki to modify the local monkey and make humans to do the work for them. Let us tie this back to the stories that aliens have come from somewhere in the universe because there are minerals, material, something special in the soil that inter-dimensional space traveling aliens need. This is our 20th century understanding of building. Elixirs, potions, physical and tangible things like chemistry that we use to build everything we sit, drive, live in and vacation at. As if Merlin waved a wand or mixed a potion.

Is it more likely that this post flood story is a great example of one of the last, known visible lines of advanced humans on Earth "publicly" seen. Meaning, the most advanced pre-flood humans may have split opinions on how to move forward after multiple cataclysms and particularly this last disaster approximately 13,000 years ago. The Anunaki may represent a faction that chose not to retreat and to allow the natural tribes of humans to continue near them. The tribes that were around Sumer pre-flood, post-flood moved into the scattered remains of a more advanced human city. Some of the advanced survivors took some of their remaining technology, remaking themselves as gods. It is very possible, with the ability to modify genes, repair cells, use 100 percent of the human brain, they could control a lesser conscious human population. They anointed themselves

121

and pulled out their remaining tech to remain in power for thousands of years. They would need machines repaired and maintained. Humans could do the slave work of mining and smelting for a small group of humans presenting themselves as gods. Either they could only maintain themselves or chose to only maintain themselves in the aftermath of a cataclysm.

KILLER PARTY TALK, FOR NERDS. OR FORTNIGHT PLAYERS

3-D printing in these are done by external machines, Kurzwell describes the not so obvious and sci-fi version of nano machines self replicating, producing objects from a swarm of nano sized factories working together to produce something else as big as a building or as small as nano objects.

Here is your killer party conversation in Nerdville. If you can build anything out of atoms, whatever you want to build, gold, metal, whatever, what would you build? Imagine if you had the coolest 3-D printer ever, billions of nanobots that hover around waiting for your commands. 3-D printers are an emerging technology, nano factories are real. Imagine this nano 3-D printer can print working things with internal parts on a quantum level. 3-D printers now are printing ears, skin, taking living cells and printing them into medical solutions. 3-D print gold with your quantum printer. With control of the atomic structures and material science anything is possible. Gold, like any material has properties internally and on the surface. Material sciences looks at many things, one of those things is the surface of a material has properties different than that of its internal structure. Your 3-D printer prints factories, in turn they build things or builds more factories. After a mathematical point, there will be so many nano factories that when something comes to mind and you want to print it, you will give a command, the nano factories will build something from the smallest to the largest item you may want. Conceive it, will it, build it. It would appear out of thin air. No one from any planet goes anywhere for minerals. It is a 20th century level of understand earth, water, fire and wind. Aliens travel for funzonium. We are at a precipice of understanding our post flood myths lead us in circles and keep us trying to fit these myths into a coherent story, when all it is is a story. There are still enough people with VCRs and oil lamps that can touch back 100's of years as there is millennials that only care about social media. Neither group cares about quantum switching and the details of quantum mechanics yet it is in our future and our past. The applications of our fully conscious brain and quantum technology with ancient high tech interactive megalithic buildings, roads, communication equipment would be badass. The problem is the ruins would not look like much to us now. Our mind allows for aliens giving us a hand or thousands of slaves pulling stone up a ramp. Meanwhile we are not grasping that a highly advanced human race is at a quantum technical level and it is solely our past achievements.

There are examples of functional machines printed from particular materials supplied to print the designated item, in the future or deep in our advanced past, printing could be of a golden material or simply called from the either and on a nano or quantum level made into the cells or material required for the printing. Only the formula for the atoms required would be needed. No more digging, no mining.

Back to the killer party, when your done talking about this new car you were describing or creating with a friend in dialog over a drink, you get up and walk out and get in your newly nano built car that is waiting to take your home from this same party. Imagine a swarm of nanobots, ready, at your control, able to deliver things or food, anything from atoms in the air. This has a number of moral and potentially self explanatory reasons to how an advanced society could destroy itself. An advanced human society could ascend into a non physical body. The particulars of controlling an atom and it's parts is bananas. Your ability to repair or handle a single broken or hurt cell, to enter the cell, reprogram the DNA. Stop all disease. Genetic tech later...in a chapter coming sooooon.

We are and were human. We know this. Applying the Victorian template about gold is the result of our understanding of now. People liking shiny things and making bracelets. Humans are amazing story tellers and when you live amongst the ruins of the gods, how do you not come up with some fantastic explanations as to why we are where we are? Gold may have been really important to our ancient advanced ancestors but the stories that Gods, immortal beings needed gold falls right into our medieval understanding of the world. Our own understanding of sciences. By defining it as Gods we mystify. We see temples, worship, we no longer even conceive that it is technology. We are not looking at communication towers that used frequencies, we see watch towers for invading armies. We constantly pick up the pottery shards not seeing the giant earth circuits, we see beautiful worship rituals of the people making geoglyphs on the circuits of the Nazca lines. Not the birds, the kilometers long lines. The pieces we find show advanced complex sciences. Earth sciences on an avatar GIA understanding....just gonna keeping beating that horse. The reference is there for our alternative researchers, we keep analyzing the post flood stories and putting a new spin. They can't be relied on the foundations of ruins that could be tens of thousands of years old.

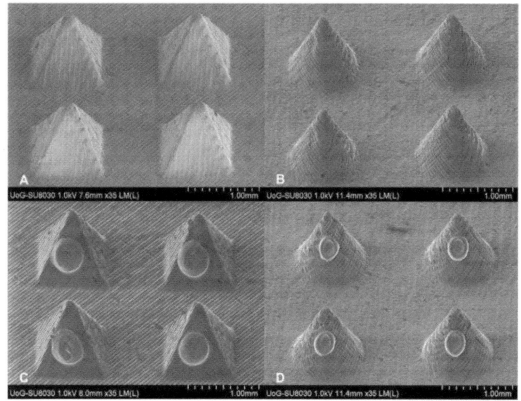

Imagine being at an ancient site, an archaeological Tell, digging, sifting through sand for bits of bone or material, then being told to send the sand and dust through another sifter, a scanner bed built for seeing nano structures or nano bots this size. Then piecing them back into the buildings, machines, or structures they were once apart of. Or in a short lived technological window, we reactivate an ancient bio weapon.

In "The Singularity is Near," Kurzwell describes some of the finds and advancements in 2008 including wifi enabled nanobots that could be swallowed or injected. The creation of nano factories that could take up residence in a body. Made of 85 to 175 atoms they could kick out even smaller nano bots. These nanobots could enter a single cell and repair or modify that single cell. Since 2008 we are here in 2019 with nano targeted cancer treatments that can head toward the sick points in the body and attack cancer. They can target specific diseases. The idea in our vernacular that we can now do this and Kurzwell describing the repair process in a cell to a complete replacement of biological cells to be perhaps diamonoid crystals. You could be that man of steel, we could in the future, meet up in a virtual or physical location, have a discussion and be present with all senses while simultaneously experiences rock climbing on Mars. The need for a physical body or being in just one place would be history. There is over 600 pages on this in The Singularity is Near and the digression as to all the implications of this is worth a read.

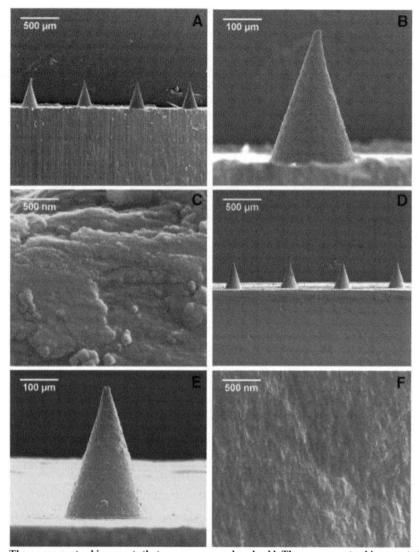

These represent achievements that are now over a decade old. These represent achievements that are not classified by governments. What lies under the sands of egypt, Tiwanaku or any other mud masked, ancient disaster site.

As we reconnect the dots, applying quantum technology, we see that there are elements of the physical world working in ways that appear magic. Particles appear as waves, waves appear as particles, particles appearing at two places at once, instant transmissions of information and many weird witchcrafts. Take Quantum Locking or flux pinning, this is a great thing to look at on YouTube. Starting with a chemically inactive disk of sapphire wafer, coating it with a superconductor called yttrium barium copper oxide, then chilling. Like liquid nitrogen cold, they conduct electricity with zero energy loss. Normally this is not something copper can do. On a track, the absolute zero disk is set in thin air. In the example, it's shaped and about the size of a hockey puck, whatever angle they set it at, it floats above or below the track. The track is a circle in this case. With a slight push, the frozen hockey puck floats around the track. From that example it is then set at an angle to the track, in mid air, it appears that something is holding it, "locked" in place. Then the disc is placed under the track. It appears to be floating but hanging now below the track. Again whatever angle the puck is placed it appears "locked" in place, it doesn't spin it doesn't act like a spinning top, no wobble, locked and moving in thin air.

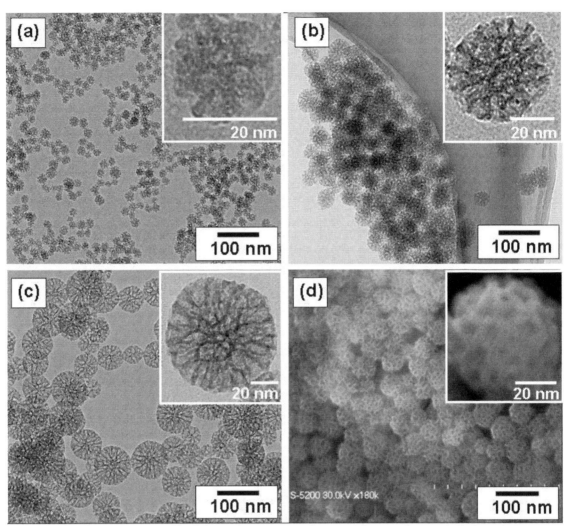

Post flood myths, our current world religious and power systems have created new needs or wants. In the ancient past they have, for unknown reasons, failed us today. Looking down and into the known sites as fast as we can will reveal our future also. A future we may want to redirect as we rediscover unknown nano technologies that would look very magical to a simpler people if the above nano machines suddenly manifested a car or a gun, or a statute of the David.

If you can lock in space, anything you could float, or move any object. The Moai of Easter Island were said to have walked in place from their carving. The large stones in Egypt and in Indonesia were said to have floated in the air and built themselves in place. As we rediscover these technologies the ideas about our past become less magical. This isn't to negate a spiritual connection, however again, imagine going to a yoga retreat at the old Chernobyl reactor and talking about how mystical and good positive energy is while doing a yoga class at sunrise or on an important post flood mythical magic day. Your doing your downward facing dog on the site of a nuclear melt down, not magical fairy factory.

MONATOMIC GOLD SHOULD OF COURSE INVOLVE THE BIBLE ORME (ORBITALLY REARRANGED MONO-ATOMIC ELEMENTS)

In the Old Testament, God provided Mana to feed the peoples of Israel while in the desert. There have been interpretations that Mana was real nano style food provided by God or others have theorized it was intervention of an advanced non human race to "help" humans.

This digression is important in that it is in either that Monatomic gold is a chemistry recipe to live immortally, it is also a great example of us in a post flood world grasping on to a post flood myth and focusing on reinventing a chemistry cure for death and the lot of human ailments. This is a distraction from the true ways the either/quantum world works and helps hide some of our living advanced ancestors.

Manna or mana is according to the Bible, an edible substance, that God provided for the Israelites during their 40 years in the desert following the Exodus. The story goes a couple ways on the manna, it was available everyday and the Israelites were to gather it everyday for each of them to the tune of approximately 3.64 liters but not extra, less it rotted and became full of maggots. This manna has references in the Yahwist and Priestly sources of the Bible. You know now that these are not sources Christians quote, or even

127

know of. There has been quite a buzz about this on the internet and for alternative researcher radar. The idea that there is a type of gold that can make you immortal or cure disease or put you on the road to a phase shifting multiverse Rick and Morty style.

They, them, and the internet have also theorized that Manna as referenced in the Bible was really monatomic gold. That Sumerian kings list has these kings living up to 36,000 years and this elixir was one of the reasons. Allegedly. According to the Sumerians, the Anunaki had an atmosphere that only gold could help or keep the planet alive. Allegedly. In the Bible god gives the Israelites "mana" in the desert to survive. One theory is that the direct translations of mana is, "what is it" that it possibly means "what is it". The theory then goes on to say that the Bible is the "mythical" or story handed down to explain what was really monatomic gold of the Anunaki. Which was used to keep themselves alive for thousands of years and save their planet's atmosphere.

Sooooo Mana, What is it? What is monatomic gold? In the 1960's and 1970s a cotton farmer in the phoenix area had about 7000 acres. Part of the farm was in Arizona, he had 1200 acres and they had a problem with black alkaline. It's salt that builds up on the soil. Cotton will not grow well. David Radius Hudson discovered Ormus. This is his short story...

David Radius Hudson was extracting gold and silver from the salted bedrock in the Arizona desert. He is getting sulfuric acid to process the salt in the soil. There was another substance with the gold. It does have the craziest of properties according to Hudsons testing the substance. It is not on the Periodic Table of Elements. There were elements in the soil that disrupted their cotton growing. Using cyanide, many metals separated, Iron, Aluminum, Gold, silver, silicon. Essentially this isn't some wizard alchemy, yet. As he was experimenting, there was unidentifiable minerals, or substances coming out. It appeared close to gold and silver but something else they couldn't identify was being produced. Hudson got a Ph.D. Of Chemistry at Cornell University to undergo an atomic emission spectroscopy analysis or AES. They seem to have found Aluminum silicate which should not have anything to do with Silica or aluminum in the entire process.

Until that point, Hudson had only been burning (boiling) the sample in the AES for a period of 15 seconds (as is common), but decided to prolong the exposure for up to 300 seconds. The beginning of his experiment went as expected. Readouts identified the sample as having trace elements of Iron, Silicon, Aluminum, and Calcium. After about 15 seconds, the test results became silent. Then, after a prolonged exposure of 90 seconds, the machine began producing unexpected results. According to Hudson at around 90 seconds, Hudson's sample was being identified as Palladium (Pd). At 110 seconds it read as Platinum (Pt); 130 seconds read Ruthenium (Ru); around 140-150 seconds read Rhodium (Rh); 190 seconds read Iridium (Ir); and then Osmium (Os) at 220 seconds. Had Hudson just discovered the material long sought after by alchemists and mystics throughout the ages? Most scientists say no, that this is a natural sequence of the progressive boiling temperatures for these substances, but Hudson was not satisfied with the findings as of this point. Hudson continued experimenting, through a series of experiments he tested very deep earth samples of gold. Deep gold finds. Through these experiments he created or rediscovered Monoatomic gold. With a researcher from Germany, now dead, he was able to measure through heat experiments elements in the process that showed up only after a burn time of 15 minutes. The Russian Science Academy has differing burn readings after extended burn experiments. Hudson duplicated those long burn time experiments. Ultimately showing to him, the proof that he had created and or rediscovered monoatomic gold.

Hudson is now internet famous for this ORMUS discovery. Here we are with the idea that a single element, or elixir can save, fix or heal you. The problem again is looking at post flood broken, ancient advanced technology and patching it back into the human experience. Quite possibly Hudson's experiments may have touched into the either and rediscovered these different possible states of metals.

Here we are again with the Sumerians, and other religions speculating that humans had a great jump by gods for gold. This is possibly a great reference to fallen advanced humans and that may be the sliver of truth in the Sumerian or biblical stories.

Is it more likely that ancient advanced survivor humans live secretly influencing individuals or governments to simply help keep the rest of us safely out of their advanced way? Meanwhile we sheeple ourselves on the next bingable season of a Netflix show. We have to consider that the records we have and are interpreting, are showing more than one advanced human race, they may have separated from each other pre or post flood.

Discerning what of the Sumerians myth stories could be true may simply be the age of the anti-diluvian flood kings. That long lifespans were possible due to external technology and human gene technology. There maybe a relationship with the Biblical stories for ORMUS. The Bible mentions Gilgamesh, the Sumerian flood story and Noah are almost identical. Spending a lot of time on the idea that an alchemy of gold can expand your life or cause you to see into other dimensions is a rabbit hole for post flood researchers. It's a bit like being fascinated with Victorian culture and societal traditions that have been forgotten about the Wild West and how cowboys actually spoke. A lot of time can be poured into this side channel of research.

One of the things that is a repetitive theme of all researchers today is the template we keep working from of any past sciences or mystical idea. In this case alchemy is a respected methodology by some and complete nonsense to others. The idea that a single element can repair the code of the body, the DNA, that elixirs, incantations can help... as we look at the cells, we see that they do vibrate, there is a frequency to everything. We have nanotech that is going into the individual cells doing actual repair work. With the mention of Mana in the Bible, are we really looking at nano tech given to an ancient people that kept them alive in the desert? Was it a more benevolent advanced ancestor handing out red cross aid to a disaster stricken tribe? The other possibility is that the story of the mana for the Israelites is just that, perhaps no one was helped, or just a handful. The story survived in the Bible because it is good narrative. It may have had a delivery system in a food or plant base. This is speculative, but here may be post flood evidence for another, more benevolent ancient human society, helping us to guide us back from our genetic amnesia. Having the mana story maybe there to put us back on the path to pick up our more complex sciences. ORMUS may have a place.

Genetic tech is the chapter to delve deeper, for now there are still too things to discuss, alchemy has its roots in our post flood attempts to create something from our desires. There are many traditions and famous people a part of secret societies which include alchemy and therefor mystery. Mystery creates a fog of stupidity around a lot of ideas. If your trying to do one part eye of newt and two parts iron and spinning in a circle trying to make gold for 2000 years, someone is going to take it seriously and realize, you just have to add one part frog leg and a pinch of cow dung. This sounds ridiculous but these are some of the filters that are put on the physical remnants of our past. Instead of seeing nano factory's in crystal formations of megalithic constructions, we see the constellations, a temple, and beautiful flower headdresses on hippies feeling the energy at Chernobyl. Monoatomic gold may have unique properties and be a valuable contributor to health or to future research into other technology. Looking at it with an eye of alchemy and potions ignores our complexity as humans and all living creatures.

CYMATICS

Ever wonder why there are so many patterns? Not 42, just the intricate patterns of cloths from Indians, India, or Asia in general. On buildings we attribute to the Greek, Romans, Etruscans. I developed an interest in the past and even as a kid walking through the institute of art in Minneapolis I imagined that the reason there were interesting patterns was because they had nothing else to do. As we see the lost ancient advanced past, clothing became complex because its a type of technology backup. As we reframe the past the idea that only the complex patterns would remain of a higher technology is possible. Through the ages there would be a slow loss of the purpose of patterns of circuits or formulas. Patterns and layouts of complexes like Nazca earth circuits, pyramid complexes and other ancient sites would just be well laid out streets and cause ways. The true purpose of the layouts and complex patterns lost, just intricate traditions now. Your Persian rug and the design may have the dimensional space algorithm for inter-dimensional travel or DNA sequencing an animal.

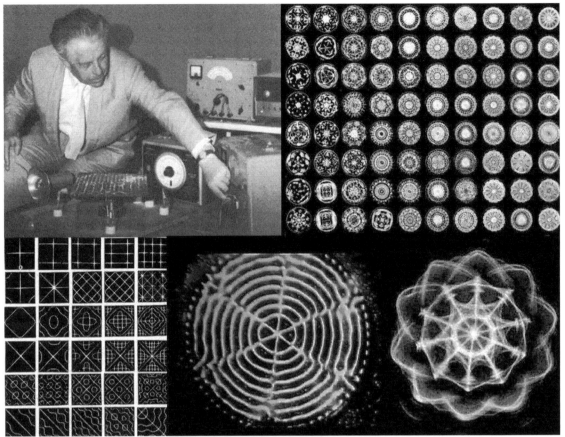

Hans Jenny started experimenting with sound and noticed that frequencies had unique patterns. There is still a debate that there are particles and waves in a theorized "duality". It is being proven almost without doubt that there is no duality of particles and waves. Fields and either are all part of the same basic principles perceived in magnetism.

Cymatics is from the ancient Greeks. Hans Jenny, a Swiss researcher published his work in 1964 called Kymatic about waves and frequency. To simplify things, it's a model of vibrational phenomena. He coined it cymatics. There are many musicians and artists that have developed an experimental music and visual artistry from this field of science. Surfaces of a plate or a membrane is vibrated and patterns are made visible by amplifying different frequencies. Using sand, paste, liquids, heat, flames, even mercury, the surfaces are displaced creating striking and accurate patterns. By accurate I mean patterns that look like every complex clothing pattern or Tibetan sand picture, Greek or Hindu design that you could imagine. Hans Jenny used Om, the ancient Hindu representation of the universal sound. The pattern on the sheets looks identical to the ancient representation of Om. This is a significant thing to figure out. Ancient patterns representing a sound that there was allegedly no machines for had an established symbol. Wouldn't that mean that there was once a higher technology?

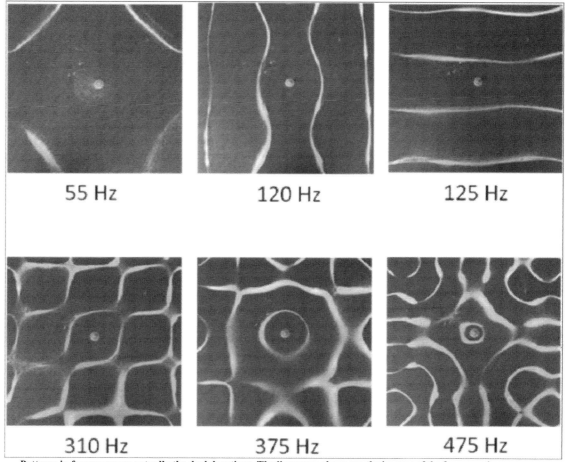

Patterns in frequency are actually the dark locations. The lines seen above are the inverse of the frequency's pattern.

My old way of thinking then thinks, once upon a time they had a sheet and 100's of monks chanting or a table and someone noticed the pattern formed on the surface that gave them the representation of Om. They spilt flour or rice and while the monks or chorus chanted or sang, someone noticed a neat pattern.

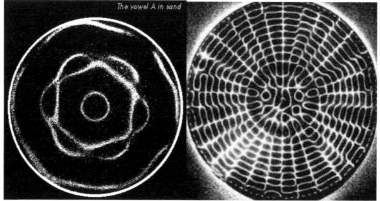

A particular frequency could have been delivered to an individual person or through a machine to lift an object, tune an individual or possibly tune thousands at once.

The idea that sound can heal, cure, that all cells, that all things have a vibrational quality is known now. Jenny is the first in modern times to really re-experiment with vibrational sound. His book became available in the 60's, this is pretty recent. The patterns on the plates change depending on the geometry of the plates and the frequencies being used are incredibly similar if not identical to many ancient patterns.

The Chinese Spouting Bowl, the cymascope, and Chladni Plate are all examples of vibrational mystical sounders. Jenny's work was filmed and can be seen online. The patterns that are formed as you watch the videos look very much like our complex patterns in ancient clothing and ornate pillars and columns from Malta, Rome, Greece, Egypt and China. The patterns look similar to to Tibetan sand drawings and the detail lace on clothing from many cultures.

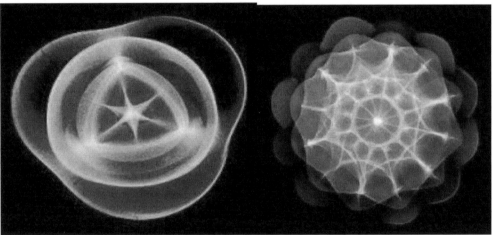

Levitation, moving with sound, healing with sound, the sounds the very machines would make doing all that... all of that would look like magic and the very memory of that machine may be reduced to a sound that could be described to an observing group of simpler humans or to descendants of the original makers of that kind of machine. The pattern of the sound could be woven into cloths or carved in stone like a Rosetta Stone for sounds.

Since the fall, the final smash to put us in the dark ages around 12-13000 years ago, we have forgotten and mystified our past technology. Can't produce the frequency anymore, weave it into a rug. Maybe at first to not forget the frequency but then later it is just a nice rug pattern. Or an ornamental garb that was once a technical achievement laying out the cymatic wave to cancel earthquakes in a specific area is a priestly robe. Or the vibrational frequency to destroy a brick wall or worse, kill is now a repetitive Corinthian column leaf pattern. Now the pattern is the laced marriage gown of a tradition as old as the culture wearing it and nothing to do with technology. Now it's something to revere and respect for it's cultural significant. Not that it was the pattern to a pre-collapse ancient high technology death ray or medical device, nope, now it's just pretty.

The complexity and exactness of the patterns of frequency when viewed through Jenny's work makes a very good comparison to quantum locking and the ability to exact a frequency and use it like a tool in a tool box. Depending on the job pull out the specific frequency wanted. Need to lift something with sound, we can do it, we have done it in a very crude way but we can do it again. Would you like to rip a particular cell to shreds, we can do it. There is obvious evidence that this was once a wide spread knowledge and incorporated in ancient technology. IF we only had ohm as an example. We have large stadiums, half shell amphitheaters in Rome, Greece, in South America that appear to be for frequency receiving and sending. We paint a primitive picture when we look at them and assume that it was for entertainment or public announcements and parades. The most recent evidence is showing something else completely amazing. This will also lead to a possible use of the Costa Rican Stone balls. (Shout out to Hugh Neumann and D.H. Childress's Stone Balls)

SEISMIC METAMATERIALS

Your about to read nerd stuff that is some of the most mind blowing things we now know about our ancient highly sophisticated relatives...

Just recently published by Stephane Brûlé, Stefan Enoch, Sebastien Guenneau on April 9th, 2019 a paper titled "Role of nanphotonics in the birth of seismic megastructures."

> " *The discovery of photonic crystals thirty years ago, in conjunction with research advocates in plasmonics and meta materials, has inspired the concept of decimeter scale measurfaces, coined seismic metamaterials, for an enhanced control of surface (Love and Rayleigh) and bulbs (shear and pressure) elastodynamic waves.*" Continuing, "*...nanphotonics, can be translated in the language of civil engineering and geophysics.......should not make us forget the heritage of the ancient peoples. Indeed, we finally point out the striking similarity between an invisibility cloak design and the architecture of some ancient megastructures as antique Gallo-Roman theaters and amphitheaters.*"

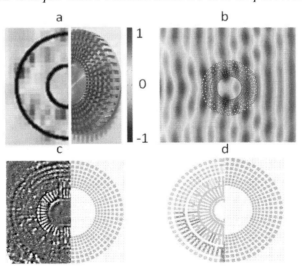

The most important work to date about ancient frequencies technology and earth system control is coming from some absolutely brilliant scientists. The imaging above shows that the colosseums and amphitheaters themselves were created with earthquake and sound and vibrational control or tuning in mind.

Let's translate, what they found is foundational structural components in the subsoil and above the ground that help cloak or mask or cancel the effects of an earthquake in a city setting and in these amphitheaters. They go on in their paper to point out that the, "white region in the center (e.g. a park) would be a safe zone where people could gather and remain safe during an earthquake. One could also envisage building a large structure (e.g. an amphitheater or a stadium) in the white area, and provide its dimensions are different from those of the buildings constituting the cloak, it would be protected from the shear component of the earthquake. This is their actual findings in tests. This information is new as of April 2019!

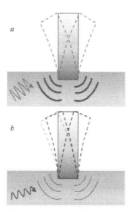

FIG. 4. Building under seismic disturbance and inertial interaction represented as a secondary seismic source, before (a) and after acting on the initial vibrational excitation (b). Acting on the input signal allows to influence, and particularly with the aim to decrease, the emitted vibration by the structure.

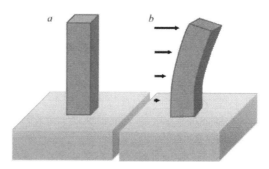

FIG. 3. Deformation of building on a thick plate: (a) Building at rest. (b) Elastic deformation for the first fundamental mode of the building.

In their closing statement in the paper, "While working on this review article, we realized that there are striking similarities between an invisibility cloak tested for various types of waves and sky views of antique Gallo-Roman theaters....It seems to us that such architectures are more resilient thanks to their unique design. Perhaps this is the reason why some of these megastructures, as amphitheaters, have remained mostly intact through the centuries? This deserves to be studied in more detail, and we hope our preliminary observations will foster efforts in the search for more analogies between engineered electromagnetic and and a new type of seismic metamaterials we would like to call 'archeological metamaterials'."

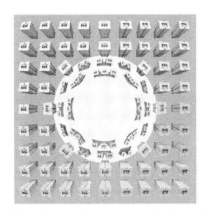

FIG. 6. Top view of a megastructure made of a set of above-surface bending resonators (cf. FIG. 4b). Here each resonator is a tall building. The typical size of the seismic cloak is 1 km.

The idea that archeo metamaterials with engineered soil, not just under a single structure, but over the course of sq. Kilometers to control the safety of a living populations and providing the same cover with surrounding trees and vegetation shows a for site and depth of planetary consciousness that makes me want to throw out my stainless steel straw.

They go on to show a picture of a more recent building in Mexico City. They then compare the more recent construction to the ancients, "On the contrary, recent constructions such as the one shown in FIG. 16. do not share the same resilient features as Roman amphitheaters. The future of seismic metamaterials might be brighter if physicists and civil engineers, not only draw useful analogies with design of electromagnetic metamaterials and metasurfaces, but also take a closer look at ancient architectures and learn from these beautiful and amazingly resilient designs."

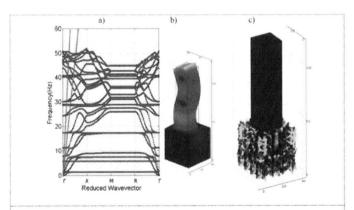

Figure 3. a) Band diagram for a concrete building (20mx20mx80m) atop a concrete homogeneous plate (40mx40mx40m); Floquet-Bloch conditions are set on vertical sides of the plate and stress-free conditions hold elsewhere. Flat bands correspond to eigenmodes of the building around 1 Hz, 9 Hz, 17 Hz etc. that couple to the flexural band (lowest band at Γ). b) Representative eigenmode of a) at 17 Hz. c) Eigenmode with suppressed building's vibration around 17 Hz when the plate is structured with auxetic metamaterial (4³ elementary cells with bars making an angle as in Fig. 2 c)).

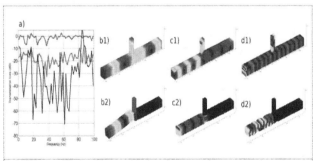

Figure 4. Quantification of energy loss a) with red (resp. black) curves representing transmission through a building atop a concrete plate (resp. a concrete plate structured with an auxetic metamaterial); Magenta curve gives the total displacement field stored inside the building above an auxetic-like metamaterial normalized with respect to the same total displacement field above the homogeneous plate. Representative out-of-plane displacement without (b1),c1) and d1) and with (b2),c2)) and d2) auxetic-like metamaterial illustrate how seismic protection works at 1Hz (b1),b2)) with the impedance mismatch between the homogeneous plate and the auxetic-like metamaterial ; at 9Hz (c1),c2)) with a local resonance ; at 37 Hz (d1),d2)) with the Bragg gap.

Lots of important squiggling lines. The picture on the left depicts a building with and without nanostructures or meta-frequency controlling structures keeping a building from shaking or moving. On the right it shows displacement in the soil having been groomed to help a tall structure in the center from moving with a disaster wave. Engineering the soil itself over large surfaces, not just pre-compacting existing soil but engineering and adding cymatic shapes that cancel or harness or distribute waves and frequencies as desired. This is the frontier of our past and future. It appears we have, by all evidence been doing this already.

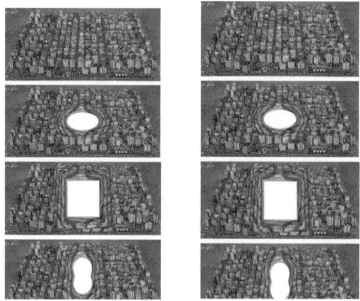

The shapes you see in these examples represent different results of what would be a safe zone depending on the style and shape of the buildings you use to control or manage the frequencies of earthquake and other wave disturbances.

One of the other cities they site is Bologna, Italy, which by all accounts looks like it had ancient skyscrapers, some of them are over 100 meters. There are approximately 22 left of what could have been more than 180. Said to have been built in the early Middle Ages, they are not complex, or megalithic in size, however the math on them possibly as seismic maskers is referenced in this article about the location of these buildings being part of a wave canceling zone. The center of a city, perhaps a park, surrounded by these buildings would provide the cancelation vibrations to elevate the safe zone which could be a park or area mathematical to the wave cloaking or an amphitheater.

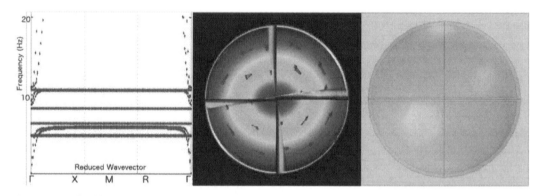

FIG. 5. Same as Fig. 4 for 8 pieces connected together and to concrete (host medium) by 20 evenly spaced steel ligaments of length l_i =0.03 m and diameter h_i =0.02 m.

It has now been studied, that various configurations of stone spheres, some halved, quartered, some with steel rods in them or rubber layers have all shown to have various cloaking, wave dampening effects on various frequencies. The chart is showing various stress points within th sphere and it's abilities to absorb or deflect different waves and frequencies.

There is so much to unpack here that is mind blowing and exciting! What if in sitting in this large perfectly tuned amphitheater the vibrations and frequencies resonating in this space was once used to wash over a crowd and heal or cure with vibrational energy? The acoustic properties of these world wide amphitheaters and other megalithic structures are astounding and yep, there is a quickly rising science of archaeoacoustics. The dolmens all over the earth have acoustic properties, some seem like they are almost sound cannons pointed all over the earth to receive and send waves. Yes, exactly like kids playing with two tin cans and a string in the middle. People stand in an amphitheater and talk or snap their fingers and talk about the ability to project, no one really thinks much about the idea that an amphitheater is there to receive and absorb waves. It's always about how everyone could hear Plato talk or watch a play. This the first scientific paper where the proof in the physical structure of highly advanced frequency ability is present and it is so obvious that they have to point it out. We are also talking cloaking from weaponized waves and communications. This is highly advanced ancient technology of our human ancestors. This paper is so new and so detailed, it's observations so stunning, we have to stop and reevaluate every site and surviving body of ancient times for our high technology linage.

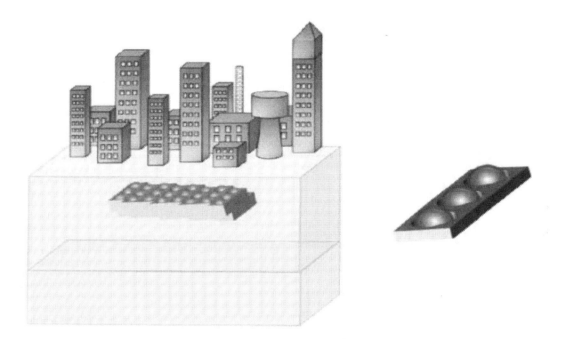

FIG. 1. Schematic, not to scale, representation of a seismic wave shield consisting of a periodic array of split-ball resonators placed underneath the foundations of a large civil infrastructure. Such inertial resonators shield wavelengths much larger than their typical size thanks to low frequency stop bands associated with local resonances.

These are the spheres suggest as above for wave shielding. Possibly the giant stone balls that are found buried all over the place and on the ground, often described as concretions, perfectly constructed and often found to be of multiple layers of material. What originally was the building or buildings that these ancient stone balls were under to create wave shields?

Let's talk balls now, big stone balls. The Costa Rican stone balls are found all over eastern Costa Rica, they were found in California digging for trains, Bosnia, Russia, Scandinavia and all over the earth. Considered by mainstream science to be perfectly round balls called concretions. Made by volcanoes throwing dust and bits in the air, causing, apparently, perfectly round balls to fall from the sky. Like stone snowballs rolling down in an avalanche. For our advanced theories, they appear to be cast in a mold and could easily, like obelisks, be mounted on stands like a power pole. Being in size from a couple feet and a few pounds to over 64 tons, they could depending on crystal content, other make up, be receiving, sending, deflecting waves or foreign frequencies. Some stone balls could be for one or two functions, others might be strictly defense. They are everywhere and anything that has ever held them up has long become dust. On Easter Island, the most holy, sacred and special object on the island is a stone ball. Not the big Moai, the stone ball is the most sacred thing on the whole island.

Stone spheres that were unearthed in Costa Rica and placed on a lawn. They are unprotected, unresearched and thought to be something to throw into a grave next to someone important in antiquity.

There are the findings of Royal Rife and his Royal Rife machine. He found that he could kill cancer cells and eliminate other diseases by focusing waves of energy at different frequencies at the cancer or viruses. Royal was experimenting in the early 1900's. The machines he was using were very powerful using plasma energy. The amps needed to produce a wave that would penetrate the human body is significant, commercial applications right now are not remotely close to the original machines.

Rife's work was significant and his work was stopped. He accused the American medical association of a plot to discredit him. There are machines sold now, computers, devices that are allegedly delivering frequency ranges that the original Rife machine were. The issue is that there has to be a carrier wave to deliver high RF sideband frequencies that were responsible for actually destroying the microorganisms that were part of his famous 1934 clinical trial where 16 patients were cured or recovered. These patients had TB and some had cancer. The original high RF primary frequencies would be needed along with the carrier waves. Buyer beware.

The United Fruit Company had banana plantations as early as the 1920's. The soil was incredibly rich. Doris Zemurray Stone (ironic right?) and Samuel Lothrop began in the 1940's to dig the stones up on the plantations.

Currently you can get on the internet and spend thousands to get a royal rife machine. Or a computer program that will give you the frequency of the disease you want to kill. The problem with these machines is that they do not produce high enough frequency to penetrate the human body. The real machines that Rife used did destroy diseases. Think tuning any string instruments. When out of tune, you tighten or loosen a peg and the frequency you want comes back. The cells of any cancer, or virus vibrate at a certain frequency. Rife found that he could shred or rupture the foreign cells with different frequencies. Conspiracies go bananas about the suppression of his research and that his machines were dumped in a river and everything was done to destroy his research. You don't have to look very long on the internet to find Royal Rife's notes or the original news articles of his success in killing diseases. Digging to the part that you recreate the intensity of the frequencies seems to frequently be left out of the new machines abilities and details. They have not been approved by the FDA. Here in Rife's work we have an example of the reapplications of frequencies for healing. His work has documented results. We have this new stunning paper about cloaking of buildings and spaces for safety and health in April of 2019 and Rife's work in the early half of 1900 doing cruder but effective disease work. The following is the evolution or modern applications of cymatic work in medicine.

Here they are with a sphere. They were being found in size between a few centimeters to over 2 meters. Ranging up to 15ish tons. They have weathered, they are made out of various stones including limestone and gabbro which is a vary hard stone.

Just like our modern and very recent seismic meta material study, the stones are found in the ground. We have had flooding, catastrophes, many possibilities range why the stone spheres are close to a surface or out. Recent cultures could have found them, mimicked them, or repurposed them.

They vary in size and shape. Some are more oval in style. They are also found all over the earth. The seismic wave and nano cloaking with the terra preta soil combined with the size and shape of the buildings going above these spheres would require different size and shaped stones.

The material and layers of these spheres need to be studied and sampled. Protection came in 2014 as a world heritage site. Work on the stones had a pause for over 50 years after Stone and Lothrop looked into them in the 40's.

The size is a easy one to grasp. The fact that they are in engineered soil and spread all over the earth is another one of those proposed "mysteries" that standard academia doesn't really want to solve.

When Dr. Semir Osmanagic started digging and working in the Bosnian Pyramid complex. Other archaeological anomalies appeared. Like 64 ton stone spheres. Smaller ones also. Layered with multiple materials and largely unstudied as of yet.

They vary in size and shape, some are hollow. Based on the seismic stresses seen above it would be many of the advanced pieces of technique required for wave and frequency control for a highly advanced ancient society.

They are found in New Zealand, California, Italy, Russia, close to the North Pole, so many places you'd have to shake a pointed stick.

Over time, from Bosnia to Mexico and any where a stone sphere was found, various legends and myths would identify the spheres as having gold and or treasure in them. Thankfully there where plenty of greedy people to blow and hack some of the spheres open. Had they not, standard academia would be thrilled with letting them alone. They would be protected and topical research or observations from behind a velvet rope would be about the only thing allowed. It appears that some are hollow. Perfect reverberation Chambers to change, harness or transfer various waves and frequencies.

Various stone spheres laying in situ still.

There are islands in the northern most regions of Russia bordering the North Pole where tourist can stop and look at the stone spheres. As we have seen from various maps reconstructing the past shorelines and various sunken lands, we have no eyes on what population or manufacturing centers would be open around an ancient advanced megalithic world.

This sphere is found in China. Nope, not one, many. Engineered soil all over the earth, engineered buildings. A new total map has to be made to account for these similar constructions.

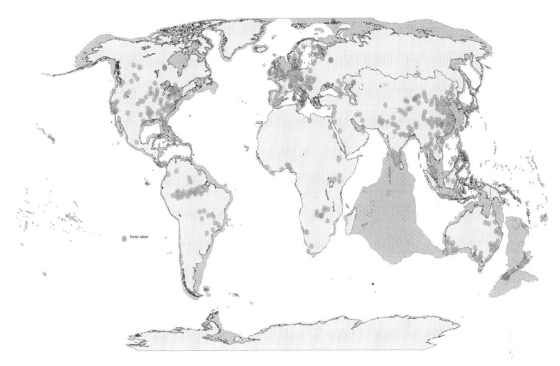

The locations of the stone balls and terra preta

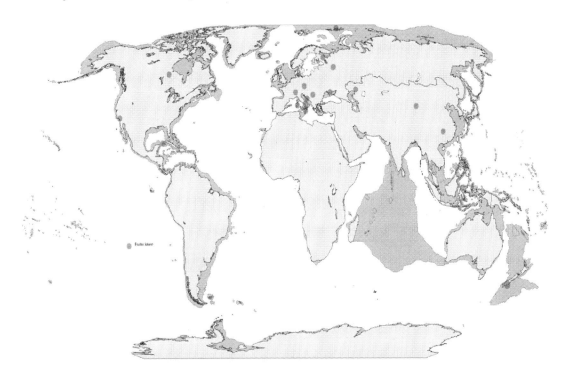

The locations of the stone balls across the world.

JOHN CHANG & MO-PAI AND HIGH INTENSITY FOCUSED ULTRA-SOUND

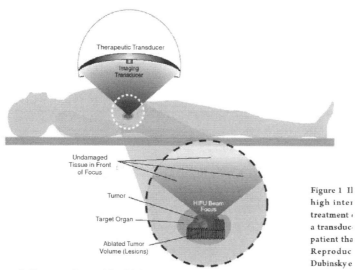

A diagram of a working high powered sound wave blasting cancer cells.

The Guardian, Sat 31, Oct 2015

> *"High Power sound waves used to blast cancer cells." British doctors can target and kill tumors without surgery. The Institute of Cancer research at the Royal Marsden hospital in Sutton are already using the tech to kill deep in the human body. " The technology is completely noninvasive and allows us to monitor changes we are making inside a person instantly" Thomas Andreas, therapy director at Philips. With ultra sound you can snap a picture of an organ or a growing baby, guide surgery or needle tests to a point(haha, point) so with a power of 10,000 times that of baby ultra sounds, "when we pick up a target tissue to kill off, we need to heat it up to about 55c for at least a second. That is enough to kill it off," sad Ter Haaretz, "....more important we can do it at places that are deep inside an organ- while leaving tissue on the surface unaffected.""*

HIFUS has been used in England for 5 years at this point. Wim Hof and Stig are teaching people to control their autonomic immune system and here is simple mindfulness making people healthy. This isn't good for fundraisers for cancer that never gets cured or anxiety meds that need to sell, or inflammatory medication that breathing can just take care of.

ANTHONY HOLLAND: DESTROYER OF CANCER CELLS

Associate professor, Director of music technology Skidmore College, DMA, MM, MM, BM, President Novobiotronics, Inc. Expert in digital electronic signal design, synthesis and analysis for biological effects and most importantly is the discoverer of the ability of Oscillating Pulsed Electric Fields (OPEF) to destroy cancer and MRSA cells.

Let's back up and talk Royal Rife. Rife built a frequency machine based on electrical waves passing through a gas (plasma ray) and found that he could shatter cells. Rife figured out that wave frequencies onto electrical fields and found that some 40 microorganisms could be destroyed. These include cancer cells (2 specific cancer cells at the time Rife tried). Holland found the inventor with the patent, Dr. James Bare and was able to assemble a new machine. Holland used the 11th harmonic. It is a mathematic multiple. They start killing 100's of microorganisms and this is viewed by fellow biologists whom had never seen anything like it. They literally can't believe their eyes. Holland goes at pancreatic cancer, the cells start growing biological antennas. Cancer is 1000 hertz and 3000 hertz and then he goes at leukemia and he shatters those cells also. Holy Shit, right? They completed, and continued the experiments and killed 25 to 42 percent to high as 60 percent and slowed growth to as much as 62 percent. He goes at ovarian cancer, killing them again. The work Royal Rife was doing is showing now through Anthony Holland that it is repeatable. Holland says " The math behind it is mind boggling, but we are closing in on a new scientific paradigm."

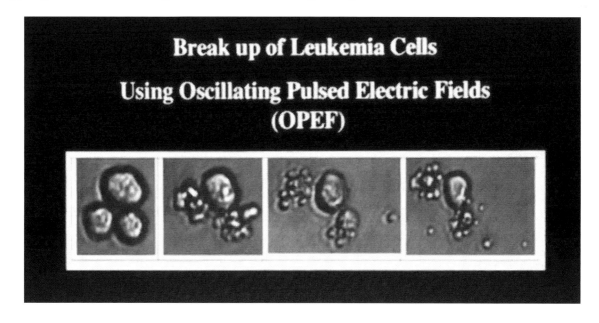

In MRSA, with killer sound waves, they were able to slow it, and add a drug that now made MRSA die. Holy shit! Seriously where is the running nightly news report on this research? Rife must have been right about someone trying to kill his research. If Rife was a fraud, so would be Holland, however there are a couple Ted Talks to show his work and opps, it's harder to kill that obvious evidence isn't it?

Cymatics may be responsible for being a future study umbrella over cymatic polygonal construction, our vibrational life down to cellular structures and material technology that has just turned to dust. Let's not forget the walls of Jericho were shaken down. The fundamentals of everything being vibrational and frequency is just beginning to be understood just like quantum theory disrupted the physics world when it came along. Here we are with quantum either and frequencies coming out on top over particle theory.

Spintronics is the science of quantum mechanics and basically it's called spintronics because it is the theoretical ability to control or spin an electron in a direction giving it a "state". In a computer, binary code is negative or a positive, on or off, one or zero. The quantum has many more states leading to infinite possibilities. Yes, binary offers a lot too, nothing like quantum so spintronics is getting us closer to quantum computing.

Quantum locking is cool, it's just one aspect of what has many material applications. Different products from basic fiber and glass to plastics are being used to create non moving switches for future quantum computers. This is the on off binary thing. You need switches to set the information in a machine. There is speed to process and then there is access to existing data. The idea that computers are on a wafer thin board could give way to cells themselves being able to do information storage and act as active memory. Wether plastic, or organic matter, it could control information or become a factory to create or 3d print anything. As an example, it would appear that someone could lift a hand and make something out of thin air but what they really did was send the build plans of a toy plane to the nano factory's floating around him and they grab particles from the air and build the toy plane. All you would see is the wizard in that hat. This is easily the case for a primitive people that have lived along side a more advanced culture. The more primitive may verbally passed or through a written language tell the story of walking or floating Moai and the the walls of Jericho tumbling down from the playing of the horns by the Israelites. This is one of Erik von Daniken's main points about the walls of Jericho and the ark of the convent. The Israelites walked around the city of Jericho and played trumpets that the ark amplified. Von Daniken theorizes that the ark was a piece of ancient tech that was used as a weapon and it vibrated the walls to rubble.

How hard would it be to create portable machines that simply play as an instrument and create field perturbation to lift, move or heal? Instruments today including frequently used harmonic ranges in top musical hits could actually be deep human memory of a higher functional use of those chords or sounds when used as the healing, levitating or other machine they once were.

If you can control a subatomic particle, to beat this horse a bit more about any alien race intentionally coming to earth for minerals, if you can travel in the craft of the sciences that allow faster than light travel. Or even cooler, space folding travel through dimensional space. This is technology that requires exacting mechanical application of spintronics to your body, machines, and engines of your society. If you're trying to resolve any of that by digging in the dirt on a planet not as close as the moon? Your at least an idiot alien. Or maybe like Captain Kirk, being tested on a planet with a captain from another ship and you need to create a rudimentary cannon to kill the lizard captain.

Sure, maybe you crashed, needed to rebuild and leave earth. Our planetary super collider is big. In the future maybe it will be the size of a microwave. Is it more likely that our own race of humans, advanced to be able to do what we have figured out. Really, it took 100 years for us to get where we are. Anatomically correct humans leaving boot prints 300 million years ago? Maybe it took them the same 12,000 years? My point about the math and ancient maps is that the broad range of sciences needed to have achieved the insight we have had would not have been possible without a higher, more cohesive society. I believe that we can do more, implying a societies level of achievement by looking at the math, maps, and structures.

PI

"Quantisierung als Eigenwertproblem" (Quantization as an Eigenvalue Problem)

Pi and the Pyramids, the two harmonies pyramid and stadiums and stone balls. Why incorporate an equation that wasn't needed to build the pyramids at Giza? However a world wide network of healing, communication, defense and interstellar communication or radar centers would need math for infinite things like waves and frequencies.

One of my questions is what type of metal would connect to the vibrational frequencies of communication or energy for the buildings? It's not a matter of just earthquake control and cloaking from other waves. The type of metal may conduct energy between polygonal blocks like an antenna or for amplifying sending and receiving data from all sides. Copper not initially being thought of as a superconductor but there it is in the right element locking in thin air with crystal and spinning like mad in our quantum locking scenario.

One of the first and best uses of quantum computing and nano tech could be to move like bacteria or a virus through soil, rock, and analyze what components are left. For the first time, the very dust around an untouched site could be rebuilt. Imagine crushing a bridge of concrete to gravel. Imagine a new breed of archaeologists coming to Machu Picchu, and coating all the walls megalithic and the later stone rubble additions to the site with a powder containing nano bots. At that point the bots crawl all over the rubble fill in analyzing the surfaces for what is there, mold, lecithin, angles. Even the round rubble wall fill in. The archaeologist spends the rest of their time setting up camp, they sit down on one of the edges of the site, looking out to the spectacular views, pulling up the nano data which is giving all sorts of new info. The rubble appears to be mostly from other fallen structures, a quantum computer would analyze quickly the locations of where those bricks and stones really belonged, showing hypothetical models of the missing structures. Building back the correct megalithic structures with blocks that would be accurate for the gaps. Also there is a big gab in what we are not going to talk about till cymatic polygonal masonry which is the frequency effect of the polygonal construction. For now the nano tech is analyzing the LIDAR and unburied ruble and adding that into the factors for where all the rubble goes. Separating what the Incas rebuild and what our ancient high tech ancestors built.

THE PYRAMID COMPLEX OF GIZA (IT'S EIGHT SIDED) PI FLAVORED CONSTRUCTION

The Great Pyramid of Giza is 8 sided, and so is Menkaure. If you closely look at the 3 smaller pyramids by Menkaure at least one of them is 8 sided also, why? This is barely pointed out by anyone. It's the most significant structural element for re-engineering the technology of the structure, other than there are geopolymers present.

In 1940 British Air Force pilot, P. Groves saw the pyramid for it's actual design. He flew over it and took these now famous photos. The angles are subtle and can only be seen from the air and at certain times of the day. If we were not unraveling an ancient society with advanced technology then we are just looking at really over done tombs. It is more likely that the math on this pi based pyramid to have more vibrational and frequency reasoning behind it. Animation after drawing puts this structure with 4 sides In books with loin cloth builders and movies and documentaries. The indentation to create subtle sides however at the length and width and height of the pyramid would give the pyramid a star shape. Menkaure has the same feature on one side from ariel view photos. In dealing with pi and looking at the great pyramid complex as a more complete complex, you could see that it takes on a different personality with 8 sides being confirmed. The middle pyramid, Khafra is on a piece of bedrock raising it approximately 33 ft. making it look like the biggest. I made the assumption myself that it was the tallest. Menkaure is on the far side. The many issues of this being a complex adapted for use by the Egyptians means that they may have repaired or worse, been responsible for pillaging stones off the pyramids for other purposes blurring the true facts. There are records of some later middle age rulers taking the stones. If pre-flood and in original use the complex had two 8 sided pyramids and the center pyramid was a true four sided, then perhaps it was reflecting signals to either pyramid. The outside pyramids were using the center as a reflective unit. The use of the complex and individual structures is too early to say, however how can you get a true assessment without a better picture of the physical structures and a better idea on the surface material or plating that is missing. It is assumed it was stone. It is more likely that a nanostructure or plating for frequencies and wave energy was present. There are knobs or "stuff" nodules that appear on some of the exterior blocks. They appear in Machu Picchu and many other places around the globe. It is possible the "knobs" on the Great Pyramid give support to increase shear strength for

an exterior plating of some kind. On a surface this big, no matter what kind of adhesive used, these nod points maybe for higher frequency or vibrational communications between surfaces of the structure and or for shear strength of that exterior surface Simultaneously.

The pyramids are perfectly oriented to the cardinal points, and how about it's neighbors? How does it line up with them? There is a reference by Robert Bauval about the Orion mystery. That the pyramids shafts point to stars and the layout of the complex mirrors the star system Orion. We have

already covered this. What about star systems past Orion that a highly advanced society would see? What about alignments that go way beyond what is physically seen in the night sky to other planets beyond, only to be seen by ancient advanced satellites?

The golden ratio, pi, and Egan values equate quickly that the math for these structures align with energy, communication, tuning the earth, tuning humans and nature, or possibly more. Not just super straight temples and tombs.

On the grounds of frequency, we have looked at the many ways everything vibrates. Frequency and resonance of cells, the chamber in the chamber of the Great Pyramid, if it was for humans, would be a tuning center? If the Great Pyramid was energy and communication as the math of the pyramid indicates, it is more likely that the chambers of the pyramid and the work they do in resonating would effect individuals differently. The shafts in the Great Pyramid would adjust. They could be up or down based on the tubes or shafts of the pyramid being like organ pipes. There is a reference that the shafts in the Great pyramid are ceremonial, that they point to stars. Frequencies could change based on air in the shafts if you look at them as giant tuning shafts. Air that changes including nanoparticles in air that change its focus and center for the application in the moment of use. The combined vibrations of the stones above the kings chamber and the shaft vibration would change the surface vibrations of the pyramid and those on either side. Oh remember the other two pyramids that are almost never mentioned, like a Frame for the picture of the Great Pyramid. So think of the surface of the great pyramid as a drum. The shafts as organ pipes. If it was industrial and medical, we have to start breaking down the tech. If we are looking at an advanced civilizations that could live in definitely and manage cellular regeneration with the aid of machines, then this could have dual purpose. We have no material left of the interior of the machine and worse it could have been repurposed to be scepters or gold chains. What we have in scale is the shell of your favorite 64 stingray, no interior, no engine. But what if we had a shell of a transmission box, and a shell of an engine? All we gotta do is reverse engineer everything else. Easy, right?

Many ancient sites resonate on key harmonics. Most of Petra Jordan. The site has room after room, to 320,000 cubic sq. ft. rooms and they resonate perfectly. Also interesting at least from Ariel maps Menkaure and Khufu may not be the only 8 sided pyramid in the world, and the smaller ones next to Menkaure appearing to have at least one 8 sided pyramid indicating a high technology lost function. How do we know? Dynastic Egyptians build with mud brick, re-stacked ancient fallen buildings and never talk about star shaped buildings or build them or hieroglyph them.

Is there a correlation to the type of stone and corresponding obelisks or did one building being rose granite or sections being a certain granite help receive, send or channel energy, communications, etc.? There is also a magnetic signature to the material blocks. On one hand it could help blocks stay together while under earthquake or other stress or generally to keep them together. On the other hand it could be a side effect of transferring energy between blocks while being used as communication tools.

Speaking of waves, the energy of water could make has been researched by Georgia tech Z.L. Wang. Three volts now to 10,0000 volts independent of weather, day or night. In other words, one wave of water equals 31 terra watts more than we need can be produced from kinetic energy.

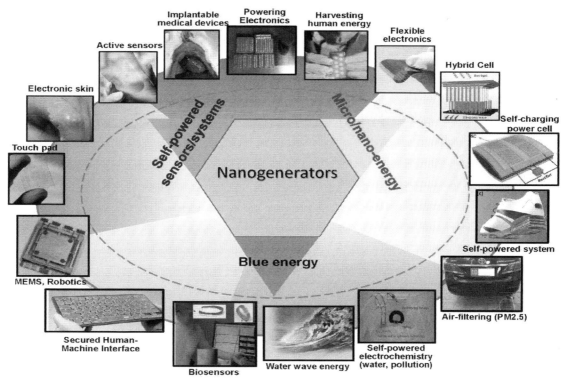

Z.L. Wang is responsible for all these advances. How hard or should it be required in future archaeology to look for versions of this technology?

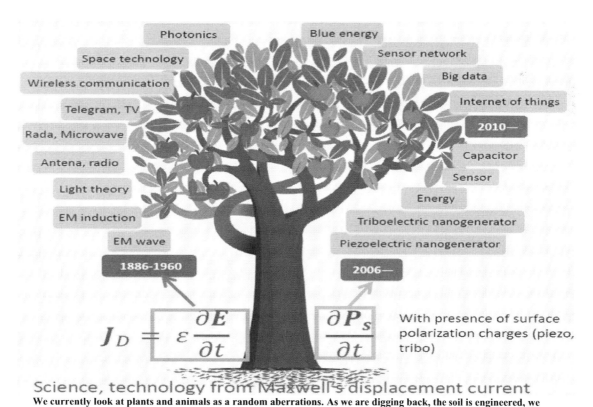

Science, technology from Maxwell's displacement current

We currently look at plants and animals as a random aberrations. As we are digging back, the soil is engineered, we seem engineered, trees, plants and animals may be part of what really is a high functioning planned system. To this day it averages that over 5000 species are found new, annually for over 30 years.

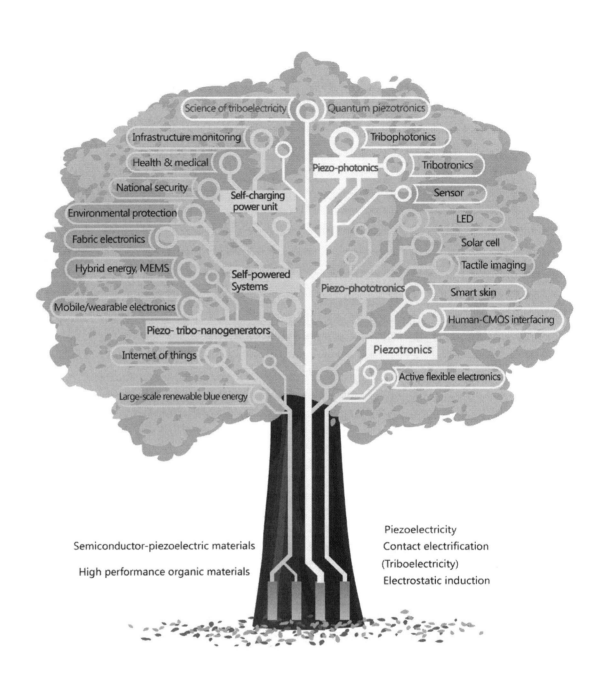

Trees, animals, fungus & bacteria could all be connected to filter, manage internal and external threats while simultaneously creating energy. Communication between "animals and plants" and polygonal cymatic constructions like obelisks could be possible.

Curiously some stones which ring like a bell have no other purpose than to indicate the position of treasures hidden in the earth? As a result of this idea, various rocks containing bedrock mortars in Chile have been ruined, and the interesting ringing stones near the port of Eten, formerly called "Las piedras del Capitan," were broken in pieces. In Ecuador, wherever one finds rocks marked with petroglyphs, or even with natural cracks which might possibly be taken for artificial designs, one sees also remains of excavations in search of treasure, which naturally have been uniformly fruitless. Stone pieces including obelisks, having tuning, frequencies are found from Asia to America. Like Singing Rock Mountain. It is an avalanche of ancient singing stones, perhaps once a large building or many buildings.

Sound or archaeoacoustics is relatively a new field and raises more questions to the standard beliefs of academia while showing more than hints of incredible ancient advanced technology in sound. It is so easy for standard academia to find old things that we have established as "facts" an idol for worship, a temple, a summer solstice to dance around and always another temple. Not vibrational technology of a more advanced society. That ancient technology is now the pattern to someone's yoga pants. The first thing any conventionally trained priest of archaeology wants is to do is humiliate and discredit this new information in order to keep their own job. Spending any amount of time with quantum consciousness and vibrational technology now, has allowed some researchers to discover the lost technology in the very buildings and city layouts like Bologna, Italy. Amphitheaters that could receive or cloak a building or an area is terrifying and exciting all at the same time. The sciences showing that we can effect quantum level particles or either with our thoughts, should be a lens to review all of the ancient structures we have found. Searching through post flood religions should be clues to help us answer the growing body of evidences that a highly advanced group of humans made it through the last cataclysm. Devil is in the dust and the quantum either.

Chapter 7

WATER TECH EMOTO GRANDER AIDS STRUCTURED

Quantum consciousness, we could go down that rabbit hole forever. Your thoughts, creating vibrations, creating something in the universe on a level we can not see. Water is god. Consciousness effects water, or is it that water reflects consciousness? Water is flammable, bridgeable in air, can lift heavier than water objects when cooler, freeze faster when it's warmer and harder and denser in ice form after starting warmer. It seems to communicate on a quantum level with itself and it heals, cleanses, creates energy, life and these observations were made before and during Schrodinger, Planck, and about the same time we had a steam engine.

There are a few researchers new and old that are making and have made incredible observations about water and it's complexity. These observations about the world of water are immediately beneficial to us today in ways they are not

Viktor Schauberger

immediately shared in mass. Water is one very universal thing we all need and we look for in space and on other planets. If there is water, there can be life, if there is one living bacteria or piece of slime on any other planet, modern religions of earth will lose their monkey minds. In looking at water we can again, reevaluate the ancient structures of our past. The incredible researchers we are about to look at and their amazing research into water is only equaled by the shallow observations we have made about H2O. These great discoveries come really to us as rediscoveries. What they observe seems to coincide with our ancient advanced ruins.

VICKTOR SCHAUBERGER

"Implosion is no invention in the conventional sense, but rather the renaissance of ancient knowledge" - Viktor Schauberger

He was born in 1885 and was initially an Austrian forester. He died in 1958 as one of the greatest naturalists, philosophers and inventors, ever. His first job was managing a forest of 21,000 plus hectares of trees. He loved natured and studied every aspect of it. He began noticing incredible personalities of water that can only be described in the quantum world. There was a spring that was once covered by a stone hut, once torn down the spring dried up. When the hut was rebuilt, the spring returned. This is not the only incident like this. Water has had a history of appearing when needed at places that never had a spring before.

The Romans covered springs with stone, leaving only the opening free to attach an outlet pipe. Side note on Romans, they, like the Dynastic Egyptians, came to a place from Tartaria, or possibly they were Etruscans, found the cymatic polygonal walls, fallen columns, remaining megastructures including the colosseums and amphitheaters and rebuilt. The water tech including aqueducts and in some cases just needed some patching.

Vicktor noticed that springs were common in deep forests, rock clefts, rivers and streams seamed to shade the water from bushes and trees on the banks. While thaws in spring, rising floodwaters built up banks of debris only to be carried away when the air cooled on clear nights. He concluded that water could carry and had a kind of suction power. When water was at its lower temperatures and flowed undisturbed. He would apply these observations in 1918, there was a shortage of firewood due to the Great War. There were no animals or not enough to carry the wood down from the hills.

Schauberger was ridiculed that water being off a 10th of a degree would not matter in the flotation of heavy logs down chutes. Yet a 10th of a degree can easily indicate illness or disease in a human.

Schauberger proposed using a small, rocky mountain stream to transport the wood. In the coldest hours of the morning, they moved over 15,000 cubic meters of wood down from the mountain. This proved a lot of critics wrong about the transport method and later, was a technology incorporated in his log flumes. It was always assumed that the heavy logs would not move but sink. Schauberger's observations about the temperature of water was one simple yet never understood before his modern observations.

Schauberger was fascinated by trout and salmon that could just "float" stationary in fast moving mountain water. Below the surface was a current, yet they just could float stationary in one place. Was this also water temperature induced? He placed warmer water up from a single trout, not much and it caused the trout to move and not be able to maintain its position. This was another repeatable experiment where water was showing attributes outside of wet, frozen or evaporated.

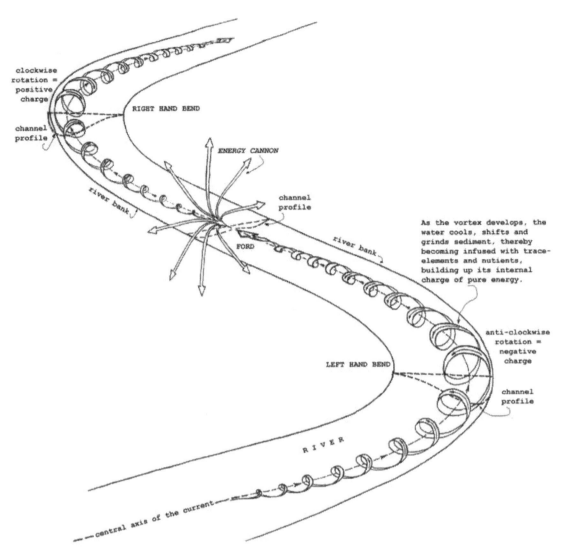

Schauberger deduced and diagramed the "health" of water and it's nutrient and energy Value here in this diagram. Water shoved through city pipes in a straight line loose all their energy values and many of the health benefits of water that gains mineral and energy values when traveling in a vortex. There are pipes now made to mimic vortices and to help water maintain its healthiest benefits.

The egg was a great shape geometrically speaking for vortexes. Inside a hyperbolic vortex and water makes vortices, eggs are an easy thing to move for water. He saw us miss using one of two forms of energy found in nature. Outward expanding flow that is used to break down or destroy and inward-spiraling which Nature uses to energize and create. The combustion engine is the not most effective way to create energy. Move an egg shaped stone, heavier than the stream it is in, just wait for vortices and at the right temp, up rocks go and float.

Schauberger was ridiculed by hydrologists when he said that the log flumes he built to float the heavier than water logs down the flumes relied on a 10th of a degree difference. He also changed the flume flows after observing a snake swim on water. Schauberger changed the temp and flow, achieving something that had never been done.

Shauberger was making quantum level observations about water with his eyes and possibly common sense deductions. It wasn't just a chemical compound of H2O. Water should not be just pumped through pipes, chopped in turbines, and definitely not bleached, chlorinated or needlessly heated. A human gets sick if their temperature is off even tenth of a degree. Proposing water had to be within a tenth of a degree was witchcraft according to the victorian scientist of the day. The idea that the earth was connected, like it was one giant entity? Here he is making quantum observations that quantum scientists were observing in their experiments.

He had antigravity inventions based on vortex energy theory. Thank you National Socialist Germany for keeping him locked up under threat of death to keep him researching during the war. Allegedly. Schauberger wanted to rebuild water-courses that revitalized rivers and keep them from flooding, clean their own banks and not have soil erosion. He patterned water barriers of braking and helping rivers or any waterway move in 1929. He was well aware that dams abilities to hold water were effected by motion and temperature of the water.

Late in his life, the hydrologist Professor Forcheimer gave Schauberger's ideas a go after being one of the religious academic critics. He had nothing to loose, being in his 70's. There was no standard academic that could threaten Professor Forcheimer into retracting support for Schauberger's ideas. He became a believer. Mind you this isn't supposed to be a new religion. This is a revolution in re-discovery of our powerful connections and abilities from our past. We are living with amnesia, we have no mind again that we control the very atoms in the air around us.

Funny time to bring up the Bosnian Pyramid. The geologist Robert Schoch, Michael Tellinger, Sylvie Ivanova, Brien Foerster, Graham Hancock, many more have gone to see what may be the largest pyramids ever found. This of course caused a stir as Dr. Semir Osmanagic has continued excavations on and in miles of tunnels being found. I could geek out about all the pyramid factors. That make this or not this a pyramid. Shoch says it isn't. How this relates to Schauberger's work, is that around the Bosnian pyramids and through the medieval, Roman, and small villages that have been in the area, all are planted near the rivers. One of the main videographers for the Bosnian pyramid noticed that the rivers look intentional in their weaving, and there are signs of geopolymers. Even if the structures of the Bosnian pyramids were not full pyramids, the area is in the heart of elongated skulls, the Tartaria, Etruscan and deep rock cut roads regions of middle earth.

"Humanity has committed a great crime by ignoring the use of cycloidal motion of water," Schauberger said, "For example, the current water-pumping devices were not only uneconomical, they cause water to degenerate by depriving it of its biological values."

Schauberger in practice and designs had seen in water some of the higher prevailing forces that were once part of our consciousness. It's temperature, abilities to move in a vortex, it's high mineral health affected if it wasn't moving naturally down a happy river or stream. Water lost its ionization in city water pipes and became sick. Schauberger was not the only one seeing the natural world for the first time again and the central role water had in it.

LET'S KEEP TALKING ABOUT GERMANS, WELL AUSTRIANS

Johann Grander, two things to say about him right off the bat: According to some court rulings, mainstream academics, he is a complete fraud. Grander water filters and/or "revitalization" filters are nothing but B.S (you know B.S, they give you degrees with this title at mainstream indoctrination schools. You can pay, give four years of your life and they give you a piece of paper that has your name and B.S. written on it).

Second thing you should know right away about Johann Grander, The Russian Academy of Natural Science awarded the Silver Honorary Award, which is to also make Johann Grander the only Austrian to ever receive this.

Johann Grander, father of Revitalized Water

Remember the Russians? They went to space first....Super brilliant thinkers the Russians, The former land of Tarteria. Long, ancient, history with the largest megalithic constructions found on earth. Red headed, white mummies everywhere that aren't supposed to be there and land of ancient nanotechnology. The Moscow Institute determined that the nano parts found in 10-40 ft feet of a geological layer were at least 20,000-318,000 years old. In 96' Dr. E.W. Matvejeva from the Central Scientific Research Department Of Geology and Exploitation of Precious Metals are definitely advanced pieces of technology. Rabbit hole to our highly advanced past.

Johann Grander was observing what Schauberger had investigated in water. Grander had found a spring in an abandoned copper mine, he studied the water from the mine and noticed a high mineral content. After many experiments, he ultimately created "structured" water. Healthy water with high mineral content, good ions, "energetic" "structured" water. In his observations this water could revitalize water that Grander thought of as "dead" water. The water coming from a city or a well is forced through a straight pipe, chemicals, bleach, chlorine were added, by the time this water gets to the tap you use, it was mineral-less, no negative ions, nothing that really helped us, essentially dead water.

Grander had a theory that water had memory, that if you could expose "sick" water to healthy water, the water would pick up on the healthy attributes and convert itself by exposure to the healthy example in the filter. Austria, Switzerland, German swimming pools get less algae, chlorine, or as calcified as before by incorporating Grander filters. Less rashes and skin irritations were reported by swimmers. In industrial applications factories had costs in chemicals, cleaning and changing the water. Grander created a filter that reduced the bacteria to the point that the factories reduced the water costs, chemicals and cleaning by half. A laundry uses the Grander filters and they started saving over 15 % on their bills. The examples were coming in from people using Grander products. Grander credits his information in just observing the natural world. Water is not just H20. Electromagnetic field, wifi, cell services, random waves in the air, water is all over and exposed to these waves. Acidity in water contributes to arthritis pain and inflammation in joints. The filtration and water revitalization products were working in factories, businesses including homeopathic remedies, over all many successes including that Russian award he received.

There were all the standard complaints from mainstream academics that structured, revitalized water was not real. It was determined in court. Well, he also won the Honorary Cross for Science and Art from Austria. So I guess water in Grander and Schaubergers' experiments, despite actual observable provable experiments, they are left as mysteries, oddities, quacks or very well meaning men. Of course quantum mechanics just keeps getting everyone squirming and uncomfortable. The proof of these men are in their actual accomplishments. The results of both these men's work was economic, observed and tested and continues so.

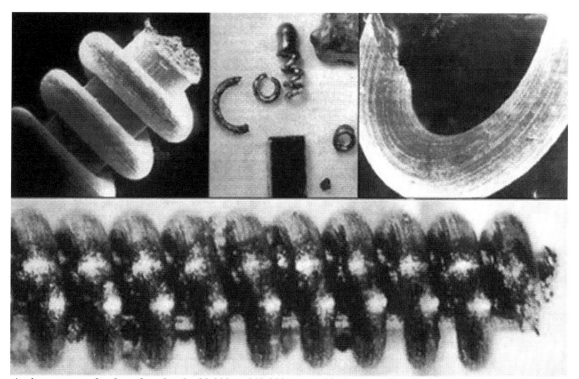

Ancient nano technology found to be 20,000 to 318,000 years old. At any archaeological site parts are sifted for, however looking for nano technology would require a reinvestigation of every bit of sand or dirt uncovered or yet to be at every site. If this technology is at this one site, it could be at more. More importantly this research has been stopped or forgotten like sunken pyramids off Cuba.

Oh, about those Nano parts of high technology that were maybe 20,000 to 318,000 years old, they were studied in Helsinki, St. Petersburg, and Moscow. The work ended when Dr. Johannes Fiebag died around 1999. The article and pictures of the pieces float on the webs. Just apparently not anywhere else. Ancient nano technology parts, alien or human machinery?

DR. EMOTO MASARU

Emoto is a researcher that took the words, thoughts, prayers and labeled them in multiple languages on bottles, jars, containers etc..of water. Freezing the droplets after multiple timed exposures to the words, thoughts, prayers and seeing what came up in image. The structure of the water made what could be described as beautiful snowflakes. When the words and thoughts directed at water were negative, "I hate you, die," words like murder, disgust, anything that was negative, irrelevant to language, the water was reviewed under microscope and photoed. The result was melting yellowing, pretty gross looking water. It was pretty close to healed severely burnt skin, not pretty.

Dr. Emoto Masaru, creator and experimenter of water having consciousness.

Dr. Emoto created a rice experiment. Three glasses of raw rice, each filled with water about even with the raw rice. Then each bottle labeled with words. One bottle, I hate you, one, I love you, the third, just ignore it. Not labeled ignore, just literally ignore it. Every morning, or at least once a day, go up to the three bottles shout or think "toward" the water just like the water is labeled. For the hate bottle, throw some nasties at it, ignore the ignore bottle and sing some loving praises to the love bottle.

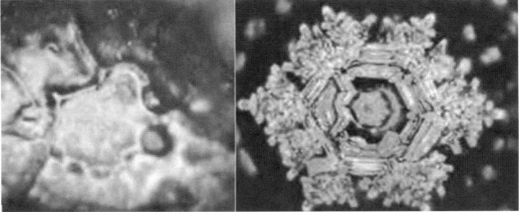

In the above experiment water is exposed to various words. Dr. Emoto found that the words in any language didn't seem to matter. After negative or positive words were applied to water in any language, the water would have consistent results as seen here. Negative word on the left and a beautiful crystallized structure if a positive word was used.

After thirty days, the water labeled, "I hate you" looks the worst, with the neglected bottle coming in a close second with molded, rotten, grossness growing in it. The one that has been sung loving words and praises, is sweetened and fermented nicely. This experiment was repeated all over the internet. Of course that validates it, right? Many worked, many skeptics converted, then there is the group that site there were no double blind examples, that the experiment could be tipped or faked to show the positive results. There is the simple facts that these examples are not repeated in standard academic environments and this is just pseudosciences. Worse, they give Emoto, Grander, and even Schauberger the complement of being well intentioned men. That they mean well. If you want to just touch on conspiracies, if we were on track of coming out of the amnesias we are in as the survivors of a more advanced past, wouldn't a group that is trying to keep us all sheeple not outright lie or put down these experimenters and researchers directly? Would it be better to use these incredibly subtle knocks, half true observations to discredit research that puts on track for our own awaking and realizing that some of our advanced ancestors are still living among us?

Emoto continued his work, treating in his estimates, over 15,000 patients with various diseases that were all given conscious water called, Hado. This water has been given various treatments, mineral, words and prayers of kindness, labels on the bottles of water like healing, wellness, and happiness. All under the theory that the water is picking up the memory or intent of the words, thoughts, and prayers of the provider as described by quantum theory with directed intent. The patients say they experienced healing with the use of this water. Homeopathic healers have described rashes and various skin ailments leaving where all other treatments have failed. Some of the reasons for this success is due to the idea that most living creatures are made two thirds of water. The logical assumption that not all water is equal can be easily demonstrated in Flint, Michigan. The water there is a nightmare.

Assuming the truths of personal testimonies, the water is helping by directed consciousness. By standard science and medicine, there is no truth to it. But these are the people that didn't know there was a DNA double helix or a quadruple helix, Eurasians with naturally born elongated heads and what, a fourth state of water?

Solid, liquid, vapor and.....fourth phase of water, PLEASE STAND UP?

Gerald Pollack of the University of Washington, discovered the fourth state of water. Water can arrange itself into a hexagonal crystal lattice. Water in a living organism is different from basic water. In a living being the research is showing the water is structured and with unique substances. Water consciously structures itself into an organized way. Water begins to arrange itself in a human body and become hydrophilic. It becomes very pure. In a layer only a 1/4 of a millimeter thick, it purifies itself due to electric forces, small particles are driven out. The water in this state has an altered electrical resistance, a gel-like viscosity and a different Ph balance with a negative charge. This is absolutely a new transitional state of water, between frozen and liquid. What was obvious was this state of water is important in living organisms. Light was the reason this state of water could be reached. Sunlight and infra-red light could expand and grow this new found state of

Gerald H. Pollack, the discoverer of the 4th state of water. We thought that DNA had a double Helix, then it turned out to be quad-helix, what about water's newly discovered 4th state, could there be more?

water. The water was storing the sunlight as energy in the form of energized hexagonal crystal structures. Their research is showing that water is apart of our biological process, not just an element.

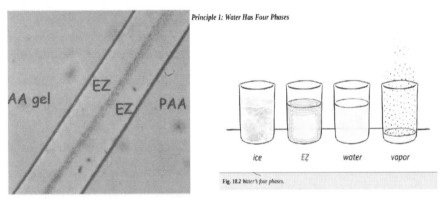

In this diagram water in it's fourth state is shown on the left and in it's known states on the right. The state of our most abundant element and understanding it is far from being understood. This is more proof that we can be technologically advanced but still lack the understanding of the underlying principles. Many of the "sciences" we have work but on theoretical theories. Despite our lack of knowledge, we produce cell phones and cable TV. No problem.

In recent experiments, cut flowers were dipped in water, live plants were dipped in water. Droplets were analyzed and the droplets mimicked the shape of the items. What was even more interesting, was that water was able to know whether the flowers or plants were alive. Whether or not they were cut. There was a presence in the photos of a black or dark center in the droplet if it was cut. If it was a living plant, the droplets had a bright energized center. Both droplets showed the pattern of the varieties of flowers and or plants used. This is just like Dr. Emoto's work. The ability to discredit the overlapping research is looking ridiculous at this point. If it was one research with one angle that would be one thing.

BURN WATER BRIDGE WATER

Water is not supposed to burn. However, no water, no burn. In the greatest find in maybe a 100 years John Kanzius from Pennsylvania, was looking for a way to fight cancer. While doing the cancer work he found that radio waves could split salt water into hydrogen and oxygen and burn water. This is not an explainable thing. Physicists don't have an answer on that. Radio waves burning water still may not have the benefits of Schauberger's vortex but it is nice to know oil could go to hell.

John Kanzius, discoverer of burning water. Water has a fourth state, it can burn, what else can water do that we don't know?

Here in the experiment water can be seen actually burning like any other flammable liquid.

Water had the ability to create a bridge. Discovered by Lord Armstrong in 1893, water will form a bridge between two glasses of distilled water. This work is continuing with Dr. Elmar Fuchs at Wetsus-Centre of Excellence for Sustainable Water Technology. What is weird about the water connecting this way is that when you put two glasses of water together, a bridge forms where the water is going to connect. The water, when given current, doesn't try to connect on the other sides of the glass, or on the far side of the glass and just "boil" over to the table. Instead, it starts "bridging" to the other glass. Where the two glasses touch no less. This is not explained. Water should not being creating bridges. The water has a different structure and density. The water is showing consciousness or our intent is also directing the water and the water understands what to do.

What other ways is water functioning on a quantum conscious level? If you exposed water to electromagnetic fields, it should not be a variation that bacteria could "feel" yet the bacteria can tell the difference between treated and untreated water. Molecules themselves take on the personalities of the water they are in. The identical molecules are different, even if related but placed in another volume of water. Depending on the researcher, the very handling of the water changes the outcome. How quantum and frustrating is that? Or are your good thoughts, prayers(un-mystified), and intentions part of a quantum world that is the true law of the universe and as beings in it, are we

Here John is pointing as the experiment is splitting salt water into hydrogen and oxygen and burning. There is not a known explanation to this by physicists. This again points to the fact that nature is complex, conforms to laws and technically we can achieve results that while the underlying principles escape us as of yet.

affecting negative or positively, not just good or evil, are our intentions actually shaping the world and the things in it. This doesn't make your average scientist happy, which is why most wished the quantum world would have went away, or more accurately never been seen. It didn't, they saw it and nothing is sitting right in Newtonian land. : (

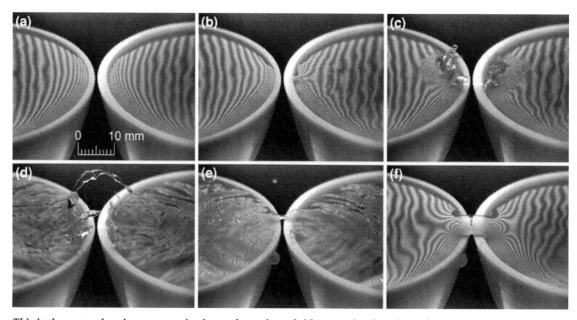

This is the water charging, communicating and creating a bridge exactly where it needs to to connect with the other cup. The water in the cups is not trying to connect to another side of the cups, or at the bottom, just at the exact correct spot.

171

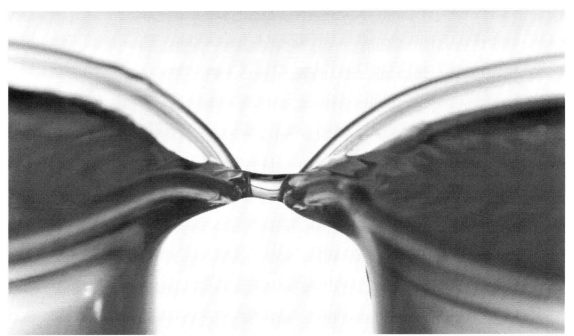

This is a closer look of water "magically" bridging in thin air to connect to the next cup. This is one of our first clues that in the natural world, magnetism and field modalities need to be studied even closer. The gravitational and magnetic current is spinning strong enough to keep the water in a coherent state.

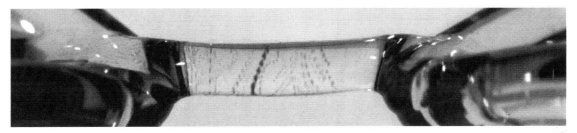

The very process to keep water spinning and coherent like any other magnetized object may lead us down many new field research areas. It is quickly accelerating in awareness that there is no duel particle wave theory. There is either, magnetism and it's states and expressions. Here is water expressing the coherency of mother nature's laws not theories. Mysteries only to our understanding.

WOOD, TREES, FORESTS, CONNECTIVITY

The quantum world, the only world, has particles in two places at once, observable influences of the observer on the out come of a test and the binder, the substance that seems to connect the universe is water. We are quickly learning that it is not a particle world but an either world. Think giant swimming pool.

Water is conscious, or is it that all living things are apart of it? The maps of the world 50,000 years ago, the lakes of the Mediterranean and the lakes of the Caribbean are gone, flooded into the ocean. The view of the world would have been very different. Engineered soil like Terra Preta and Chernozems indicate that the world population was very big, and well fed. It is a possibility that trees and much of the earth was intentionally designed and maintained.

Giant red woods and Sequoia trees were once all over the earth. We don't know the weight capacity of the logs these trees could manage. These trees at one point look like engineer soil to have been placed intentionally to manage disaster and wave frequency cloaking for ancient advanced human populations. Their size applications for an ancient high technology society could create whole homes out of one tree.

What is almost never discussed are the trees. Cymatic polygonal construction seems to be a foundation. Either everyone in an advanced ancient society were in the great outdoors all the time, or the missing top halves of all ancient construction are what's missing. A cymatic polygonal construction would be the perfect foundation. There are no buildings left with wood that are over 8,000 years old.

This has been a common problem. Massive cymatic polygonal blocks would be the only thing left after thousands of years. Plaster on stone would turn to dust. The wires would dust. If it was nanotechnology, for instance like Tesla roofing tiles or painted nano technology it would not be visible or recognized on an ancient structure for being that. Remember, researchers only find what they are looking for. We have nano paint that can collect solar energy for us. Currently it's a concept for mass market but it has been applied and has been experimented with.

Plastic, would eventually turn to dust. There is a long list of material products we understand; materials we can imagine building with. We have no idea how an ancient high society would have created finished surface materials to work in an ancient highly advanced conscious environment. We know the ancients abilities in cutting andesite and the other hardest surfaces on earth appear unparalleled. To polish and manage stone the way they shaped it is one side, would it be safe to assume a highly advanced ancient society could be conscious about their wood use? Would it have been exceptional?

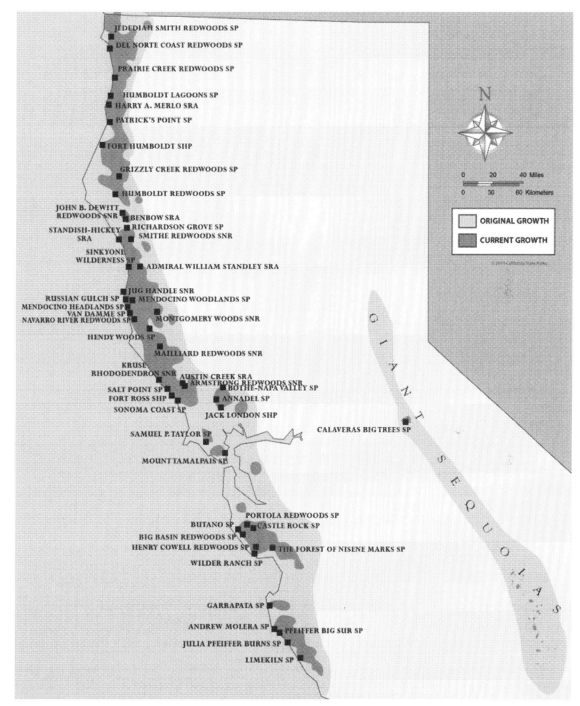

This map is showing known locations of Sequoia in this known growth cycle and life period "recent past and present."

Let's look at Sequoia National Forest in California where some of these massive trees are left. There are black and white photos of tunnels being cut through them and people driving through these trees that are incredibly large. It doesn't need to be the Ewoks and Return of the Jedi to imagine living in trees. There are tribes that do it now. If you are cutting stone basalt, granite, andesite, and other incredibly hard stones like nothing, and moving them, how hard would it be to work with incredibly large trees? To cut them paper thin, create walls, beautiful carvings? Building on the cymatic polygonal walls like the ones found in Peru or Bolivia or all over the earth could have been capped with giant trees. Trees that were as easy to move as 1000 ton megalithic blocks.

From the United States government:

"Ancient ancestors of the giant sequoia (Sequoiadendron giganteum [Lindl.] Buchholz) were widespread throughout much of the Northern Hemisphere during the late Mesozoic Period. Climatic conditions changed, forcing the more recent ancestors of present giant sequoia into the southwestern United States. The native range is now restricted to the west slope of the Sierra Nevada. Although seen in 1833 the effective date of discovery by the Europeans was 1852. Soon after that specimen trees were cut, and then extensive logging removed about a third of the big trees. Preservation of groves started in 1864 and gained momentum in 1890 with creation of Sequoia and Yosemite National Parks. Numerous scientific studies have been conducted during the last century from paleobotany to genetics of these great trees, but much is still unknown."

"To show the world that California really did have such huge trees, selected trees were stripped or cut down. The first to go was augured down in the North Ca- Laveras Grove in 1852. It took a crew of 25 men working 10 days to drill enough holes to send it crashing down"

From Wiki, "....make resolving the specifics of when and how *Sequoia* originated once and for all a difficult matter—especially since it in part depends on an incomplete fossil record.

Paleontology of the redwoods....fossil record shows a massive expansion of range in the Cretaceous and dominance of the Arcto-Tertiary flora, especially in northern latitudes. Genera of Sequoioideae were found in the Arctic Circle, Europe, North America, and throughout Asia and Japan. A general cooling trend beginning in the late Eocene and Oligocene reduced the northern ranges of the Sequoioideae, as did subsequent ice ages. Evolutionary adaptations to ancient environments persist in all three species despite changing climate, distribution, and associated flora., especially the specific demands of their reproduction ecology that ultimately forced each of the species into refugial ranges where they could survive.

Did you catch back there that they grew in the Arctic Circle? Piri Reis Map anyone?

I think it's important to understand the awe that goes with being able to cultivate these trees... John Steinbeck wrote about the redwood, "The redwoods, once seen, leave a mark or create a vision that stays with you always. No one has ever successfully painted or photographed a redwood tree. The feeling they produce is not transferable. From them comes silence and awe. It's not only their unbelievable stature, nor the color which seems to shift and vary under your eyes, no, they are not like any trees we know, they are ambassadors from another time."

Can you imagine our highly advanced ancestors, creating a society worthy of silence and awe? Can you imagine building with these trees? Think of the forests of the world now. Most you could look at as weeds. Look in a city, most are small, some Dutch elm survive, but trees are not like the forests that once were. Could you then imagine a wood structure? Cymatic Polygonal work would likely be the structural base to buildings that could have risen beyond tree lines of forests that were 700 ft tall. Building with large sections of the trees. Being able to shape with 1000 ton stones, one could imagine 1000 or 3000 ton tree sections, set on cymatic polygonal buildings to rise above and become living quarters and great spaces.

The sequoia once rediscovered, were a wonder, there is evidence that vast forests of these trees were all over the earth. One of these trees took a crew of men in the 1860's five days to cut down. If you can build the foundations of Baalbek and the Great Pyramid, you can cut down sequoia in large usable sections, sections weighing 3000 tons? The beams you could fashion would be as large as the foundation blocks of Baalbek. You could build as tall as you want. With a foundation that is unaffected by earthquakes.

THE STUMP and TRUNK of the MAMMOTH TREE of CALAVERAS.
Showing a Cotillion Party of Thirty-two Persons Dancing on the Stump at one time

Cutting wood panels, or plywood would be well in the scope of an ancient society. We make beautiful wood panels using laser cuts, we put images on wood, could you imagine a giant, organic living billboard advertising the next amphitheater event while receiving your healing energies and returning?

This is Hyperion to scale with the Statue of Liberty. Hyperion allegedly was not found till 2008. The scale of this tree is the exception now. It was not the exception in earlier human occupied times. In an advanced human past, trees like this would have been the norm. Fast growing and for many purposes.

This is Hyperion relative to the forest around it. Notice the sheer size difference in comparison to the other trees.

HYPERION- A redwood not discovered till 2006, it is 379.7 ft tall.

There are crazy properties to these redwoods. They are incredibly resistance to decay, redwood is used for house framing, heavy beams, ties and trestles for railroads, steps, table tops, veneers and furniture. There is significant evidence that the coastal redwoods were the largest trees in the world, before logging. Many trees were reported to be over 400 ft. With ranges between 400 and 425 ft they will grow beyond within a rainy fog environment, which the trees seem to create.

In "prehistory" these trees were everywhere including Asia, Europe, all over South America, and possibly Antarctica and the North Pole, before the pole shifts. Bark for these trees are found in subway constructions and tar pits. Massive petrified trunks and pieces of the extinct Metasequoia Occidnetalis, the Sequoia Occidentalis, made up most of the badlands in North Dakota. The trees were old and thought to be prevalent from the Cretaceous and Miocene, then they were discovered to be even older. You can drop the term "living fossil" and a high five for these trees. The Metasequoia is a deciduous tree, like bald cypress. Known for thick buttresses, fast growing to 130-150 ft and over 6 ft on the trunk. Metasequoia was found in 1941. Thought to be a fossil, in 1944 in Modaoxi, China, a couple researchers find a new tree. In 48' Arnold Arboretum sent an expedition from Harvard to collect seeds. They seeded universities and conservatories and arboretum worldwide for trials.

Hyperion is tall and big, the versatility of this wood and it's use makes you wonder, was it that we found uses for this "natural" material or is it within it's "planning" as a natural resources for ancient advanced humans, like planned soil.

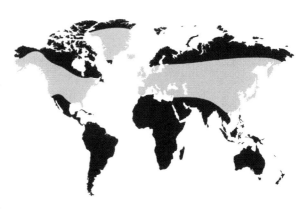

This is the known locations of the ancient trees. This is the world that we think of as abnormal. When you hear the term mega fauna, you think dinosaurs eating big leaf ferns, not a mega tree network made of trees easily worked on by an ancient society working daily with cymatic 1200 plus ton stones and engineering soil. Engineering trees not in just size but placing them and the very soil they were in.

TREES ARE CONSCIOUS

Pando is considered the world's largest living organism. Not every forest has been searched. There is a possibility that certain bacteria, viruses or fungus may be the contender for largest organism. Pando is very big, covering a massive amount of land and would be able to communicate a massive amount of aerial, ground and underground information to a highly advanced society that could speak and or program organisms like this.

FROM FORBES Oct 18, 2018, 11:41am

The World's Largest Organism, Pando, Is Dying

Trevor Nace

Contributor

Largest living organism that we think we know about...

The largest organism in the world is in Fishlake National Forest in Utah. It is 1,000's of years old, and is dying.

The organism is named Pando, Latin for I spread, and is a massive grove of quaking aspens. You have seen quaking aspens if you've visited the mountains of Colorado. They are known for their bright yellow color in the fall and make a quaking sound as wind passes through their leaves.

47,000 aspens all originate from a single male parent aspen, sharing an identical genetic makeup. The single male aspen genetically cloned itself and has been doing so for thousands of years.

In total, the grove of aspens cover 106 acres. It's not clear why and how this specific grove of aspens grew to be so large. The grove could have outcompeted other trees in the area, with the ability to rapidly reproduce and grow. If you have visited Colorado during the fall and gone to see the brightly colored aspens.

PETER WOHLLEBEN: TREE OR EARTH WHISPERER

Peter has written a very popular book called "The Hidden Life Of Trees: What They Feel, How they Communicate - Discoveries From a Secret World".

In detailed scientific research and in his own terms, describes what biologists already know. Trees talk, they are social creatures. They can learn, remember, count, and nurse sick trees to health. How about how they get on the "wood Wide Web" sending each other signals of danger. They use a fungal network and communicate amongst each other. Trees keep stumps alive. They make and send the stumps and each other food.

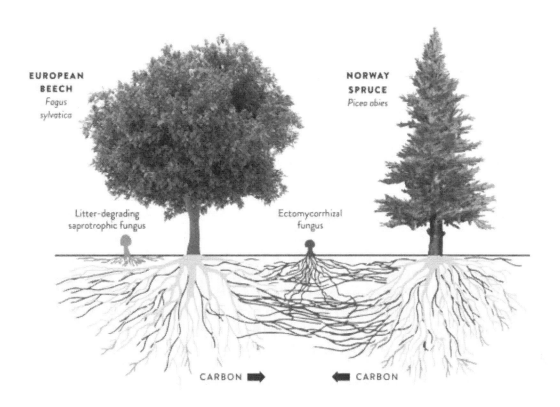

This is a visual of how two trees of different species could share nutrients, communicate and use a neurological like fungus network between them. If trees could do this inter species, why not animals and humans, or fungus and humans? There is the real possibility that the slivers of truth in many myth and legends that people did once speak with animals may have truth.

Research from Bonn University shows that the trees have "brain-like structures" at their root tips. The roots analyze toxic material and other soil conditions. Then communicate and change the root growth. The roots change coarse and grow in other directions. Monitoring whom is eating on them or their bark, trees can emit tannins, they can make a tree toxic to the animal eating it and send signals through a pheromone release to trees down wind.

Plants are not out of this, just like dipping them in water and the water knowing if they are alive, cut or dead, plants are being studied for speaking and or making sounds in the roots. Monica Gagliano experimenting at the University of Western Australia has gathered evidence that this is happening at 220 Hertz. We will not hear it folks. Maybe the actual question is, "If a tree falls in the forest, who doesn't hear it, us?"

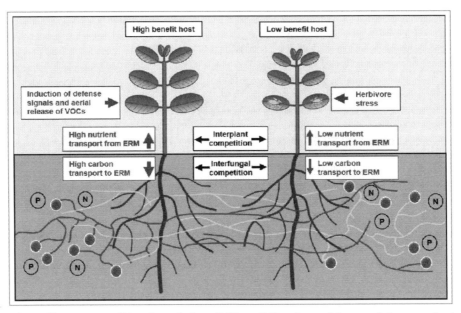

Plants, like trees are talking through the soil. The soil if engineered for growth by an ancient high technology society would have accounted for communication to and from all layers of this well groomed world they were creating and maintaining.

Suzanne Simard of the University of British Columbia in Vancouver have been making so many discoveries about trees in the Pacific Northwest. Like Cedar and maple on a single "network" while Hemlock and Douglas fir on another. The findings, along with Wholleben's observations have upset standard sciences and of course the logging industry. Just like the Native American was a savage, nothing more, that there were no advanced societies in the US prior to pilgrims, we can't have trees having feelings, or plants, how would all the vegans feel now? Screaming plant salad anyone?

Suzanne Simard has made so many discoveries we could discuss them in another book. Remember, on average we are finding 5000 new species a year. Yet we keep talking about most everything on the planet is dead.

The consciousness of any plant or water loving structure and its level of love or pain or connectivity to each other is important. We are looking at a new science, the relationship of plants and trees to each other, themselves and the earth. This is relevant if we truly want to be sustainable and understand our human history on this planet. This is another unknown relationship to the Earth that may be an ancient advanced human engineered and cultivated network. The trees and plants could be part of a network, that is sensitive to sunlight and many other ultraviolet and unseen waves. This earth system could connect, decipher and communicate to all other creatures.

http://www.peter-wohlleben.de/ an introduction

Engineered soil all over the earth, advanced constructions, cuts in genes in all creatures and now, if you missed it above, due to an incomplete fossil record, mostly unknowns. It's an unknown fossil record with no origin for the largest trees on earth. Taken on it's own, along with the missing fossil record of all plants and creatures...because there lost, it's just another bunch of anomalies that we should shrug off? Is it looking more like intentional design? The Siberian 3000 ton megalithic wall stones and Baalbek's 1000 ton stones are signs of the scale we once built at. We are living amongst the trees and plants of our advanced ancient past. We look at people who feel or sense trees or animals or are too "emotional" and we drug them or put them in therapy. The consciousness of the trees connecting, the plants, the animals, is this the biblical sliver of truth that we did once speak with them all? There constantly appears a series of possibilities that engineering of the earth having been intentional. The rivers that wind, are they or were they at one point sustained or groomed that way? Does water make its way into a dry well or someplace new to be a fountain for new human settlement. Can our intent to be healthy or our very thoughts transfer through water? Revisiting the fossil record and looking at our ancient structures shows more and more connectivity in ways that we didn't consider in the modern archeological world. That water could be unhealthy affecting the trees and plants and us. Rivers, streams and ancient buildings, perhaps to know more about the organic structures that are gone or what was once the metal structures, we need to look again with satellite and LIDAR images to dusted rivers in Egypt and other suspected truly pre-flood sites and we won't just have gold nano parts from Russia. Well maybe. We will just have more all around.

This is a close up of one of the many funguses that communicate, feed and connect plants and trees. There may be many organisms with external and internal neurological and physiological networks between them that are waiting to be discovered, let alone understood. Again.

Chapter 8

GENETIC TECH AND ANCIENT ADVANCED SOCIETY

Scalar waves

"50 million years ago you walked upon the planet so, Lord of all that you could see just a little bit like me, walking in your footsteps.... walking in your footsteps." - The Police: Walking in Your Footsteps

There are many cases of foot prints being found in stone that were once sand including boot prints! They have been dated to 500 million years old, 300, 120 million and walking with dinosaurs. Literally foot prints and dino prints being found side by side. It's a mystery right? It appears we have been walking on this planet for at least millions of years as Homo Sapien Sapien. How many times over could we rise and fall, post flood stories aside? Our modern reengineering of the megalithic ruins that have been studied show that the advanced level of building and energy knowledge would be equaled to their genetic knowledge. The evidence presented so far is that we terraformed and engineered a good portion of the soil, plants, trees and animals on the planet. The size and scale to what we could build was unlimited. It appears that it is all connected. With a modern understanding of material sciences, cymatics, a more advanced level of quantum and nano technology, our very consciousness was plugged in to this global system. It is in our ancient math and maps that are left for us to reverse engineer. Math in cymatic polygonal construction that we don't understand completely yet. Fortunately, we have that recently published paper on Seismic cloaking. The earth grids of Peru, Bolivia, Jordan and Asia appearing to connect our very buildings to a living network are being

A platform in the Paluxy River bed near Glen Rose, Texas. Excavated by Geologist Dr. Don Patton around September of 2000 revealing 136 consecutive tracks, proceeding 400 ft. Not far from these tracks, considered the finest example of a dinosaur tracks preserved anywhere in the world, are tracks with perfect human foot prints in them with dinosaurs!

photo'd and study more than they have ever. There is evidence that our bodies were once capable of so much more and possibly living indefinitely. We are capable of what is labeled now as super human abilities, either in moments of dire emergency or with training they are rearing there heads again. Training that allows a human to lift 1000 pounds in a dead lift or the once impossible under four minute mile are two modern examples. Now we have genetic research showing substantial anomalies in our genetic code and individual humans doing superhuman abilities reactivating some of what was mystified as God like abilities. We will walk through the finds that taken together reveal a truth we haven't quite been able to grasp or verbalize yet. It's not aliens, it's us. They or we ancient advanced humans are here still. The genetic evidence of a highly advanced human society are here in our historical, genetic & medical record and in eye witness accounts have shown we are interacting with them. Ancient advanced humans did not all die off, they survived and live here on Earth. We have a historical record that points to them now and in our past. Let's take a look…

EXTRA EXTRA BRIEN FORESTER

Supermen or super genes, which do we talk about first? The very thing we are afraid of, Frankenstein sciences. CHICKEN OR THE EGG? Which came first? Didn't think we would answer this too right? An advanced ancient human culture would have as advanced medical and genetic research as the ancient building sciences like composite geopolymers, placement and mathematical ratios with PI and the golden ratio, Baalbek's scale and complexity, the maps of the past, etc. The genetic inquiry is always assumed the answer is chicken, maybe the Egg. Either way, you can't have an egg all

Elongated skulls from Peru above, elongated skulls are found all over the earth, thanks to researchers like Brien Foerster and his genetic testing we know these skulls are from a race of humans from the Black Caucus Region of Crimea in Europe.

by itself. Someone engineered it. There is no proof or record of a dual animal laying an egg and a baby at the same time. Then one day it went to just eggs. There is no example of this in all of our biological knowledge of any species ever. I love that amoebas just spilt. Squirrel! If you are engineering animals and creatures, yeah, you can program cells to give birth with a creature programmed to recreate with eggs. Easy. We built a lot of theories about cells before we knew of the double helix of DNA. Then we recently discovered that our DNA is at least a quad helix. What does all that do? Lots of rabbit holes and all I can say on that is we are Quickening our understanding of every aspect of science, just not or abilities to relate to it except by established theories. Theories are theories are theories. We filter facts with theories when it should be the reverse, by "standard academia" standard, the weirdest and most obvious out of place art-a-facts like skeletons, tools and DNA should be our foundation for theories of our origins, timeframes, technologies and histories. In our DNA and in the animals around us there are indications the planetary story is mysterious. Sorry, I couldn't help myself, a mystery in prehistory yo. We are going to look at some genetic facts that point to a more complex past for man and beast and likely plant. Which finally brings us to Brien.

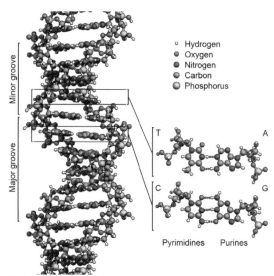

This is a diagram of a quad-helix

Brien Foerster, is a researcher and historian that unlike established religions of science had the balls to get the Paracus skulls of Peru tested genetically. These elongated skulled people represent some of the oldest "naturally" preserved mummies in the world. They have been found to be as old as 9000 years. Genetic testing the origins of these elongated skulled people has NEVER been done by mainstream science. Accordingly Brien in his book, did mention blood work done off the detailed textile burial blankets, had very odd results. The blood work should have had only one blood type, O, they had instead many. This is not possible if the established history has anything to say about it. The blood type of everyone in North America at this period should be O. This study was buried, it was done in the 70's. If a cover-up is done in the open is it a cover up?

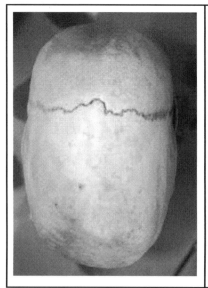 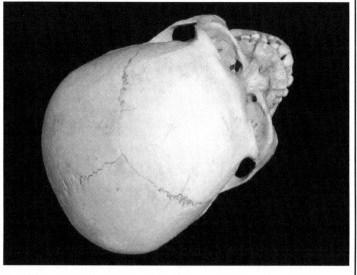

On the right is a typical human skull, on the left is a Paracus elongated skull with a single suture line. This along with a number of other anomalies are naturally occurring in the Paracus. Brien Foerster's genetic testing in 2019 has shown at least six unknown genetic markers to the standard human genome.

185

The suture lines on the skulls do not form like normal humans. On the Paracus, they are different than ours. These people didn't have boards tied to their heads to make them look like cone heads, they were born with these elongated heads. We keep talking about the elongated heads and no besides Brien ever seems to mention that their neck and spine attach completely differently. I personally showed pictures of the skull and where the neck would attach into the human body and both surgical nurses first words were, "that's not normal". They saw the suture lines and the blood and DNA results published by Brien and they couldn't believe it.

The bodies of these ancient Paracas people would be different. As these people walked the earth, tribes would see them, mimicking them with flattening their children's head. Possibly killing a few adults in attempts to do it. The mimicking of human cultures is common, the head binding is an example that actually is seen all over the earth. What about the African tribes with elongated necks? I was fascinated as a kid seeing these tribesmen and women with rings placed around their necks to elongate their necks to double the length. I wondered how they did it? Through x rays of these people you could see the great strain on the skeletal system the process had been pulling the spine up, causing their ribs to point down, causing all sorts of damage to the body. They did it for "beautification" according to anthropologists. This would be a great culture to maybe label in close proximity at some point with more advanced humans that had modified their own genes creating the elongated head and having a longer neck. It would be helpful to paleoanthropologists to revisit what that living society saw in their own verbal folklore to mimic the long necks. This is only one feature of the Paracus. They were taller and along with an elongated skull had a taller neck. In the tribes that mimicked the appearance, it would be interesting if there was a way to get a genetic history of these tribesmen and see where they map around the world.

With over 3 years of work, Brien Foerster with Nassim Harrrim, a genetic scientist, tested soft tissue, genes, and hair. Yep, straight from Nassim, he explained to me directly that the tissue they took included brain and optic nerve that was soft tissue. This is not generally the case when any mummy is almost 3000 years old. Mummies are not supposed to have soft tissue. Could this be due to a superior cellular level building technique not available to how we live on this earth now?

The mother's DNA comes back and there are multiple unknowns. The results, NOT human DNA. Not that it couldn't be human DNA, it just isn't any known human DNA, ever found. Let's back up and identify the next thing they did find, the origins of the DNA they could identify placed the Paracus in the Black Caucus region of Crimea. Eurasia. This is a cover of National Geographic and Smithsonian and British museum worthy. Well, above worthy. I will put money that at the time you read this, months or a couple years from publishing there will still be no buzz.

The Academic model says a land bridge about 40,000 year ago, must be the only way anyone came to America. Let's add up some of the anomalies again: Virgina Steen Mcintyre's find of 275,000 year old camp fires in northern Mexico or all the anomalies across Canada to South America, LIDAR scans from just 800 sq miles of Guatemala and on and on in annum. Now we have capstone genetic proof. Yeah, white mummies with red hair in Mongolia and now gingers with elongated skulls, crazy suture lines, spinal columns connecting in the wrong place in Paracas with at least six unknown genetic markers unknown to any human. There were other mummy finds showing they mixed with locals eventually, however the elongated skulls that were born that way were Euraiasian. European, Gingers!

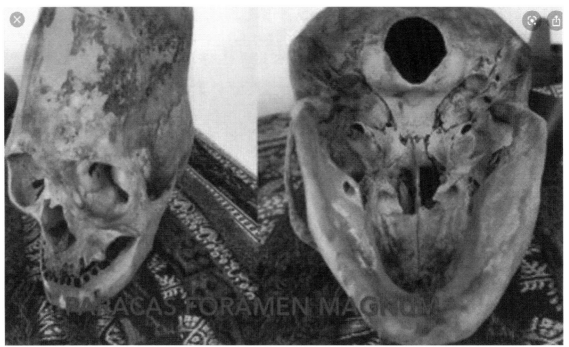

On the right is a normal human skull and the location of the spinal column. On the left is a Paracus spinal location. This is not a deformation. It is entirely different and the surgical nurses and doctors I have shown it to have no explanation. Brien Foerster's book on these skulls and genetic testing is a must have.

The bone structure of these people, including their very neck to there body attaches entirely differently. Their DNA shows six none human genome markers. This was the point we started with, so the quick alternative conclusion, it's ALIEN! Close the book and throw it if I had stopped there.

This is the crux. This is not the only time our genes looked messed with. The DNA that was found is not human as we know it. There for it is frequently a talking point that it must be alien influenced. Clearly they stopped on the way through the universe and helped us a little. Is it more likely that an advanced human race, developing technologies that appear once "installed" as species of plants, soil, animals, geopolymers, cymatics and wave technology, wouldn't ancient advanced humans develop DNA inserts or modifications over the thousands of years they had the technology? There are many splits in people and animals that have or appear to our technology now, cut and modified artificially. Why the different races? Redundancy in case of catastrophe or work specializations? Why giants? If a person can train today and lift a 1000 pounds, what would a really fit working giant lift per the Bible and other post flood stories?

The Paracus of Peru is one example of our ancient high tech society possibly taking a step away from their own ancient advanced society. Maybe a core group, left a post flood or catastrophic area in the Crimea past and moved to Peru to start over. For you movies and sci-fi fans, the Paracus pulled a new Battlestar Galactica TV series mod on their larger ancient society, moved to Peru and started over with no tech. There should have been a spoiler alert but you should absolutely watch the series still. This is one theory that is easy to see when you start getting your head around the fact that we advanced to a very highly technical ability, then fell, then rose again, maybe fell again. It is easy to see if your in control of high medical technology that you'd become different races.

Up to now, post flood mythologies and histories control the theories of our pre-flood origins. Genetic splits that show changes in the human DNA have been found before that appear to have been modified to serve a specific need at some point. This genetic evidence is used over and over to point out that we were monkeys or cavemen pounding rocks till the Anunaki or other alien race came along and modified what was a simple human race. This requires a presumed theory about being as advanced as we have ever been today and never more advanced in the past. Also, that the earth, in its state for life, evolved randomly, that this planet is not or has not been intentionally shaped and terraformed. Starts to sound like a creationist theory right to the balls right? The classic assumption is random splashes of planet sweat grouped and formed very motivated bacteria that had a dream, the dream to be a cool swinging monkeys one day right after a few million billion or so years of random evolution. Then there is the ever more terrifying idea, we walked upon the planet so, having been from some other world. Maybe placed here intentionally. Maybe intentionally coming here. We may have developed into a highly advanced society millions of years ago as the Vedas speak of and the physical evidence show. We then tasked ourselves with populating the planet. With an advanced understanding of energy, of the universe, we created the tuning needed to stay on a revolving rock and travel through the universe living in harmony. Creating what appears to be natural things like animals, bugs, and soil to support us, communicate with us, and read and filter cosmic information.

A human hand on the chicken and the egg, soil itself, genes, to our simple 14 % or so conscious selves actually all an intentional man made machine. This is blasphemy for some, heresy for established theorists, and now crushing to those that want it so badly to be anyone other than us in the universe that pulled us up. Not realizing that it was ourselves that pulled us down. But we are awakening. You can still love nature by the way, even if it turns out your trees and water are zero and ones on a giant motherboard. The motherboard of all motherboards might just be Mother Earth. Brought to you by ourselves truly. Possibly with epic mistakes. It will hurt those that want to believe that nature is just this random design by the happy happy joy joy fairy goddesses. Look at the golden ratio again and tell me how it's not exact and toroidal field again.

WIM HOF, THE ICEMAN AND STIG SEVERSON BREATHOLOGY

We are becoming our super human selves again. There was a man that searched all the mystical things the world had. Hinduism, Buddhism, Christianity, and yoga, were all on his radar for the one true thing. Wim went all over the world searching and he speaks 5 languages. He holds over 26 World records and is the first man to do what modern science says is impossible, control his vagus nerve. Wim Hof has shown to have conscious control of his inflammatory response, his autonomic immune system. Wim has accomplished this through cold water exposure and a unique breathing technique to control the mind and the body down to its ability to heat and cool itself.

Wim Hof, the Iceman. Is seen here running in twenty below. He has run barefoot for 26 miles, in shorts, at 20 below and maintained his core body temperature multiple times. He travels the world teaching anyone how to rediscover and control their autonomic nervous system through cold and a breathing therapy that also reconnects you to the earth in still unknown yet instantly amazing ways.

Wim Hof with five languages has one thing to say about our actual super human abilities that are now dormant, "FUCKING DEMIYSTIFY!" No woo woo, no religion, no Misty Mountain Hop, "Just do it!" He says.

I met Wim the first time he came to America to teach his method in San Francisco and watched him answer yogi questions and other breathing experts, "do you breathe through your nose or your mouth?" He says it for the first time again " NO, in through any hole out through any hole, you like holes, you know what I am talking about! We can all do this! We forgot, FUCKING demystify, you want a fucking prayer? Here you go...." He rattles off a Hindu chant. Wim adds that in his opinion, people mystified what was once easily accessed human abilities. Creating religion and ritual around our higher forgotten functions. It isn't that yoga or physical methods of developing the body isn't apart of the overall picture, but we have somehow mystified and blurred the lines to train our brain and body to its higher functions leaving the ritual and not the ability in the end. He is convinced that we have the ability to control our immune systems and more and he is proving it! When we need to be warm, we can control our inner fire. He proved it more than once. Like running a 26 mile marathon in 20 below zero, barefoot and in just shorts. Climbing Mount Everest quite a ways with only shorts and boots. His point is that for the last few thousand years, sitting in a secret temple, with a bunch of other monks hasn't helped general society. Yes Tibetan Tummo is a meditation that has been documented and filmed where the monks sit with just a basic cloth on their waist, they are given a frozen blanket, it's been dipped in water and frozen, then laid on the monks back. At that point the monk meditates using their breathing technique and secret way and heat themselves while sitting in the extreme cold. They heat themselves to the point that the blankets melt and dry while they sit meditating. It has been filmed with infrared to show the heating of the body and it is an amazing feat. There is nothing wrong with having religious or mystical beliefs. Wim's point in demystifying is being put to the test by actual universities studying him concluding that he is consciously controlling his immune

response and heating himself and cooling. The universities include Rotterdam, the University of Minnesota, Stanford neuroscientists and many more. Why? What he does is not possible in a medical textbook. Like controlling your inflammatory response after being injected with dead form of a bacteria that should at a minimum make you violently ill. Wim meditated through it. Then they said he was unique, Wim essentially said fuck you, we all are capable, gimme your researchers! 14 researchers and 10 days training later were all injected in a laboratory setting and all subjects meditated

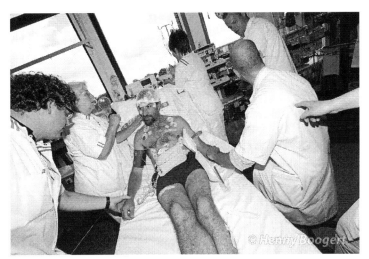

Wim Hof has been studied all over the world, he is being monitored here in an experiment that proved that he could consciously control his autonomic immune system. This is medical textbook impossible. Wim went on to train the researchers and the experiment was repeated after only 10 days of Wim Hof training with the same injections. With monitoring include blood draws, all the researchers repeated the inflammatory control.

through the immune response. Blood tests, full monitoring of the process and video documented to boot.

Wim Hof repeated this control experiment before I had met him in the desert, moving 50 miles, no water, controlled his body temp and kept it from overheating. There was a warning from the Stanford Professor at our conference with Wim who stated, "...learn the method, we are studying it, we don't understand, it's real, the human body has great strength in cold, however the margin in a couple degrees in heat is death. Do not repeat the desert example Wim just did!"

In another example Wim took an inexperienced senior who didn't know the method, taught him the breathing technique, then took him up Mount Kilimanjaro. They took blood samples and he and the student not having been climatized to the height, had their blood adapt to the climb as they went without having the body needing a climatizing over a couple days and then climbing. The body adapted and the blood on the climb and they did it without issues.

Wim has sat to his neck in ice, breathing and controlling his body temperatures while talking to people. Having conversations, not tucked in a mountain temple concentrating so hard he needed to remove himself from society itself and keep a secret code. He is in public, with a crowd, laughing and joking and pausing to focus at some points but connecting to others has he practices his techniques. You have to ask yourself if the "practice" of any mystified version of the mechanics of the human body is still locked in a temple somewhere, is it really applicable? Religion always has a perfect alibi, you aren't faithful enough or your not trusting in your faith, you haven't reached the right "level" etc. They will always get that pass. Here is a man that is training the old, the young, and the sick, to give them control of something we have forgotten, neglected, and replaced with traditions, rather than trust in our sleeping 85% consciousness, only seeing slivers through drugs, or emergency. Instead, Wim Hof, is part of a growing group reawakening the human powers within us.

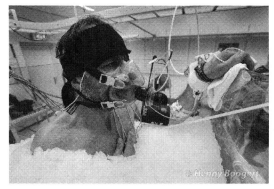

In monitoring Wim, he was able to consciously warm cold spots on his body while fully submerged in ice. He also repeated these tests in heat, moving 50 miles in the desert and controlling his body temperature. Many practitioners of the Wim Hof method have reported, sensing there body in "tripping" like ways, including seeing geometric patterns and feeling "connected" to the earth in unknown ways.

Being a practitioner myself, someone who practices the Wim Hof Method, I can tell you it isn't a parlor trick, it has been looked at by the best debunkers, they are converts. My personal experiences, include ice cold showers while in the meditated breathing having my eyes closed and experiencing bright orange geometric patterns, almost like blankets in the shape of tetrahedrons, others have reported white light. My patterns were organized, shaping and moving as every inch of my body was sensing something beyond the describable. I could feel the very pulses of my blood flow and nervous system on a level that felt like I was hyper aware of everything around me. It isn't always the same. There is plenty of explored benefits, pain relief, calming, sensory enhancement and I continue to experience more. No matter what you read from anyone, personal experimentation is a must, what you eat, how you move or exercise has to be dialed to where you are mentally and physically at. There is no right or wrong, the Method can be learned at Wim's website quickly.

The method in 15 minutes will likely be an experience you have never had meditating siting and staring at a candle or at a yoga session. There is a connection to your physical body and higher senses and your body seems or feels like it is just an antenna tuning you back to your higher self. This is truly an amazing sensation, you can learn to do it in a 20 minute video Wim has on YouTube, and if your ready, just go straight to the Wim Hof method website and sign up for the courses on line, if you breath and are alive, this is for you. It isn't the solution, it's a method on a path of self exploration to wake you up and help you tune in and live in a deeply present way.

For Wim to continue to experiment and to be experimented on, the medical world and the paradigms about the human body are changing and this is good for all of us. This is an awakening as even Wim describes, the connection through the cold, breathing, and yoga mixed with other physical movement training is an exciting real and practical way to bring ourselves back from the ancient catastrophic fall we had.

STIG SEVERINSEN: BREATHEOLOGY

Danish, Ph.D. in medicine and a degree in biology, Stig becomes obsessed with holding his breath under water at 6. Goes on in 2010 to break Wim Hof's record by swimming 236 ft under ice. Mind you Wim did it in 2000, and Stig beat it by only 47.6 ft. The feat on it's own isn't just a demonstration of one bodily function in stress, but in control. Stig also held his breath for 22 minutes in 30 degree water setting a Guinness book world record.
Like Wim Hof, there are documentaries about Stig. The Discovery Channel called him " The Ultimate Superhuman" It was originally broadcast on the Discovery Channel in 2013. Both Stig and Wim have been featured on Discovery, History Channel, BBC, and 60 minutes.

Stig, like Wim Hof, practices a similar cold therapy and breathing technique. In Stig's practice, he set a world record of almost 22 minutes in almost frozen water, comfortably sitting on one breath. Other people have tried doing this without truly practicing a method as a parlor trick reporting incredible discomfort. Do it with practice and the experience even after one time can seem "zen".

The breathing work also mixed with cold exposure eliminates stress, helps some with PTSD, cancer patients and their pain, and general relaxation and sleep. The intangible mental benefits and control over your autonomic immune system is still intangible for a medical textbook or a scientific explanation. This is outside their wheelhouse, it is also outside the secret temples of mystified traditions that may actually have their roots in basic human higher advanced consciousness. After thousands of years it's just a beautiful ritualistic pattern.

Stig is teaching athletes, has been invited to TEDX, again, at the time of this writing to explain his breathing technique. Combining yoga, cold, exercise and the breathing is reactivating our higher functions and bringing back some of our consciousness. It isn't that having the body oxygenated for 22 minutes isn't incredible, it's the relationship we have with breathing and or any bodily functions. According to their research there is a direct correlation to lung strength and aging. People developing these incredible external physiques and having poor or minimal lung capacity which in turn is causing aging and complications leading to death. The lungs, like the heart, need youthful training.

SELF DOMINANCE

Idol Portal and Erwin Le Corre are part of the worldwide "movement" culture. Oh, yeah, this is another huge rediscovery and revolution. Our relationship to fitness is off, to eating, to ultimately living. Each man has a very different background, Ido is from Israel, he is at the forefront of "movement". Given the title as founder of the movement culture it in tails all things movement, breathing, fighting, dancing, sitting, playing, all movement. Google him and watch as he holds a one handstand and can move fluidly in circles as if his entire body is on wires. He has been gifted the title "the man of self-dominance" like our superhuman Wim Hof. Ido is a super human experimenting with all physical, eating and any practices that has allowed him to personally achieve self-dominance.

This is Georges Herbert himself. The founder of the Natural Method and as it quickly went across Europe prior to WW1, it was quickly forgotten after the war due to the chaos and death of many of the teachers. This method when practiced produced decathletes in approximately 6 months with abilities beyond the normal training. Abilities including safely jumping from 2 and 3 story heights and comfort in extreme temperatures. Herbert found over developing a muscle group for looks was useless while developing the whole body to work together produced results like the ones in these pictures. With no weights.

In one example to explain why movement isn't fitness, or rehab or a sport, Ido explains that when you specifically train to do handstands, your good at that, but it's a specialization. When you train repetitively to specialize in a particular sport you are "specializing" think tennis elbow. When you specialize in movement of the whole body, everything becomes strong. Ido says he is a generalist. You can be specialized but the sacrifices include repetitive motion stresses and trouble with joints and muscles around the constant specialized sport or activity. Or running, have you looked at a long distance runner? They look like Mr. Burns from the Simpsons. Movement is the world, fitness is just a small portion of movement. Specializing in it is not allowing a full connection to your entire connection physically and mentally to the earth. Watching Ido and the movement crawl like lizards across a beach or gym, it's cool. Being able to bend over and not be so built in one direction to "appear" strong and throwing out your back picking up a pencil is one of the many more important points. Becoming a generalist in fitness allows for a lifetime of strength and broad abilities that can lead to complete physical dominance of your body. Imagine one day being able to learn how to do an iron cross or a complex tumble that would take a gymnast 2 or 3 years to do and you crush it in a session. You just had to be taught how because you grew up practicing movement.

Erwin Le Corre is considered the "fittest man on Earth" by Men's Fitness. Erwin is another modern father of movement culture. Erwin rediscovers the book "La Methode Naturelle" by the French General Georges Hebert. Rediscovering Herbert's training method for fitness and real movement, Erwin has brought it to the masses in the form of Movnat. Georges Herbert had one core philosophy for the natural method of movement, "be useful". What is the point if you can not assist or help your fellow man? In some cultures your not considered a man if you can not help others.

During a rescue operation Herbert observed large muscled men tire out during activities while leaner, more flexible and "cross-trained" men were able to run, jump and help others without tiring. Herbert developed his method to train troops and test the results. The equivalent fitness level after using his method in six months of training was that of a decathlete.

"A man so "muscle bound" as the saying goes, is not in possession of a power. The power owns him." Edwin Checkley.

Before we talk about Edwin, you're going to have to youtube "bodybuilder try's muscle up" you'll see this incredibly defined man that can't really do anything useful. It takes all his pretty exterior to make one muscle-up happen.

Back view of General Herbert.

Edwin Checkley, London born, American settled, absolute greek god physically (1847-1922) at the time of his death, was 75. The examining doctor thought Checkley to be a strong fit man of his 30's. Sadly there was a gas leak that ended his life while he slept. Edwin was one of Georges Hebert's inspiration for the Natural Method. The Natural Method is available online now in a 3 parts. It was broken up into 3, it is not a trilogy, just one big book but broken up for modern readers. Completely worth it, useful and informative. Edwin's book A Natural Method Of Physical Training also advocates almost no weights and bodyweight training only. Checkley could lift 3, 150 pound plus men and carry them a hundred yards for show. Edwin, like Wim Hof and Stig Seversen focuses first on breath. The over muscled, "chiseled" chested strong man may have weak lungs. Sound familiar? Where is Stig and Wim? Not born yet. Checkley believes to many people were focusing on the exterior view of strength and not the full wholistic body and mind. Observers of Checkley in action, saw him lift hundreds of pounds, preform feats beyond trained strong men of his day(like Ido's idea of a generalist), and resume lectures with no heavy breathing, no loss of breath. His lung capacity was so beyond your

Edwin Checkley developed the one of the earliest methods of a natural method. No weights. the body and breathing, as Stig and Wim discovered needed to be developed as much as the muscles of the body and heart. The lungs contribute directly with the continuing strength of the body. When examined at death, Checkley was thought to be a man in his 30's or 40's yet he was 75.

professional boxer, wrestler "fitness" athlete he could do all that and go back to a lecture. His all around fitness was godlike and through natural non-machine exercise. Edwin is an important rabbit hole, he is someone that is a reference for Georges Hubert, that is a study in for Le Corre, Ido Portal, and anyone today interested in movement. Take a minute to look at Edwin and Huberts physique, compare it also to their range of flexibility and movement, lung and breathing strength, weather adaptation and you have a historical record in modern times why Le Corre and Ido, Wim and Stig seem super human. In Checkley's book, he explains, as does Hubert how to become truly fit in life. Mix these with Le Corre, Portal, Hof, Severinson and self experimentation and you will evolve in real time, whether or not you can give a Hindu chant or a Sun salutation.

Le Corre modernized and developed Herbert's work creating the Movnat program. Now thousands are doing it, Le Corre has trained athletes, Special forces, and the average person. Barefoot running, jumping, climbing, moving with nothing but a pair of shorts. Movnat points out that expressing yourself genetically in a positive direction involves eating naturally, being in nature, your very life living with constant movement! Pushing adaptation, maneuverability, getting out of a gym and adapting your body and stimulating greater brain development in movement complexity is part of the better training methods for conditioning which is in "nature". Now doing these things in the giant earth grid we were meant to connect with may have always been apart of the intelligent design that we just forgot. Erwin points out that movement in the moment, in nature doesn't allow room for your mind to wander, making you more present to where and how you are feeling now. Erwin points to the mystification of yoga, it's ingrained traditions as being useless outside of a studio. Sound a bit like Tibetan Tummo? Didn't Wim cover this too? Fucking demystify.

To be away from our natural world makes us sad, depressed, off balanced, angry, a host of negative emotions, even if it's barefoot running, connecting the feet to the earth and the actual "Grounding" that occurs. Christopher Mcdougal goes over it in his now famous book "Born to Run". There is a connection between the electrons of the earth and being barefoot. a review in the Journal of Environmental and Public Health looked at a number of studies that show the electrical connection to the body and earth have health benefits. People slept better, chronic pain elevated, improvements in the brain, skin health, moderated heart rate variability, improved immunity and all from being barefoot. A study in The Journal of Alternative and Complementary Medicine found that walking barefoot increased the surface charge of red blood cells. The cells clump less. Soooo less blood thinners, more walking or running barefoot?

There seems to be outlets, connectors in our genes, organs like our Pineal gland that have functions that are just being re-stimulated through all these activities. Wim Hof, Stig Severinson, Erwin Le Corre, and Ido Portal are connecting us in a real way back to what we now call super human abilities, back to a time when it was normal, not godlike. When we were all super human probably like Herbert and Checkley.

WELL, ABOUT DE-MYSTIFYING...JOHN CHANG, THE IMMORTAL

Chi Kung Master Burns Paper With His Hand - John Chang, yep, you're going to have to youtube this. Kota Danaos, author of more than 150 publications, having experience as an engineer for General Dynamics, a martial arts instructor in jujutsu and tai ch'i China, traveling frequently to Indonesia and the USA, wrote a book about John Chan: The Magus of Java: Teachings of an Authentic Taoist Immortal.

John Chang, is interviewed, videoed and tested by physicists, medical techs and general debunkers. He is documented performing what you would basically look at and call magic. John performs pyro-kinesis, starting newspaper on fire using what he calls Chi, electrifying and spontaneously combusting the paper. With the ability to be telekinetic, levitate, telepathy and other paranormal abilities John simply calls himself a healer. Attempting to stay away from the public eye, eventually John agreed to be interviewed at length. The video documentation of his abilities are there for all to see on youtube. The discipline is called Mo-Pai. The documentary is called Ring of Fire made by Loran and Lawerence Blair and was well received when it came out in 1988. Chi, or we might call it bio-energy is documented as John Chang creates electrical current within his body to heal the filmmaker of an eye infection. Kosta Danaos was the second of 5 students John accepted after the documentary went on to be an international success.

John, according to Danaos, is the direct heir to the lineage of the sage Mo-Tzu, a sixth century sage and Confucius's greatest rival. As usual, here we are, in the present, and truly great practitioners of lost abilities now called "arts", actual medical knowledge, and energy knowledge lost to the "west" is separated by simple communications. Mo-Pai has never been studied by the West. Danaos is the first to write on it, study it directly as a student of the master.

In my opinion, here is an example of the West meeting eastern mystification of ancient high technology. Technology that is in the form of what we would call magical abilities to start fire, control electrical current having amperage yet no voltages, healing people with no western scientific sense behind it. There are many interesting points and observations in this post flood world of our once programmable bodies to heal, cure, connect to a greater conciseness directly observed and experienced by Kota. We keep diving into Greek myths, connections of post flood religions and looking to see if they tie to one religion or one origin. They do, they are post 12-13,000 year cataclysm. It's one giant society picking themselves up out of the mud and many of those left standing were not ancient highly advanced people, they were just ancient co-existing tribes and communities.

Kota goes on in his books Appendix 2 to discuss something really interesting. The subject is cold fusion in the human body and cellular health, repair and energy sources. Kota believes a possible explanation for John's Mo-Pai abilities may be nuclear excitation. Researchers, Kevran, Komaki, Pappas, Hillman, Goldfein have suggested that the forces driving the sodium-potassium transfer in a cell is a constant state of cold nuclear fusion. In turn, John's patients feel the electrical shock, the healing benefits, but the mechanics of the energy that John's transferring is unknown to modern science and definitely unknown to the post flood faith that gives it mystical names of Ying and Yang and yin ch'i etc...it's been labeled that, it's real, but by any other name is a rose a rose. The High tech cellular technology that makes us is outside of any one book, the awareness now is that it is high tech, engineered, and likely ancient high technology of ancient humans past.

There is one article, one of many on the general subject of electrical stimulation in changing cellular processes and healing tissues. In the Journal of cellular Physiology 234 (1), 816-824 2019 titled, " Effects of biphasic and monophasic electrical stimulation on mitochondrial dynamics, cell apoptosis, and cell proliferation" they explore after stating sciences to this point doesn't know the effects of electric stimulation on mitochondrial dynamics and processes that there are measurable effects that require continued study. If this didn't put you to sleep before you read the paragraph, then fist pump to you! The idea that ancient post flood people mimicked in sounds, chants, religious practices, healing and mindfulness techniques that are remnants of our powerful past are evidenced in our research now. Like Wim Hof is saying and doing, de-mystification techniques that with practice we are falling on the ancient technology. The religions and "practices" like Tibetan Tummo and yoga are mystifications of technology. It's a bit like trying to start a 747 and sitting in the captain's chair just pulling and pushing buttons till something groans on or blinks thinking that that is the best it gets. Then building a 1000 year religion or "practice" around the pushing of buttons. After a thousand years, you get someone to believe the button room can fly.

For the people whom went to John Chang for healing, they got it, for those looking for learning the method, they too are on a journey of rediscovery. The way we continue to relate the body of evidence that we were once more advanced, to these abilities should clear a fog of mysticism to reveal ancient lost high tech genetic knowledge. We have an inner power that needs conscious awareness that we can do it and answering who we are by seeing past post flood traditions.

MARK SISSON, ROB WOLF, DR. ALEJANDRO JUNGER, DR. JOE WALLACH, ...MORE AND MORE

There is a growing group of Doctors and self experimenters that have accomplished through various motivations including personal tragedies medical or otherwise and difficulties having achieved incredible results for the human body. Connecting what should be obvious mechanics to mainstream science that some of them have been trained in that are not addressed by standard academia. It all falls on the"mystery" side of things. From fixing the human body to a newer term, "positive gene expression" and leaky gut, each of the above names and their individual works could aid on almost every page of their work in your personal journey to be happy and healthier in a substantial way. Their research in our bodies digestive and physical abilities add to a monumental pile with Wim to Ido on how to develop our lost abilities and former superhuman selves.

Mark Sisson will talk paleo all day, having been a professional athlete, now trains them and normal people on diet and exercise. With millions of books sold and the flag ship the Primal Blueprint is a must read. Essentially training and educating people about eating real food and why would that be needed. I had a kidney specialist tell me all I have to do is eat, the body just sorts it out :(

Here is how we eat, imagine being your favorite high performance car and once a day, once a week or after every meal, you walk out and hit it with a hammer. Maybe on a door, how about a sledge to the engine? Would you put oil in the gas tank or radiator fluid in the windshield wiper reservoir? We treat the human body that way. If I were a Bugatti I would not do that. Putting a hammer to your digestive system is nuts.

One of the biggest reasons to include the above researchers is that our ability to reconnect spiritually, and to our true past is laying dormant in our genes. Yes, I finally said something about being spiritual and more to come. In reconnecting we are using the body and mind and earth to jump start our buried memories of our histories. We could have many more books on paranormal experiences, near death experiences, and past lives. Our genes, our DNA, seems to have past memories that may kick on occasions during some activities and deja vu rears its head. In some moments it feels we have been in the same place doing the same thing, or a premonition about a pending event or location of someone. In other cases it's ayahuasca, or peyote or some drug hot wiring our current access panel to our memories stored in our genes or jumping the pineal gland for a fraction of a moment to connect us back to the earth or human conscious network that sends us a memory or vision of something happening. We chalk it up to Gods speaking, whew whew, or some divine connection to goddess Mother Earth. Time for us to step back from assuming that it is mother divine goddess of the eggplant sending you visions while hopped up on goofenthol. No more white robed covens staring at a new summer solstice, full moon or equinox and dancing with flower wreath headdresses. Imagine if that is how you had to start your car or smartphone? Do a thousand plus year old dance, and the car starts. Demystify, seriously. Positive gene expression has been achieved through exercise, real food, meditations that are useful, and healthy balanced lifestyle. Positive gene expressions can include unexplained medical observations of individuals thinking cancer away, regrowing missing bone, muscles healing or even their sight a million WTF's here. It can be eliminating diabetes without medication, that is getting to be common in the paleo world now. These are modern tie ins to the genes we are only starting to really re-understand today.

In the world of self experimentation and paleo, details of nutrient values are looked at for there pro and cons to cellular expression. "Positive gene expression". Mark Sisson, Robb Wolf, Dr. Alejandro Junger and a host of others are detailing micro nutrients. For instance, if you have tomato that looks ripe and beautiful, but it is grown in sand, how many nutrients can it have? Most of our commercial tomatoes look amazing and 90 percent are grown in Florida, in sand. How many nutrients are in sand? To make it to a market in Minnesota from California you have to gas the vegetables or fruits, there is no other options other than to produce them closer to a market. If not, they are picked early and gassed to fully ripened while in transit. What quickly is established in the last decade of paleo research is that not all meats, fruits, and vegetables are created equal. Hormones, feeding animals a food like corn when that is not the natural diet to a cow or a chicken. The research shows that feeding animals theses foods is changing them, and also us. Not for the better. Animals and plants have specific diets, supplementing the foods and nutrients is no good.

Garbage in and garbage is being established. Down to the mitochondrial DNA can change depending on the foods, and the associated chemicals that are being introduced via our farming and animal drugging methods. I have personally heard expert doctors tell me that your body just figures it out, to just basically eat good....what is that? Dr. Alejandro Junger has sold millions of books about how the human digestive system needs care. His work is great for anyone wanting to be healthy starting with maintaining properly the approximate 3 1/2 pounds of gut bacteria that digests for you.

Let's tie this back to engineered soil. Perfect Garden of Eden growing conditions for plants. It is likely, ancient advanced humans engineered the soil to produce food that was so nutrient filled it could cure you simply by eating the harvest. We seem to have intentionally engineered the trees and animals and the food we eat. Take those screaming or talking plants, they are absorbing information from each other and the frequencies and waves coming to the planet and around the planet. If animals and people once ate plants exclusively as stated in the Bible, is it possibly more for information. Layered information from the environment, from the soil, through the plants and the animals transferred to us and them to each other. Also, if we repaired our cells, if they never shut down, is it possible that the information gathered from the very cellular consumption of these plants and animals are now unreadable data. Basic nutrients are absorbed still but the higher information is not being absorbed and translated to our conscious selves.

Dr. Joe Walloch, author of Dead Doctors Don't Lie, has done over 20,000 autopsies. His research, like Viktor Schaubergers, is on observations in the field. He established that we were just not getting the nutrients we needed. There are over 60 nutrients yet about 3 were making it to us despite organic foods, that the soil is depleted. Nutrients saves cells by providing the needed building blocks for repairs and maintenance. This alone is a rabbit hole for your enjoyment. These missing nutrients can be added back into a liquid and delivered to the roots of plants through aeroponics. Is it possible to locate the richest remaining Terra Preta or chernozem soils and re-engineer them, maybe. We haven't yet. The nutrients of every level of everything, is compromised. The absolute positive of Dr. Walloch helping thousands and his continuing years of research is bringing us back.

These above human and life explorers are worth looking into and studying for your own personal advancement. We need to continue and tie in some curious gene splicing and look at some of the post flood myths that have some slivers of truth in them.

Our post flood histories in religious records document immortality of man and god.
The Paracus have DNA that is unknown, the star child has unknown features, what are those aliens people say are grey, big eyed, cow killing white Gumby looking aliens? Let's look at the Bible and longevity shall we?

IMMORTAL IMMORTALS IMMORTALITY FOR ALL

We will have to give a mention to the Greek and roman gods, whom are really just the Greek gods renamed, and say that humans post antediluvian story tellers are very creative. The Sumerians speak of the Anunaki and Gilgamesh. Gilgamesh is in there stories and in biblical stories, along with over lapping ages of kings and people like Adam and Eve. The Hindu Vedas are old by the millions of years. The Bible, "western" religions and myths along with many cultures including American Indians, Maya, Inca, and the Aztec have their stories that include a great flood. In all their myths their maybe slivers of truth. Let's look at some religion and how post flood beliefs might tie also to what genetic markers may be showing us.

The Bible for some is taken as literal truth. For others there are stories that are parables within it to live a clean good life. Adam and Eve were created to walk and talk with God, to live forever with animals they named and could actually talk too. Originally not eaten by the way. That gets glossed over. Animals were to live with us, and eat plants also. This blows some people and christians away. Here is the excerpt before the antediluvian cataclysm and God's word on how we were all one big happy planet...

ISAIAH 11:6–9

The wolf shall dwell with the lamb,
and the leopard shall lie down with the young goat,
and the calf and the lion and the fattened calf together;
and a little child shall lead them.

The cow and the bear shall graze;
their young shall lie down together;
and the lion shall eat straw like the ox.

The nursing child shall play over the hole of the cobra,
and the weaned child shall put his hand on the adder's den.

They shall not hurt or destroy
in all vmy holy mountain;
for the earth shall be full of the knowledge of the Lord
as the waters cover the sea.

Live happily with the animals, everybody eat plants. God planned for us to talk, get along with the animals and only eat plants....then the flood....

Genesis 9:3

Every moving thing that lives shall be food for you. And as I gave you the green plants, I give you everything.

Pre flood, the story is the animals and man eat fruit and plants, post flood, it's a Free For All in a Higher Sense Ted Nugent style and everything for itself. Why not talk about this when we were talking about Terra Pretra and Cheranozem? Because we were once vegetarians like it or not, and we may have been non eaters all together. The focus now is on immortality with God in the Garden of Eden. We fall, we flood, we eat it all!

One of the things that fascinated me as a kid is the age of people in the Old Testament, Methuselah lives to be 997 years, Jared, lives to be 994, then the ages drop, 660, 400, 200. 147 for Joseph, etc.. Why were the ages always declining? Also, there is no mention prior to the flood if the animals were to die or not either. IF we were to have been immortal before Adam and Eve bite of the tree of knowledge. Were the animals planned also? Here we are post flood and god instructing everything to eat everything. FYI no more talking to animals, this isn't explained or why do the animals have to die? What would be a point to talking to animals? Information about planet maintenance? Intergalactic incoming frequencies messing with the running of the earth?

The Sumerians king's list. This is a list of kings that ruled post antediluvian and pre-antediluvian for the Sumerians. The list is in the form of a stone tablet that is rectangular or triangular stone or clay post. There are multiple copies and one place it's been found is Ore that's one city in ancient Sumer. The list literally states, pre flood kings/post flood kings. This is where it gets interesting about the Bible. The flood story of the Sumerians is similar to the biblical flood story. Both cultures acknowledge Gilgamesh. In the Bible we have these ages listed and they decrement down, while post flood Sumerian Kings list shows a very close relationship with ages of kings slowly reducing down to 20 years of rule.

In theory, the post cataclysm of 12-13000 years ago destroyed the last of our ancient earth maintaining machinery, the earth power grid, was shutting down. The fertile Terra Preta and Chernozem was not being maintained or producing the required nutrients for one, the balancing and harmony produced by our larger power structures were off. Now the only thing left was the resonating energies in the air, or ionosphere. We lived and breathed it out till it was no more like a divers tank of oxygen. The frequencies of the earth slowly or quickly like a violin in the cold became untuned.

Pre-flood there was 8 Pre-antediluvian kings living for 241,200 years.

From the kings list those 8 kings, ruling for 241,200 years, goes as follows...

"after the kingship descended from heaven, the kingship was in Eridug. In Eridug, Alulim became king; he ruled for 28,800 years

King Alulim ruled 8 sars or 28,800 years

King Alalngar ruled 10 sars or 36,000 years

"Then Eridug fell and the kingship was taken to Bad-tibia."

King En-men-lu-ana ruled for 12 sars or 43,200 years

King En-men-gal-ana ruled for 8 sars or 28,800 years

King Dumuzid, the Shepherd ruled for 10 sars or 36,000 years

"Then Bad-tibia fell and the kingship was taken to Larag."

King En-sipad-zid-Ana ruled for 8 sars or 28,800 years

"Then Larag fell and the kingship was taken to Larag."

King En-men-dur-ana ruled for 5 sars and 5 nerds or 21,000 years

"Then Zimbir fell and the kingship was taken to Shuruppag."

King Ubara-tutu ruled for 5 sars and 1 ner or 18,600 years

"Then the flood swept over."

The mainstream academia says they forgot what years were and really meant to say moons, or seasons, or dog years. Seriously, they knew how to nano coat metal to a single molecular level, build with Pi and the golden ratio but didn't know on multiple tablets that they had to chisel, that they weren't putting on the right time frame for their rulers? Unlikely. Exactly more likely we are speculating that these might be kings, or the Annunaki that enslaved human kind per the Sumerian texts, that the Sumer stories and Gilgamesh are all about. Or is this one of the first written records recording a pre-antediluvian highly advanced human culture uninterested or unable to recreate the technology that kept them immortal? Had the damage been so irreversible 242,000 years ago shut down things enough that they chose to bring up the tribal peoples around Sumer? An ancient advanced human culture where a smaller group decides to live in the open. Making themselves kings for thousands of years at a time. Could it have been from another flood, or war, or impact disaster, sure. Clearly the list is showing kings that died, or moved on, to something else.

Post-antediluvian Kings and Biblical Patriarchs have a common theme starting at the same period, they decline dramatically after the flood. Could some of the last great machines have been so destroyed that it was just winding down, untuned, unmanaged atmosphere and soil and everything else failing to function gradually? This list shows Sumer and Biblical Patriarchs declining in ages....

Sumerian Post flood kings		Biblical Patriarchs
Jushur for 1200 years		Adam 930
Kullassina-bel 930 years		Seth 912
Nangishlishma 670 years		Enosh 905
En-Tara-Ana 420		Cainan 910
Babum 300		Mahalalel 895
Paunnum 840		Jared 962
kalibum 960		Enoch 365
Zuqaqip 900		Methuselah 969
Atab 600		Lamech 777
Mashda Son of Atab 840		Noah 950
Arwuim Son of Mashda 720		Shem 600
Etana 1500	"The shepherd, who ascended to heaven and consolidated all the foreign countries	Arphaxad 438
Balih son of Etana 400		Shelah 433
En-me-nuna 660		Eber 464
Melum-kish son of nuna 900		Peleg 239
Barsal-nuna 1200		Rue 239
		Serug 230
		Nahor 148
		Terah 205
		Abram 175
		Isaac 180
		Jacob

The ages are not similar completely but they are in the ball park for possibly being the same people. Gilgamesh is recognized in the Bible, and giants, and angels.

These kings lived longer and ruled for 1000's of years? How? The Singularity and basic quantum knowledge would allow for the repair of any living cell, or it's replacement. Living indefinitely would not be difficult. If some of the higher advanced ancient humans were worker bees, they may have held on to technology they themselves as survivors of a catastrophe may not have known how to repair. Despite thousands of years, they may not have been able to re-engineer it to save themselves, instead relying on a patriarch system using local tribes as labor. We have similar accounts from the Egyptians. Herodotus remembers meeting Egyptian priests in his travels that showed him an account of pharaohs of Egypt that went back overs 11,000 years. Thank you idiots who burned the library of Alexandria.

Herodotus Histories, Book 2 Chapter 144-145 excerpt,

"....Of these gods one or the other had in succession been supreme; the last of them to rule the country was Osiris' son Horus, called by the Greeks Apollo; he deposed Typhon, and was the last divine king of Egypt. Osiris is in the Greek language, Dionysus.

Among the Greeks, Heracles, Dionysus, and Pan are held to be the youngest of the gods. But in Egypt Pan is the most ancient of these and is one of the eight gods who are said to be the first of all..."

Interesting like the Sumerian kings list, the first that ruled Egypt were gods, 8 of them. Sumer having their 8 pre-antediluvian kings. Though, from Hercules to Amasis, there were 17,000 years passed. The mystified, or "holy" texts of the Sumerians, Christians, Judaism, Hinduism, the greeks and romans all have post flood references to lengthy life spans of "gods". Speaking with animals, walking with gods, is it possible the sliver of truth is that we had indefinite lifespans, used our pineal gland and did speak with animals and only ate plants?

Oooh, wait, we have the Hindus Vedas, going back millions of years. Those scribblings. That's how that still gets handled, the Sumerian kings list is written off that they are talking about moons, the Bible ages are written off, in fact, no body touches it in a church, or general discussion, shhhhh, it's a mystery. What we have seen in the historical record is that humans are old, that primitive tools have been found through the ages are tools we could find today in any number of the over 150 known tribes still living nomadically or in remote uncontacted islands, forests or jungles. Primitive people live remotely or near more advanced people as I write this. These tribal people don't need a grocery store. When everything goes to shit, the bark eaters and loin clothiers come down to tie an IPad around their neck for jewelry and worship polished stones in a group. You pick the solstice. Give that a 1000 years and god for bid you have an archaeological team searching for our past as they dig and find things below that 1000 years.

Who were the Paracus, how did they get to South America and why did they have red Hair? Some American Indians did, some American tribes had blonde hair and blue eyes, they don't get talked about as much do they? Thank you European people settling in modern time for enough diseases to wipe out over 70-80 percent of the native populations. The bones are out there, genetic testing anyone? You might find what was found in the eastern United States, the Hopali A group, showing clear indicators of Judaism as the origin of these Indians. Yep, they are related to the middle eastern Israelites!

A German researcher finds cocaine, and tobacco, and other indicators that the Pharaohs has direct trade relations to South America. Ops, ops, bury it or start testing more mummies? Start testing the dead for a more complete genetic map or just gloss it over? We know where we are as of 2019 with mainstream science and this one.

A map has been drawn to say that early man was evolving in africa, moved out in every which direction and there are maps to prove it. They just pump out maps with arrows. We didn't know there was a quad helix till a paper was published on Jan 20th, 2013 in Nature Chemistry, about 60 years after we figured out there was DNA to even build a cell with.

A whole other story on Rosalind Franklin, whom actually discovered DNA, went uncredited. People are working to change that. It was Rosalind in the 50's that figured out DNA. The four stranded packages are called G-quadruplexes coming 60 years later in 2013, that is quite a while building medical knowledge on the part of the package. Meanwhile the out of africa theory is going strong along with Darwinian evolutionary evidence literally based on a story with a dining table worth of physical evidence.

The discovery of the four stranded G-quadruplexes is guiding cancer research, neurological disorders, a million other things and this is only a recent observation in 2013. I guess some science moves faster than archaeology right? We are moving but the topsy/turvy nature of the body of knowledge we have is used so many side way ways, we think food is for fun, not fuel and repair or higher connections.

Identifying the quad is supposed to help in handling cancer. Did you know that there is a TED talk that you can watch a scientist that is killing cancer with sound? Killing diseases with sound? No drugs, sound. Think that could be a split page article on the cover of National Geographic and the Smithsonian along with the Paracas DNA results?

HIGH INTENSITY FOCUSED ULTRASOUND

The Guardian, Sat 31, Oct 2015 "High Power sound waves used to blast cancer cells." British doctors can target and kill tumors without surgery. The Institute of Cancer research at the Royal Marsden hospital in Sutton are already using the tech to kill deep in the human body. " The technology is completely noninvasive and allows us to monitor changes we are making inside a person instantly" Thomas Andreas, therapy director at Philips. With ultra sound you can snap a picture of an organ or a growing baby, guide surgery or needle tests to a point(haha, point) so with a power of 10,000 times that of baby ultra sounds, "when we pick up a target tissue to kill off, we need to heat it up to about 55c for at least a second. That is enough to kill it off," said Ter Haaretz, "....more important we can do it at places that are deep inside an organ- while leaving tissue on the surface unaffected.""

Positive gene expression as explained by paleo guys like Mark Sisson, Rob Wolf, Ido Portal, Le Corre and more is about eating and moving in a way that gives mitochondrion DNA level information and input to "positively express" healthy configurations. Tell your cells your full of flexibility, strength, endurance and show it that it will have the building blocks designed to help it and the cells will blossom with health. Wim and Stig, & Edwin all speak, written and have self-experimented with mindful breathing, good eating, all leading to your body naturally being healthier, less sick, with improved recovering time, disease repelling, healthy gut bacteria and more benefits then we can list. These researchers are going at it by the day learning and self experimenting. This is a must and your hint about what you are taking on. This isn't about cool talking points. Research into our DNA has not explained what it does at all close to completely. We do not have control of it. We are trying, but it is more theory than fact. Completing the DNA and human genome doesn't mean we have a complete record of the human race.

What about animals? Did you know researchers have traced the North American canine to a breed we have no record of? That isn't the only record we are missing. The point here is not how true my theory is, the point is we need to see how far up theories' ass we are vs. what we know. Animals, like people only leave so much of a fossil record. Any biologist can tell you we are missing animals, insects and everything in the biological realm round the outside. We do not have an evolutionary record that is close to complete. This puts us blind. Denisovans and Neanderthal are not only being found in human DNA, we are finding that Denisovans, whom had larger brains than us, also bred with an unknown group. Not aliens, just more scrap ancient humans, maybe not advanced ancient humans, an unknown group.

Brien Foerster's work and DNA testing doesn't just represent a first for common sense research, it is one of the first finds that establish a nail on a map of our real human past. We don't have a complete history of the humanity let alone know what the DNA genetic map of the human being does. It's like having a programming language and no context for the program. It's just ones and zeros then. Calling any DNA in the human body "junk" genes is hilarious. The best Nero surgeons in the world will hold up their pinky and say, this is how much we know about the brain. Genetic understanding is at its infancy, in order to understand how people are genetically related we would need a complete sample from everyone. Ever. That has been on earth. Extracting DNA from uber old bodies is hard. Very hard and the labs that can do it are few. Look At Brien Foerster's efforts.

DNA AND MEMORY

DNA can store information. This has now been done. In one example DNA could store 215 petabytes or 215 gigabytes in a gram. You could record everything humans have done in a couple elephants. DNA could last 100,000's of years under the right environment. As long as you can write/read DNA it will last indefinitely. This starts to look like a great back up place. There is cross over with spintronics research and using single atomic components for storage, switching and reading information. DNA has been experimented successfully since 2012. We have been storing data on DNA for 7 years already. Harvard geneticists, Sri Kosuri & George Church and colleagues encoded a 52,000 word book on DNA using DNA's four legged alphabet of A, G, T, and C to encode the Os and 1s of the digitized file. The current storage ability is about 1.28 petabytes per gram of DNA. Current research suggests the storage capacity is at least 1.8 bits per nucleotide of DNA.

For all the time people get flashes of past lives, is it possible that they are recalling the memories stored in their own cells of past ancestors. What if that double helix is the storage for a backup human or everyone that has come before?

There is research worth mentioning that includes the idea of genetic memory through what is perceived as instinct. As an example, something traumatic happens to the mother and the instinct for that experience is passed to the child through the mother. In a study published by IFLScience.com these are some of the observations...

"...Your genes are inherited from your parents, and theirs from their parents before them. If these mutate, your genetic inheritance changes with it. However, changes to how your genome "expresses" itself – how it behaves, essentially – can also occur due to environmental changes, like ingested chemicals, exercise, and psychological issues.

When your ancestor goes through a period of excessive stress, this "experience" can be added to your genome. An extra layer of information is placed on top of your DNA sequences. The DNA sequence itself doesn't change, but its "clothes" do, so to speak. Generally speaking, this is known as the vaguely defined field of epigenetics, which means "outside genetics."

The authors of a new Science paper describe it more precisely as "transgenerational transmission of environmental information." It has already been seen in humans – Holocaust survivors' descendants, for example, have lower levels of the stress-hormone cortisol in their blood, which means they're more vulnerable to stress and fear.

"...Genetic expression, a team led by scientists from the European Molecular Biology Organisation (EMBO) in Spain took genetically engineered nematode worms that carry a transgene for a fluorescent protein. When activated, this gene made the worms glow under ultraviolet light."

"That's the longest scientists have ever observed the passing-down of an environmentally induced genetic change. Usually, environmental changes to genetic expression only last a few generations."

""We don't know exactly why this happens, but it might be a form of biological forward-planning,"" said one of the team, Adam Klosin from EMBO and Pompeu Fabra University, Spain.

Transgenerational transmission of environmental information in C. elegans

"epigenetic inheritance - especially because it serves as a remarkable demonstration of how long-lasting these inter-generational effects may be."

Chicken before the egg? Why do we all run, run or feel the backs of our hair rise when we walk up out of a basement? Can you think of times as a kid or young adult that you may have started walking up the creepy basement stairs and then ran. Walked then faster and faster and felt like something was behind you? IT DOESN'T seem to matter what language you speak, it is something that happens all over the world. There are tunnels all over the world, rock cut and deep. When I think of this genetic shared straight, I think about the tunnels in Turkey that seal from the inside out. Large rolling stone disks that seal door ways to underground cities that can hold tens of thousands. How long did our ancestors hide or how long did they live along side something that they would be so scared to go from walking to running from the deep lower levels of these rock cut spaces?

SYNESTHESIA REAL ABILITIES OF SUPER HUMANS OR ANCIENT ONES?

Synesthesia- a phenomenon where one sensory or cognitive pathway leads to automatic involuntary secondary or cognitive pathway/ Merriam-Webster 1. A concomitant sensation especially: a subjective sensation or image of a sense(as of color) other than the one (as of sound) being stimulated 2. The condition marked by the experience of such sensations.

People who have this ability to do this are called synesthetes. There are different forms of these abilities. Originally identified in "modern" times in the 17th century. Some of the forms of synesthesia: grapheme-color synesthesia, color-graphemic synesthesia, where numbers or letters are physically seen by the eye in colors. Number form synesthesia, numbers, months, years dates, create precise locations in space or appear as a 3-dimensional map.

Any number of ways this can be connected in the brain. Scientists do not know how this works, at all. You could be a synesthete and not know it. It is estimated that 20 % of the global population may have it.

Solomon Veniaminovich Shereshevsky(1886-1958, a Russian journalist and mnemonist was studied and written about by Alexander Luria, in his book The Mind of a Mnemonist (1968). Solomon could memorize complete meetings word for word, math problems, literature and could hear a music tone and see a color, touch would give particular tastes, and after many years he could delete memories like a file from a computer. This would be a problem in a post cataclysm environment if this one guy bites it and he is the only one that mentally remembered cold fusion.

In this example of synesthesia, addition and or numbers equal colors. If we as humans had this ability we might be able to quickly compute an angle or a change to a coworker while building or manufacturing something without a complicated math problem. We could be carving a megalithic block and see a color which is exactly an angle. As simple as having a stop light turn green, if you are in the parameters, the math shows the color as exactly as a tape measure would be used with a mark.

In Chromesthesia, sound converts to color and one might hear a musical instrument and see a colored geometric shape while another might hear the same instrument and think that it sounds like a particular color. Other synesthetic experiences with sound are called photisms. Any combination of senses can be mixed with frequencies and visualizations. If you had this ability, running an ancient construction site as you shaped a megalithic block to vibrate the correct frequency or cancel another out could be achieved through color codes. ...just an idea.

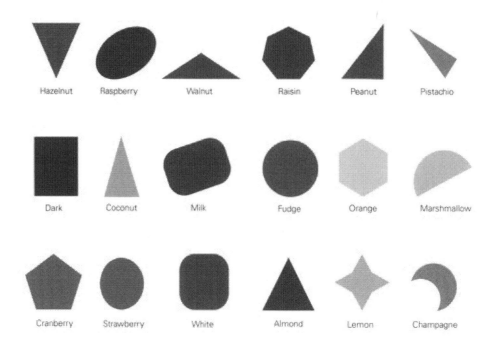

| Hazelnut | Raspberry | Walnut | Raisin | Peanut | Pistachio |

| Dark | Coconut | Milk | Fudge | Orange | Marshmallow |

| Cranberry | Strawberry | White | Almond | Lemon | Champagne |

In some cases one might hear a musical instrument and see a color and a geometric shape. Any combo of senses could be combined to experiences frequencies and sounds. In our amphitheater experience, there could be healing plays or perhaps a college class conducted entirely by symphony. Imagine going to a construction site on the pyramids or cymatic polygonal site and all your building architectural or engineering information was broadcast on speakers and to the on looker was just music, or a fellow worker whistling the next bit of information to build the very next section of the building.

The synesthetes with Chromesthesia can trigger firework shapes, move like colors in a kaleidoscope and fade when the sound is gone. The sounds change and the brightness, color, shade and even the direction and movement changes for the synesthete. Synesthetes can see music on a "screen" in front of them. Lines can move as color, width, depth, height moving all over in front of their faces creating amazing patterns.

Spatial sequence synesthesia (SSS) allows the synesthetes to see numbers in physical space closer or farther away depending on the number. These people tend to have incredible memories. Remembering details of the past in great detail. Months and dates float in space around them and time can float around them as an object.

Number forms is a map of numbers that just appears in the mind of a synesthetes whenever they think of a number. How fun would that be to do math on a mental chalk board.

Auditory-tactile synesthetes can hear a sound and it can induce sensations in the body. One might here a specific word and feel touch in one part of the body.

There is a dark side, maybe just being able to see or taste your math problems is dark but there is also Misophonia, where negative experiences are triggered by sounds. Mirror-touch synesthetes can feel the same sensation as another person. How about tasting something when you hear a word?

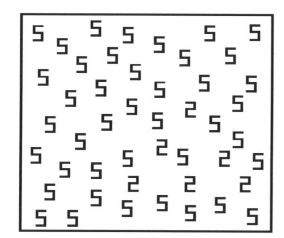 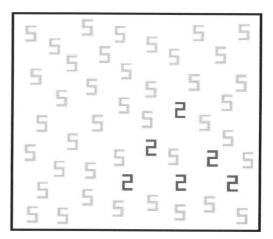

Imagine all of our ancient advanced ancestors are synesthetes and all constructions public and private are designed technically for this along with earthquake and weaponized cloaking and unimagined communications. As Synesthetes we would be able to experiences with all senses music, plays, shows, what a composer or artist would bring and collective experience would be like nothing we have imagined.

There are dozens of forms and the Greeks were even aware. Isaac Newton considered musical tones and colors must share frequency and experimented with that. Carl Jung, Georg Tobias Ludwig Sachs and Gustav Fechner studied synesthetes in 1876. Many people and many researchers are aware of these abilities. These aren't even dormant! Although, more like scrambled, old cable networks were back in the day, you could only see a bit of a show. Wim Hof and Stig tie in because controlling your autonomic immune system and vagus nerve should lead to conscious control of these abilities possibly.

Sound and color research is on going, but the other abilities of the synesthete could be part of our third eye. Possibly third eye may have become a catch all to explain all of our genetically programmed abilities. Intentional abilities. There is now international organizations for synesthetes. The American Synesthesia Association to many in Europe.

As we rediscover the complexity of genes and our own advancements to apply memories or storage in DNA, is it likely this has already been done? Are the abilities of Wim, Stig, Ido, and Irwin and synesthetes just indicators of our super engineering great greatest ancestor's research? Work our ancient advance ancestors continue to this day.

You can google endlessly the debate on Intelligent design, but more researchers are looking at the mathematical precision of DNA and feel that it is so perfectly organized that it doesn't seem "natural". That there are indisputable "cuts" in the DNA that could only be done if someone intentionally cut them. The immediate answer, Aliens did it. The first thing this does is negate the evidences we keep finding, a highly advanced human culture that could build cymatic polygonal walls would also have high medical technology. I.e., we did it.

The evidence of buried memories and "past lives" could be real. Past lives may live in our DNA and between us in a living consciousness cloud. This has been suspected for a long time by quantum scientists. Based on a possible fail safe, or desired just in case you fly into the sun, we will bring you back, the ancient humans of our past would have had many reasons and ways to make back-ups? The idea that we are each other's backups is not far fetched.

The "mystification" of past lives for instance. People have documented remembering that they lived once and can remember things that are only explainable if they were there. They locate physical places, name names of people in ancient history and have details of events they just probably knew nothing about. Speak languages they have never spoken or heard. These could be accessible by a brain that was connecting consciously to our human consciousness and although an individual is accessing them, they are not your memories but back up for that person floating in the human consciousness. We just aren't rebooted with our own superhuman selves to know the difference. There are examples of predicting the future, seeing events before they happen or seeing where a murder took place or finding a kidnapped person. This may have to do with the either we live in and our dormant third eye and senses that lay below our allegedly 14 percent conscious brain.

If evolution was straight true, and all life develops and changes due to environmental factors and we all evolve as we need to, then why the big dormant brain? Is it more likely evolution or design? The complexity of anatomically correct humans are what they are because we had already evolved and used the brain we have to it's full capacity in the past. The other option is evolution thought in this instance we'd grow into it so it gave us a brain way bigger than we needed to start with? If evolution is as stated, we only get what we need as we push into it, the brain we have would only be the size it is if it was a grown into tool from past experience.

In the ancient past after a clear amount of tragedy's either internal planetary war, impacts from space, pole shifts a combo of a lot of perfect storms, we slowly went from immortal, to living thousands of years, to hundreds, and finally to 100ish. All the while our biological tech shut off, we started eating our living RAM and companions, the animals. They started to eat each other, it was a complete catastrophe. After so long, we are left running on empty with 14ish % consciousness and living on our earthly computer board gouging the circuits.

There are documented cases of animals knowing when a tsunami is coming or when earthquakes are about to hit. When a pet owner is going to have a stroke, seizure, heart attack and many other times when a pet seems to know. It is a remnant built in code, part of our massive interconnected planetary design. A design that is ancient, high tech, human work.

Adelie penguins to the tune of 1.5 million or so. Despite an international love of them, no one noticed the party on the Danger Islands for years until a recent accidental satellite find.

How off or unobservant are we? How many times do we have to mention, we don't know much about the bottom of the ocean and more about space? How about in 2018 despite a couple tear jerking amazing documentaries about penguins, and scientists from all over the globe stationed in Antarctica and the North Pole, they missed a penguin breeding location that has an estimated population of 1.5 million or more Adélie penguins on Danger Island. This was spotted by NASA satellites, allegedly recently.

...*"supercolony were found on the rocky and remote Danger Islands after NASA satellites picked up patches of their excrement, known as guano, in 2014.*

The images prompted a group of scientists, including Oxford University's Dr Tom Hart, to arrange an expedition the following year to find out how many penguins were there.

Dr Hart told The Telegraph "This is the biggest colony discovered recently. It is a huge number of penguins.

The weirdest, most surprising and incredible thing is that, in this day and age, something so big can go unseen. They have been missed because they are hard to get to. They really have been overlooked."

EXCERPT FROM THE TELEGRAPH

The outstanding awareness of our genetic technology now, with the practical applications of spintronics, the nature of the either we live in and the reality that it is sound, resonance and toroidal field that more closely represents the atomic structure of everything is showing that aliens is no longer the next jump to answer our questions. If an ancient advanced human society is advanced in one way, it is likely they had the technology to modify their genes and go from a boot wearing ancient walking with dinosaurs peeps to a white reptilian that appears to be alien. It isn't in our vernacular to consider those unknown genes as body mods found by Brien Foerster. Simply body mods for either underground living, space travel, inter-dimensional travel, or the whim of it. After millions of years of this being home, it just isn't practical to look like the average human.

Ray kurtzwel in The Singularity is Near, discusses the advanced nano technology on the horizon and it means we could live much much longer and or indefinitely. Replacing our organic cells with diamondiod crystalline, to be men of steel. On some days the idea that we may not even want a body we could fly on consciousness alone. Our very consciousness could stay permanently in a collective cloud. As we rediscover the complexity of our own genes, we are also seeing that animals, including dogs have a genetic story that goes beyond our sight. It isn't that they just have missing link ancestor, like the North American dog, they showed up, they had a relative that isn't on the books at all. A no fossil record dog. What about the mini rhinos and hippos of Malta? There were once mini versions like Beanie Babies. We are not looking at our genetic history as one of an engineered race, it's "nature". Yet as we dig, we are seeing, physically seeing cuts in DNA we didn't make in modern times. These cuts are likely in plants. Terra Preta and Cheronozem soils are engineered and all over the earth why not the rest? Brian Foerster's testing of the Paracus show unknown genetic markers. The fact then, there is another older human genetic set, "alien" to us, likely part of a very advanced human society with knowledge way beyond what we call "hi-tech" now.

Why? There is no rule that everywhere or somewhere a planet randoms life. That there is a cosmic diarrhea of odds that pulls bacteria out of water and to land and there is a human and plants 3 billion years later. Cremo's research into the antiquity of man, and consistent finds and footprints in the stone show we have been here for millions of years. Instead of concentrating on evolution and pressing all facts into it, we should continue focusing on the revelations of new technology discoveries. We keep seeing more of the truths of our past. At a minimum, a highly advanced and managed Earth by a society that used the natural universal energies to sustain a global society on an engineered planetary system.

Chapter 9

POLYGONAL MASONRY and GEOPOLYMERS

If there is a silver bullet, if you needed proof that nothing adds up, the corner stone is literally the corner stone. Polygonal masonry and ancient geopolymers are so special, the capstone ...seriously, I am not going to stop, there is a reason we have so many "stone" references. This single entity of the ancient world is so unique and everywhere on every continent and so advanced. It destroys all arguments to whatever the penguins, the standard academia, the governments, cults, religions, religion of archaeology, archa-priests(shout out to Lauberger) can not destroy. They have all taken a chip out of our true history for their own reasons. They have destroyed, buried, burned and tried to hide our history for power and hubris. The problem with doing that

Cymatic Polygonal construction is one of the most important, obvious pieces of ancient high technology starring back at us. Over the last few thousand years it has been costumed by new cultures, rebuilt and added on to. It is all over the earth and the soil and foundation platforms it sits on represent the largest indicators of this lost highly advanced society.

with megalithic blocks, the shit's heavy. Baalbek has 1600 plus ton stones. Hard to hide.

It's easy to walk over Giza Plateau, the Great Pyramid complex, and not know the weight and total size of those platform stones. There are great great walls in Siberia that are polygonal on a scale that is no less than Lord of the Rings. This is where standard academics look like a Monty Python skit. "Say, isn't that a big polygonal wall?" "No, no, no. No it isn't." "No, I think it is..." "Nope, no it isn't, tiss a Inca wall."

We are going to look at the sciences of this technology, we have already discussed quantum, cymatics, water and frequency. Now we apply it to a thing on earth that has to make all of us stop lying about our history. Polygonal masonry isn't just tight fit and earthquake proof, it's a mechanical component in a connected ancient society that needed cataclysm protection and so much more. Geopolymars coat the ancient world, they are also high tech and would be of great use to us now.

There are specific sites that we will detail, some you have heard too much about and others nothing. I would like to start by baiting you into a chapter about this subject with examples but we are diving into the science right away. It is more important than the sites. Despite being everywhere on earth including all over Egypt.

SCIENCE OF POLYGONAL MASONRY

"Mainstream Science has to explain this!" - David Hatcher Childress

Polygonal masonry is on Ancient Aliens, YouTube, every time someone has a video there is a mention of it in the ancient world. It is very common in South America like Puma Punku or Machu Picchu, in Asia, Europe and everywhere. The first thing to say to impress anyone about polygonal masonry, being the simple monkeys we are today, is that they are 100's or 1000's of tons and then there is a pause, you can't fit a hair, piece of paper, a blade, or a dollar bill between the blocks. Then there is usually a picture or video of someone standing there next to these things all pieced together and it's impressive. Polygonal masonry is heavy, its got tight seams. Cool.

It took me personally a couple of years of research for it to dawn on me about how tight the corners are. Some of the blocks have been cut in odd sizes and have been placed together with 5 or even 10 corners or more with the other blocks cut to fit. Think trapezoid or weird polygonal shapes fit on all sides in a complex way. The precision of the fit needs to be explained in detail.

I have a background in construction, when you cut a 45 on a board, say a baseboard, as you are corning in a room with new trim, you just care that the 90 cuts made a perfect 90 degree corner where you see it. Boards are only 3/4 of an inch thick, from the view of standing in the room, the two baseboards come together. When I go to nail them to the wall, the wall itself isn't usually level, plumb, square, whatever you think, even if it was a new home, it is not even close to perfect, ever. So you put the boards in place and hope that the corner that you, the homeowner is looking at is square, at a perceived 90 degree angle. Then nail it together. Frequently it doesn't quite come together at the corner, and as you look down the wall either the board or the wall or both are not straight, ever. In their own way the baseboard is either warped and has gaps along the wall and waves out or in. Then if the wall is wavy and the baseboard is straight then the wall is revealed as not flat. You can hang a picture on it or throw a sofa on it, but you are not looking at two things that fit together. Fill it with caulk and paint or stain. Hide it the best you can.

Polygonal has many exact characteristics including joinery that is epically tight whether small or 3000 tons. Every side of every joint fits, the length, breadth and width. Why? To move with a massive quake or impact as the earth shakes, to be able to send wave and frequencies through, to, and off theses buildings, the construction must fit like the cells of a human or any living thing. Connecting from one to the next.

For years, I had heard how tight the joints were in polygonal megalithic blocks never conceiving or visualizing more than my trim example. You don't care if the back side of your 90 degree cut is touching as long as the inside of the cut appears to the person in the room as to join together and continues around the room that way. Polygonal masonry has no mortar. What had never been clear to me was the joints were not the only tight spot, the whole surface of the entire block, whether 20 or 3000 tons, is touching along every surface on all sides. Think about touching your arm to your shoulder or your heel to your butt. When you do, skin along your leg or arm comes together perfectly. The skin folds together and if you could see it transparently there is no gaps between the two surfaces. The skin fits along the muscle and skin of the other limb. Polygonal masonry is the same. Every inch whether it is two blocks 4 ft. x 12 ft. by 20 ft., bigger or smaller, every inch fits together. It is incredible.

This is our first clue to technology. The ability to connect all sides of these blocks completely. This isn't carving and carving and sanding till they are pretty close. They are perfect in a way we can not do. Unless we use concrete and pour the next block or section in a form, it would appear like a block and melt and mesh to the prior surface.

Look at some of the pictures here and imagine a couple guys, or religion of archaeology types telling you 100's or 1000's of slaves would what? Lean the two blocks apart and polish and MRI scan each block so that all sides, all perspectives fit physically together. This one task is insane. It is every joint, in every structure that you will see with polygonal masonry. Connected completely.

One purpose and function of polygonal masonry, cataclysm protection. There are so many examples down to petrified footprints in boots alongside dinosaurs that show humans have walked this earth as long as we could stand the heat. The Yucatán meteor crater is suspected of wiping out the dinosaurs. This is a good example of a cataclysm that would make you think, hey, maybe since we always plan on living here we build so big we make it disaster resistant. Maybe only rebuild a little bit.

One of our main points, one that is not argued by anyone is that there was a catastrophe, a cataclysm, it's not enough to say cataclysm because a thumb down on social media is a cataclysm for some, so we can distinguish this by saying Massive Cataclysm. Again we have the last great smash around 12-13000 years ago. It helps to point to the 19-mile-wide crater in Greenland. If by all the evidence we have had anatomically correct humans on this planet as long as it has been able to support life, then we, humanity, have lived through some terrible geological events. Having

Here is the perfect example of a later culture coming into an ancient advanced site and making it their own. Rubble stacks between large, highly finished cymatic polygonal walls. Many cultures all over the earth have adapted ruins including the dynastic Egyptians.

structures that we can reoccupy or on their base level continue to perform while under water, mud or heavy storms and weather changes. Humanity could retreat from that geological/solar event and wait. Coming up from the miles of rock cut dwellings and underground cities, the structures on the surface would be primarily intact after the catastrophic event. The Incas for instance, rebuilt and reused the material they found at sites like Machu Picchu. The wood framing above the polygonal walls and metal would be long gone. We have to look back at what may have been once forests of redwoods and sequoias. We have these buildings with a structure that could handle being hit with wind, water and tidal wave then continue to function. In the case of the pyramids as already discussed frequencies being bounced, received and broadcasted on a scale that was an earth grid. Spend a disaster underground in a rock cut city under Turkey or Bolivia or Brazil interconnected by roads and perhaps subway and wait out the cataclysm. Meanwhile above ground a super structure that can twist and turn and flex with earthquakes and water damage hit by high tidal waves, water lines, etc. Resilient construction that could function or be repaired quickly after the disaster calmed down.

The scale is lost, some of these cymatic polygonal stones exceed 800 tons and small stones can be seen stacked back into the ruin by the later cultures that occupied the space. There is a distinct possibility that the stacked stones that they rebuilt with are pieces of advanced ancient structures that were repurposed. There is also a possibility that it is a later culture's rubble and the site laid in ruin over and over from occupations over eons after the original builders and the ruins are from those cultures. The frontiers of standard and future academic research will have to walk hand in hand with a new bread of researchers to discern the truth.

The Aztecs and Inca made it clear to the Spanish that these polygonal constructions were not their construction, it was the gods. They came, like the dynastic Egyptians and they picked up ruined cities and rebuilt empires on it. This is why you are going to see a lot of polygonal masonry with essentially rubble in gaps where "newer" cultures have repaired them with a more primitive level of construction techniques.

The complexity of polygonal construction is pointed out by many researchers like Brien Forester, David Childress and many more. They appear to be laser cut, detailed and usually made from the hardest stones on earth, built and shaped to fit perfectly with keystone cuts. Along comes another culture and then rubble. Literally stacked rubble between these polygonal masonry work. It looks ridiculous. Imagine a brand new car finished off with 2x4s. Some pillows on plywood for seats, would we do that? Yet it is how we are to address all the cultures from the Aztecs and Inca, Egyptians to ancient Japanese. Megalith blocks well fitted prideful work aaaand then they got tired and stopped and just filled in the rest with rubble. Imagine the 2x4s used to finish off your car with a v8 engine and high performance brakes being from another construction site also. Not brand new but torn from something else basically Wall-E construction from Pixar on a trashed earth.

There are more than what is listed in this photo of keystone cuts and it has been beaten to death that this is the greatest coincidence or if we are being big about it the one of many open misses by standard academia, catching them up can no longer be the priority, the researchers willing to experiment and re-engineer this technology has to leave them behind. Less any stone masons, religious institutions or governments want to admit to already knowing and working on it.

Here is a keystone cut in what would otherwise be a very "complete" looking column. By research observations today, we assume that keystone cuts were poured and only flat. This example shows that a later culture rebuilt the site, not knowing what a keystone cut was, still matched the two blocks together because of the cool lego like details on the pieces setting them up and side ways. This tells us they interpreted the pieces themselves and with their own artists added to the blurred lines of these pieces true location. Standard archaeologists could help by determining if this was a particular greek style, there must have been many pieces for them to pick up and reuse. This may be of an example of a side ways keystone cut, it was set together, poured and raised up to it's current place. Ancient High technology ancestors could have had polished glass, nano paint, plastics, carbon fibers finishing this building and a sideways keystone cut would not be seen unless everything else had dusted and rusted away.

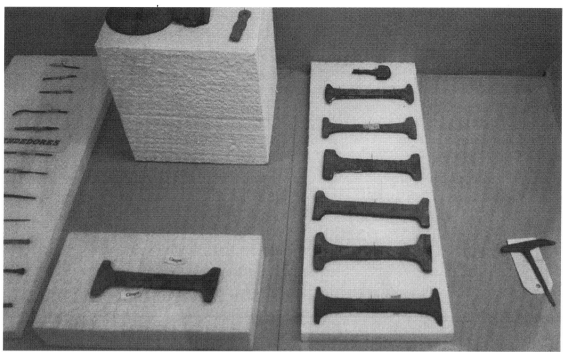

These are examples of various keystone metals. Many have been taken if exposed, maybe for arrow heads or spears or simple tools or even jewelry by later humans. The technology in keystones that is so exciting is the high crystal content of the stone used around the keystone pieces. The idea of making the stones more conductive to each other or to enhance frequency and conductivity through the cymatic polygonal construction is a possibility. The buildings that were once above these structures are left to our imagination. We are looking likely at foundations connected by engineered soil and meta structure planning right down to the vegetation and trees.

Magnetic anomalies amongst the cymatic polygonal construction is common. Field coherences are a well known science yet not understood. The keystone cut obviously appears to connect the two stones creating stability, but is that true when every side of the cymatic polygonal pieces are 50 to 1000's of tons? Is it more likely a yet to be understood "solder point" in a large complex earth circuit system that included the very buildings they once lived and worked in?

Back to the Technology of Polygonal masonry. It is amazing for earthquake control. When researchers built models and tested it against earthquakes, these buildings were able to deal with the vibrations of the earthquake by flexing and moving with the rumbling of the quake. An earthquake is measured on the Richter scale. This is a scale that determines the intensity of an earthquake. Richter is not the only scale anymore, however the magnitude scales are all designed to give numerical values that are similar. There is depth to an earthquake, as in the earthquake theory is based on the idea that the continents are on large blocks of rock called tectonic plates, these plates drift, on occasion, they either rub, slip under each other or bump down together or rise up, think about any mountain range, they are where the tectonic plates come together. The depth of an earthquake can very, it could be deep in the earth or closer to the surface and that would affect how intensely we would feel it on the surface of the earth. All the different measuring systems allow the different hypo-central depths of the tectonic plates crashing to be measured. The amplitude, the elasticity of the wave many measurements are taken. This is significant technology.

Researchers over the last few years have created physical models to scale that show polygonal, non mortared stone, could withstand earthquakes better than buildings today! This is amazing, out of this world amazing. The very fact that they put all the stones together without mortar is something we can not do. Locking the blocks together in the shape that they put them is a feat. This locking is not like what you see when you look at your bathroom floor, this isn't what is called a brick pattern. Where you start a row, then the next row is half over the seam of the row below it. The next after and after repeating. This is many sided, shaped, cut blocks fitted in multiple sizes where one polygonal block looks like it is crawling onto the next block like a slinky. And 100 tons, perfectly fit together. The technology of it is just spectacular. The "locking'' of the blocks causes them to flex move or by shear weight and connectivity to just "move'' with the earthquake.

It's amazing that the construction of polygonal masonry, no mortar is able to stand for 1000's of years and no problems. There has been failure over the years from the technology not being maintained and weathering from eons of wind and weather. Other cultures have come in and rebuilt. There is joint failure to be seen and whole sites that have been bowled over for various reasons. How long would it take to achieve this weathering? Currently there are no testing methods to date old rock. This is a fundamental problem in dating our past. Rubble on top of laser cut stone, that is too obvious.

We have two amazing facts about polygonal masonry at the high level, flexibility and durability in earthquakes and the ability to cut, move and shape every stone to fit together even if they need to be heated and fit like marshmallows or slinky's going down a set of steps. These are not repeatable achievements today. We can't manipulate the stone the way they did. This is a clue. We have already discussed frequencies, vibrational and toroidal fields, what did we just add, amplitude of the wave of an earthquake? The wave?

Here is one theory I am proposing right now. One purpose and one of the functions of polygonal masonry in the building structure is to shape the size of the stones, placing them specifically in the wall because each cut shape was designed for THAT earthquake zone and in that location of the wall. The very frequencies of the earth, were measured for that area, the risk factor of an earthquake and it's potential epicenters was considered, measured, calculated and the construction of every building was unique for how the known waves would hit that structure where it stood. That is a point I would like to make about how advanced we once were. We could read the sub earth plate tectonics. We could build impervious and "tune" each building to withstand and also use the energy it was receiving. It was only recently published that there is technology in the very foundation of the coliseums and other ancient structures to create wave and frequency cloaking. It is being credited to the Romans, that they were well aware of earthquake control, that a honeycomb like structure controlled the impact of waves and canceled the impact of the waves or vibrational energy of the earthquake. This would be very easy for an advanced culture that managed frequencies, genetic and organic sciences down to engineering their soil and communications with each other and animals.

We are looking at the Big Picture... yeah I just got another megalithic joke in. Just another angle and thought on the high technological achievement we are looking at. When you look at Puma Punku, Machu Picchu and Ollantaytambo, the blocks are big. There are places on earth where you will see a more uniform construction. As cameras pan over these megalithic sites, the comment will be some of the blocks in these walls are 100's or 1000's of tons, and it is impressive, the other point is that these stones are usually brought from 100's of miles away. Aswan in Egypt is one, much of the stones are brought from there to the Giza Plateau. It's approximately 500 miles. There are other places that get the stone and they are over a 1000 miles away. There isn't a lot of commentary on why the different sizes of polygonal constructions. I mean they keep saying this lost ancient society could take the biggest cuts and go anywhere with them. Cutting and moving the hardest and heaviest stones as if they seem to be able to fly them or antigravity them to where ever they wanted to build. Have you seen a building today? We build with the same size stone top to bottom and they are so little. Why? Why, use so many different sizes if you can cut stone at any size, shape and move it three dimensionally on all sides and with all the other pieces set them as high and wide as you want? Here in lies the third ability of our lost ancestors, the abilities to measure, estimate, conclude the exact stone for earthquake proofing structures. They measured the frequency and wave amplitude for the area and built what we see as walls for the structures were actually foundational. Would they not have also built them for accepting wanted frequencies for communication, deflecting negative waves either random from space or weaponized for destruction? Like the walls of Jericho came down with the trumpets?

Polygonal construction for example around Lake Titicaca in the Andes, has snake reliefs carved into the surface of some of the masonry. The theory goes that the stone had to be thicker, then the snake was carved by removing the other surfaces to be present on this polygonal wall. This I believe was a re-carve a later addition. There are many indications of snakes in construction fyi. Rabbit hole!

After 1000, 10,000 or 100,000s of years only stone remains and even then it could be deeply weathered to almost nothing. Metal would rust away and although wood, under great circumstances can petrify or survive in the ocean at great depths, or a bog, mostly stone is what is left. We are looking at structures where the Egyptians, the Aztecs, Mayans, South Indochina areas have all adapted, graffitied, and repurposed the buildings. It is likely that the megalithic blocks left are foundational or repurposed to foundations. The buildings in the ancient past could have had wood floors or metal or both. There even could have been plastics or materials we can't dream of.

On the surface of the buildings from South America to Egypt and Asia, there is a surface knob. It's a bump out and it can be seen on many structures in the world with megalithic cymatic polygonal walls. Now the knobs are smooth but they may not have been. They may have had sharper corners on these bumps but wore down after weather erosion and are bumps now. The Great Pyramid has these knobs around the "finish" stones. In construction today there are slate tiles that go on some roofs. Giant pieces of slated stone, like what you put on a floor. It is an older look, an expensive and eye drawing look but also makes a very slippery surface for ice and snow as it melts in the sun. Tabs, little tipped up blockers are put up to catch the ice and snow as it falls and also catch a loose piece of slate tile if it pulls away from an upper layer and slides down off the roof. Just imagine a 20 pound pizza box falling on you from two stories up. I am proposing that to keep a sticky surface even one that had a super adhesive on it it may fail over the millions of years of use from time to time. It is easily possible that the surfaces showing these knobs and nubs, are the shear strength to help hold on a final layer over the pyramids. The final

Here is another close up of the knobs found every where from South America, pictured here to Egypt and Asia. The material that would have finished the buildings long gone. Think living wood like Giant redwoods cut with the same precision as these cymatic polygonal blocks. The engraved images, statues, depths on lengths and pieces of wood that could cover the whole side to over 50 ft and for 400 ft in one board. Would these knobs add shear strength to a long lost siding? Is it possible that these knobs were once much more protruding and have just mutually weathered down all over the earth.

layer of glass, plastic, metals, wires, all the above and the nubs helped create shear strength to keep that final layer from sliding off the side of a structure like the Great Pyramid and other cymatic polygonal constructions. So the "casing stones" might be the final sub surfaces for these final coats of materials.

225

KEYSTONE CUTS IN POLYGONAL MASONRY

To investigate one more point of cymatic polygonal masonry before pulling the subject to higher conjecture we are going to look at keystone cuts. Keystone cuts in buildings exhibit a unique construction method where the blocks are set together and there is a cut groove between the two blocks and metal is poured in creating a "key" connecting the two blocks. Frequently missing is the metal from the connection points if the blocks are exposed to the weather or elements. There is locations where the metal is found and others where one can only speculate that perhaps tribal people in need of metal for spear or arrow heads or simple tools pried out the keystone metals and took and repurposed the metal. An interesting point about cymatic polygonal masonry is that it is built with large stones frequently high in all the crystal and elements for the conduction or repelling of electromagnetic waves. It is possible that the keystone cuts were not to keep the building together or even as a "starter" row or extra reinforcement, but possibly that the keystone cut and metal added connectivity to the blocks. The wall itself was able to receive information and move it through the walls to the room where the intended receiver was. Whether a computer or individual or "flash" drive, the keystone cuts could act to transmit the wave or frequencies of earthquakes to each of the blocks like a computer. The building construction from the foundation up was sensitive enough to detect and start the building countering, deflecting, even canceling the pending quake or helping the stones to stay moving together at the same frequency. The metal components appear to us to be a fancy nail.

In Egypt, in Cambodia to South America, keystone cuts are there. The possible independent development of this building technique is astronomical. You are high if you believe this was independent work around the globe. We know that there were cataclysms because you can see the keystone cuts turned and placed on their sides in the walls of buildings built by the dynastic Egyptians. This is important. Mainstream archaeology doesn't want you to look at this. A post cataclysm people came along not knowing what a keystone cut even was or forgot and just moved the keystone cuts sideways because they were rebuilding a fallen structure for their own purpose. This can be seen in dynastic buildings. One of the temples in Egypt has two blocks that could have been together horizontally, are now both within a couple rows of each other, except now they are on their sides. Did the dynastic Egyptians put plaster on these exterior walls and the indications of the keystone cuts would be hidden until the plaster fell away.

I believe one of the ways to identify the age of this world wide society is to look at all the layers that you see cymatic polygonal masonry and how often keystone cuts appear turned or repurposed.

Speaking of a dig…

Puma Punku, here is the home of the famous "H" blocks, which there are six. In this picture you can see a core drill, blocks that have shown magnetic anomalies as if to "lock" them together. Signs of excavation are seen. Brien Foerster in his research has asked why they don't excavate deeper, the response is, there wont be anything deeper. This site is covered and buried by a wave of mud. It's a lot like the Easter Island Moai that are buried to their heads yet only a couple have been dug up and only immediately around them. Who knows how much is at or below the feet of the buried Moai and this site is no different. There are only 6 H-blocks found, perhaps there are more?

Two H blocks can be seen to the right here. It is well known that the locals have and like many areas around the world have continued to quarry stone from these ancient sites. The entire sides of buildings could or might be pieced back together if a scan could be done of nearby villages and the stones that make up their structures. It is not just stone that was repurposed, small items also made of stone survived. The site above shows massive cataclysmic activity and the site is well buried. fortunately, that means many of the stones may lay safely below the mud and safely below the standard academics that don't want to dig further.

Here are two H blocks, there is an idea that they are all the same, each of the six found as of yet are individually sized. Two possible reasons, the construction capabilities of our high tech past made everything from scratch. Option two might be that they only found six, each one from a different area or row or column of the building that is now gone. The matching ones may have been taken or still buried. The magnetic anomalies represent whole new fields in archaeology that are yet to even have an "expert" in.

Tiwanaku is a site that has the famous H blocks. There are computer models showing how the H blocks would fall together to build a large building. Erik Von Daniken likes to show the 3D animation in his lectures. Brien Foerster is quick to point that there is only 6 H blocks, and they each are unique in size. We only have the 6 to study, more could be buried or incorporated in other buildings but that remains unknown. It's more likely that there were just six different blocks from six different construction points in the building they came from. The blocks are magnetic, the idea that they may have connected together, maybe locking in place is one theory. If this ancient society we are trying to rebuild and re-identify had an earth grid, and the buildings themselves sent and received waves coursing with electricity a remaining magnetic quality could be left in these and other megalithic structures. Many other researchers like to point out that the blocks fit together and would be a unique building method, this is true, but unique in that it lies in a timeline of antiquity that keeps getting masked by words, like antiquity, pre history and the nastiest of words, "mystery". The site, despite some excavations lies mostly not excavated. Seriously if you want to close this book and bang your own head, go for it. Tiwanaku, like many sites, is mostly un-researched. You don't even have to dig for the conspiracies. It is the open conspiracy of ignore it. They have done digs there but wont go beyond a certain depth and the only reason is they don't expect to find anything.

I am not making this up. There are excavations however there is no movement of the large blocks. Areas will be dug in, the site is mainly under mud, the excavation will dig in and down but never too far. This isn't 1925, digging 35 ft. is out apparently.

Old photography can be some of our best sources for "in situ" before someone messed it up in modern times or more stones were stolen. In rebuilding our ancient past we may have to engineer substitutes of missing pieces. It is sad to also see how little has changed in these sites despite their importance to understanding our true past. Many of the blocks and stones of this site are machine precise with sharp edges and sharp corners, needle like depth cuts and what can only be described as modern saw cuts.

Here are the H blocks again out of situ. They have been lined up for viewing and maybe later archaeological work, yet currently nothing on the books. Establishing connections between sites here and around the world, magnetic anomalies, crystal and material content research could lead us to not only safer buildings but more intelligent ones capable of more than housing people but also communications. Weathering on the blocks is so varied based on whether or not they were face down, face up or completely buried and protected from the elements. There are currently no way to age the lichen or moss or date stone. There is a possibility that if they were a geopolymer that organics in them could be tested for age. Photo luminescent work also has it's draw backs.

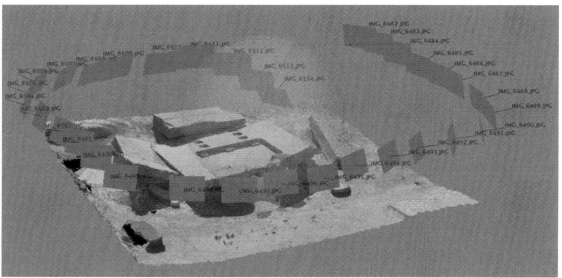

This is a perfect example and an amazing first as of 2019 of a LIDAR and geosonic work that helped image sub earth pieces to ultimately create a model of a building based on the pieces they could find. It can not be stressed enough that the communications, bio materials and man made materials like plastics and glass are long gone. All sciences have to be pieced together to connect this rebuild to the very ground the structures are in now. The soil and the consistency itself may contain meta information for seismic cloaking to a energy grid connection, think Nazca or Bolivian lines.

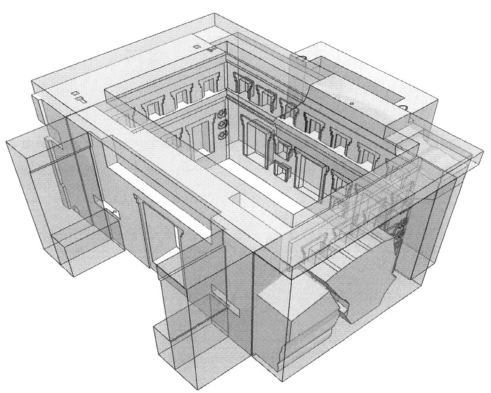

It is incredible that this group has attempted this kind of rebuild. Eventually nano technology will be able to search surrounding buildings where stone may have been pillaged to and under ground. Finding pieces as small as nano bits. Quantum computers would easily be able to compute the trillions of combinations to put them back together almost magically to to eye.

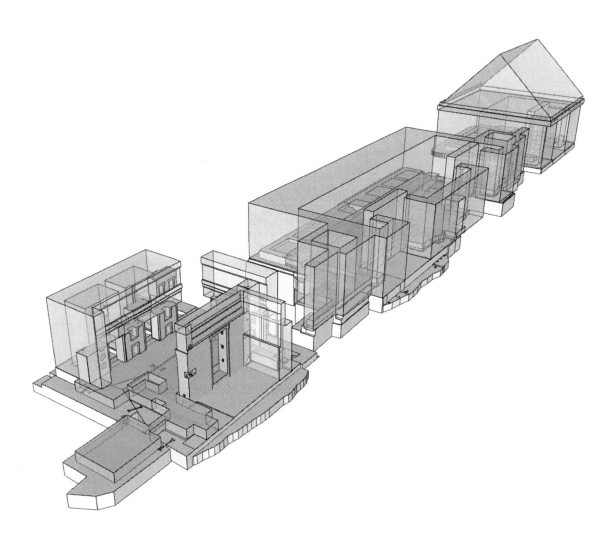

The future is exactly in these realms. The LIDAR may not be complete, the amount of stolen, damaged or quarried stone is unknown. The data set used to complete this is absolute astounding. It should not be taken as a new bible.

Around the world the disaster that hit, if natural seems to have come from a direction, which means that if the buildings were blown over from a primary wave of mud or a secondary cataclysm propelled by another, the megalithic sites around the world show one or many of these past disasters. There is extreme heat damage on some cyamatic polygonal blocks at some sites which could be from a natural disaster. The Hindu Vedas describe a war of the gods. The kind of weapons that a earth terraforming, life engineering, frequency, wave and magnetic understanding advanced human society could turn on each other is terrifying.

Recently a team has gotten creative and Radar, LIDAR and seismograph mapped at the site. Individual blocks that are buried have been "modeled" and they are trying to piece them back together with 3-D print outs of what they found under the mud in scale models. They are assuming that the undug pieces are likely to all fit together and they have even published video and articles showing what the building would look like if it was all built back up. This is what should happen at all sites. There is rubble in a building that is fill for a wall that should be megalithic. There is a good chance that those pieces are shattered remains of another building. Meanwhile, take Tiwanaku again, it is well known the locals pillaged the site for building stones for their mud huts and assorted buildings. All ancient sites have been foraged for their material including the casing stones of the Great Pyramid. There are whole stone villages in the area near by that could be pieces of these H block buildings. Where is the metal, wood the 5-10 stories above the polygonal base or H block first floor of this ancient structure? Well dust. Could Quantum computers when available be used to calculate the structures of the very sand in the ground and build back the structures, they could, in the future.

What is important about the H blocks is that they, and other blocks on the site are showing odd magnetic qualities. Not normal side effects of the type of stone, not some residual of a lighting strike and not alien. Magnetic qualities, keystone cuts and megalithic precision. These blocks are machine quality flat. The magnetic part is interesting combined with the keystone cuts and the connecting features of cymatic polygonal masonry seam to show that this may help "lock" the blocks together. So if you sacrifice the keystone cuts completely, or if you eliminate a buildings polygonal construction, maybe by adding the magnetism it adds stability with interlocking blocks like the H blocks. Our computers and phones, all electronics use magnetism, as part of the science of how a computer stores, processes and retrieves memory and we actually don't know how magnetism works.

There are magnetic anomalies in Egypt and in other megalithic structures and it is taken for granted. If you're only looking for king tut, who cares about magnets. Interdisciplinary physicists and other experts need to bring in equipment and revisit all sites on our search and rescue of our past high technology. Oh, wait, and our true past.

Cymatic polygonal masonry on all continents shaped, fitting together on all sides, keystone cuts on all continents, unusual magnetic anomaly in the stone. What else about cymatic polygonal masonry is unique beside the size of it?

I would like to detail so it's time for pictures, they are worth a 1000 words, cymatic polygonal masonry is on all continents, Malta, Greece, Italy, all of Africa, Libya to Egypt, Turkey, Ukraine, Eastern Europe, Japan, the USA, Easter Island, South America, Siberia, South Asia, underwater from Cuba to the Mediterranean and we are not done looking.

In the capstone to monumental lack of common sense and in the spirit of stupidity, standard academia has declared, all this happened, simultaneously, separately all by accident. It was in vogue, but unconscious. Everyone just wanted too. Pyramids and keystone cuts across the earth, just boom, blue jeans. Blue jeans started in the United States, find somewhere that doesn't have blue jeans. I have seen the BBC do documentaries down the amazon and there are tribal guys sporting blue jean cut off shorts.

My point is Terra Preta, Chernozems, cymatic polygonal construction, keystone cuts, giant stone balls, and pyramids. Too many things that belong together.

MEGALITHIC CONSTRUCTION AND GEOPOLYMARS

To work with the hardest stones on earth in sizes over 1600 and 3000 tons, we have but a couple cranes on earth that could lift them up and then straight down. To plan and work they way they did requires advanced instruments that would look to the stars and could also look at cells or materials. The associated sciences from Design CAD software to skid loaders and all would help in the construction of the fully completed ancient structures. There are many technologies needed to set that megalithic stone in place we keep finding. There are pieces of math, clues in engineered soil, our genes are spliced, cymatic polygonal construction, what is another? Another solid in the ground technology still found? Geopolymers. Geopolymers or concrete is used from your sidewalks to skyscrapers. They are mixes of water, aggregate, and Portland cement. In Portland cement silica, alumina, iron oxide and calcium material is mixed with limestone, sandstone, iron, clay, fly ash and marl.

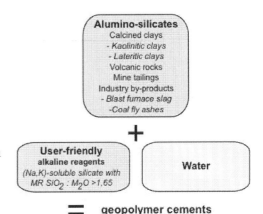

This a diagram of what we know about geopolymers, there are ancient geopolymers being found even under water with no growth on them. Ancient advanced material sciences with the foresight to include non growth of unwanted bacteria, fungus, etc.. is incredible. Geopolymers have been found at the Great Pyramid and in Tiwanaku.

Baalbek, Lebanon with two men standing to give scale. This is given to the greeks. These men are standing above the large 900 plus ton trilithons. These are individual polygonal stones that were moved to this location from over 3 miles away. We have a couple cranes on earth that could lift one up and straight down. Look closely at the rest of the blocks. They are random sizes stacked half ass. Once a plaster may have been applied it wouldn't have been a problem. The stones are clearly from a prior structure. The very bottom row of blocks looks strikingly similar to the more recently excavated subterranean levels of the Temple of Solomon.

Here is a closer look of the trilithons and of possible modifications of the stone for cultures occupying the location over the last 3 or 4000 years. There are columns on site that are single pieces of stone over 60 ft in height. These columns were cut and turned and polished and set in place and there were over 200 known to modern academics. There are plenty of columns on site that are just cut more "manageable" pieces that were stacked to the same height as the more advanced columns. Later cultures across the globe never show the same level of complexity as the earliest elements of a site showing any signs of megalithic work.

This is a trilithon still in the near by quarry, Baalbek can be seen in the distance. This stone has been photo'd with 144 people on it with room to spare. It is estimated around 1600 tons.

There are signs that this was a quarry. Uncut stones and completed stones left in transit to wherever they were going. There are "cart tracks" found all over the world from Malta, where there are elongated skulls and some of the oldest megaliths known to turkey and in many places that if we looked closely at the lowest layers of these quarry sites we might find similar ruts or cart tracks.

It can't be stressed enough that from the size of the blocks, the complexity of the cuts like at Puma Punku, the knobs, the soil, keystone cuts, engineered meta soils and materials, this is not a prior society living a simply big life, this was an epic technologically advanced world wide society. The related technologies to build like this requires power tools. Machine marks, drill holes showing revolutions 500 times faster and deeper than anything we can do today were found and acknowledged even in the 1800's by the famous Egyptologist Flinders Petrie.

237

Here is the trilithon's left corner. More importantly is the blocks directly above it. Frequently the knobs all over the earth are pointed out, these blocks also have a characteristic of something seen all over in megalithic sites. The courses on the corner look suspiciously out of place to anyone that does construction. Like the rest of the building, it appears that the blocks were just stacked back up as best they could do. There is a rectangle pattern to them. Weathering on the trilithons could have been postponed or slowed by various cultures maintaining the site.

The coarse of block that this man is standing on appears to stay level. How deep does that level go? What platform is it sitting on? What is the soil composition? Are there stone or composite stone spheres deep below this structure or did it rely on massive trilithons to keep it grounded on a well compacted surface?

This corner view shows the rectangular blocks seen from Japan to Europe. These blocks do not appear to be for this coarse of construction but were placed by later cultures to rebuild the structures. With matching construction pieces all over the earth we might need to come up with a name, the Cymatic Builders? Or Cymatic Terraformers? Looking at sites that have been rebuilt also helps us discover which recent cultures may have found various pieces of ancient high technology. It may have been found out of order.

From the other side the columns can start to be seen. This site like many is written off as having been "solved" or "explained". What about magnetic anomalies or vitrification of stone from natural or weaponized disasters? What about meta material in soil and engineered soils? The foundations have not been checked or explained fully.

The state of the abandoned site and heavy blocks adds to the confusion. On one hand you can read a hand me down translation of what was happening in Greek and roman times and imagine robed senators and Sinbad. The work to measure and see if these blocks are sitting in their original homes requires modern tools and technology to look at the weathered sides and measure the magnetic and possibly missed keystone cuts.

Here is where the stones they didn't know what to do with have been set out for study. At least they are here and available for viewing. Scanning blocks of sites or creating game apps that allow citizen researchers to play a Tetris match that really counts. Playing with scanned pieces of sites while an algorithm runs to try togive the most likely fit. Human eyes and instinct or genetic memory may have a very different idea of how the blocks fit once unshattered.

This is the famous Delphi. Like the island of Malta, the cymatic polygonal construction here is so old that the joints have weathered away. As we rediscover this very ancient lost world wide culture, did they abandon sites in their time, would Delphi be an earlier site than Egypt or Siberia? Did they maintain all the megalithic sites we have found plus more. This doesn't even address the underground sties.

If a society had enough knowledge and prior experiences to know that there were threats from asteroids to earthquakes and to survive or having survived prior disasters they would have decided quickly that it would be best to build on a scale that could withstand impacts, flooding, heating and have extensive underground networks in case the elements on earth were too violent. Whether animal or celestial or waring factions of humans Geopolymers would be developed. The great mystery stunning us even to this day is the "roman" concrete. Yeah I just did quotes, I am not implying aliens, I am implying that there was a prior more advanced society that had geopolymers along with the ability to cut and shape stone. These geopolymers are so strong they have no rebar. This is metal to put in side the concrete as it drys and helps provide strength in our modern use of concrete. In America, one can see rebar under almost any over pass on a freeway. Most of the time you can see the rebar because the concrete is crumbling away from the bridges after only being there for 5-10-30 years. They have no staying power. Concrete today still holds nothing to "roman" concrete. Holding up great domes with no rebar, no extra support.

The DailyMail on November 15th, 2018 published an article by Harry Pettit. In Donana National Park, Andalucia, Spain near the city of Cadiz they found the remains of a harbor wall. The giant inland sea has receded. Samples were taken and chemical testing in a laboratory in Modena, Italy identified a number of surprises. Dr. Giacomo Falanga said the of the samples, "These structures contain binders, like calcite. The presence of mica, potassium, and other trace minerals show proof of artificial mixing of materials, so the samples we have tested are made from ancient prehistoric concrete" Andrea Carpi, a space materials engineer from that laboratory confirmed with certainty that the samples were advanced construction methods. Which to his conclusion was "...we're talking about a civilization with very advanced technology."

Other personalities of the wall include a coating that prevented barnacle growth like modern Teflon. " That requires highly advanced construction technologies and knowledge of chemistry"

Michael Donnellan has made a film about Merlin Burrows discovery called 'Atlantica'. One of the maritime historians, Tim Akers, Head of research at Merlin Burrows said they had found evidence of a type of cement that they had not seen before as well as ancient advanced metallurgy. Some of the ruins showed signs of having been covered in metals. This is one of the first times I have seen a report identifying that the surfaces of the megalithic had a finish material. That it was possible directly coating the stone or geopolymers. On the age, they believe older than Greek and roman ruins and definitely more advanced.

We need to step back for a minute, we have to do a quick review. We have an unknown chapter(s) on this earth with cymatic polygonal walls or foundations, nano level metal coatings, math, maps, out of place artifacts by the mountain, now in our opening example, just one example of geopolymers so advanced we have never seen it? Wow right? If you can build and shape stones anyway you want with cymatic polygonal construction, when and why would the same advanced society use geopolymers, how often and in what applications? First and foremost you have to test and look for them. Second, consider modern adaptations in there use. Was it preferable to not use polygonal construction in some applications and isn't this a good indicator that we should use tests on other sites and blocks?

In another research paper from the Geopolymers Institute, 02100 Saint-Quentin, France, Escuela Profesional de Geologia, U.N.S.A., and CITEM, U.C.S.P., Arequipa, Peru, Materiaux avances en geopolymeres, submitted a paper April 25th, 2018 titled "Ancient geopolymer in south-American monument. SEM and petrographic evidence. The last example was a lab in Italy, this group is in France and tested the famous H blocks, again there are only six, un-buried and sitting together. The brief on the test results were amazing. South-American Andes monument Puma Punku, Tiwanaku, Bolivia was made of an ancient geopolymer sandstone by using electron microscopy and petrographic studies they identified unique features. Na and Fe contents in the monuments had much higher levels than in 3 other sample sites. They thought the stones were possibly cast 1400 years ago. Specifically the results suggested that the blocks consisted of sandstone from the Kallamarka geological site, cemented with an amorphous ferro-sialate geopolymer formed by human intervention, by the addition of extra alkaline salt (natron) from the Laguna Cachi in the Alitplano, Bolivia.

This is all from the abstract on their work.

The Great Pyramid was researched in the 1980's by French materials scientist, Joseph Davidovits. He theorized that the Great Pyramid's blocks were formed by pouring concrete. Of coarse Egyptologists lost their shit. No copper tools have been found, ever, that explain the pyramids construction or how they managed to carve andesite. Or rose granite. You would think that they might embrace an idea that gives the ancient Egyptians credit for something given to the Romans. Isn't it interesting by the way that the largest and oldest unsupported dome in the world, the

The father of geopolymers, Joseph Davidovits

Pantheon in Rome has patterned shapes in the dome that look like Puma Punku? Anyway, Michel Barsoum, professor of materials science at Drexel University thought, electron microscope time. No one else had...I wish I could make this stuff up. No one has checked till these guys.

The Religion of archaeology is so strong, you can look right at it and believe what they say, not what is there to research. Can you imagine redrawing the loincloth slave builders with a concrete mixer instead of ropes and wood cranes?

Prof. Barsoum studied samples from the inner and outer casing stones of the pyramids. It was a 5 year study. They found Davidovits over all theory correct, the stones were cast. The find was that not all the blocks but many were cast from Diatomaceous earth, a naturally occurring and commonly found soft sedimentary rock from fossilized algae. Barsoum seems to conclude that some blocks were dragged there but many were cast on the exterior or outer layers because they would be the finish layers.

It is within our scope to say that with many years of missing human history and catastrophe, that the geopolymers at the Great Pyramid could be from repair work. The question is whether the repair work was from damage during normal use in pre history during an advanced human races use or just like the repair work on the Sphinx that was done in antiquity during the ruling dynastic Egyptians rule. They repaired immovable monuments, pillaged other sites, re-appropriated the ancient statues and "filled" damage on the pyramid. Like the Sphinx, the findings of the geopolymers isn't as dauntingly a problem as is establishing if it was REALLY ancient repair work from a cataclysm by the surviving high tech ancient society or survivors with only user tech skills, or a long later, come out of the hills groups that may have just picked up the ancient site in the last 12,000 years and built their own dynasty on it.

A professor of materials science at MIT, Linn Hobbs went so far on Davidovit's original theory and in picking up Prof. Barsoum's work and reverse engineered the geopolymer concrete. This has not added to the calm of the hens in the story of victorian priests of history. Despite absolute proof, standard academia will not acknowledge MIT or the very inventor of geopolymers, Davidovits. Did I forget to mention? He is the material scientist and inventor of geopolymers and holds the Ordre National du Merite from the French government for his work and holds over 50 patents. Many people come along and have a theory. This one is true. Some of the blocks are geopolymers.

One more time, who is Joseph Davidovits? Inventor and creator of geopolymers, appointed Professor of Chemistry at Barry University, Miami, Florida, there he founded the Institute of Archaeological Sciences (IAPAS) to study ancient technologies and clarify ancient history, He has invented new cement blends, wining him the National Association for Science, Technology and Society (NASTS) and the Federation of Materials Societies, USA's Gold Ribbon Award in 94. He is an active member of the American Chemical Society, American Ceramic Society, American Concrete Institute, New Your Academy of Sciences and International Association of Egyptologists. He started a reference text book "Geopolymer Chemistry and Applications" that is continuously updated and then launched the "Journal on Geopolymer Science. He is the President of the Geopolymer Institute and chair of the the annual conference Geopolymer Camp, Saint-Quentin, France. For the most part Prof Davidovits' research is driven to ensure the industry's success in everything from fire resistant materials, thermal insulation, low-tech building materials, decorative stone artifacts, refractory times, thermal shock refractories, foundry applications, low energy ceramic tiles, eco-cements and concretes, composites for infrastructures repair and strengthening, high-tech composites for aircraft interior and automobile, high-tech resin systems, radioactive and toxic waste containment, arts and decoration, cultural heritage and most importantly to us, archaeology and history of sciences.

This is still not everything this man does. He has made a mission out of looking at ancient high technology, this is a bad word for stuffy got it figured out academics. This is some of the bio of the man that has made a study of the Great Pyramid. This is the man saying some of the blocks are geopolymers. Now we have a whole harbor wall representing a large port with a teflon surface causing no barnacle build up and seemingly so advanced we don't have anything like it. The H blocks and some of the large megalithic work in S. America Davidovits has determined through scientific analysis to be geopolymers also.

We are still in shock of Barsoum, a materials analysis indisputably proving Geopolymers are apart of the Great Pyramids history. How are we going to get our heads around the idea of genetic sciences that were likely as advanced as their ancient understanding of geopolymers and vibrational and energy?

OSL (Optically Stimulated Luminescence)

There are new dating methods and methods that continue to improve. One of the more recent, Optically Stimulated Luminescent is accurate to 5-10% with dating to 150,000 years. In some cases they can date till 3-400,000 years. This is a great method for non organics because it can date objects from a single-grain of minerals in sediment. It relies on ionizing radiation. The most popular version of this method is OSL or "single-aliquot regeneration" (SAR).

In the case of Baalbek, Lebanon and the trilithons, the large base megalithic blocks that the clearly tight, on the base and likely haven't been moved since built. Above the walls look half ass stacked. The dust between the layers would be significant to test. Baalbek has/had 128 rose granite single columns from Aswan, Egypt standing at over 20 meters. Lots of talk on the foundation stones that are between 800 and 1200 tons. This includes the couple that are in a near by quarry. It just isn't mentioned frequently that the columns are single pieces. Roman and Egyptian columns are stacked pieces with a finishing layer of plaster or a type of concrete these other columns are single pieces. These are single cut, perfectly shaped columns. Where are the material engineers now? Yes, they came from a typically impossible distance at Aswan to Baalbek. The site of course has been given to the romans. Some of the many issues in the crazy world we live in: One, is the clearly re-stacked megalithic blocks. The "small" stones you see above the trilithons are 300 tons. Some more, some less, but not small, not easy to lift. Two, All modern standard qaukademia say that this generally wasn't a significant site, irrelevant to the time frame. The scale of this site, if originally minor, should show Rome itself even more impressive for its day. Baalbek is a good example of a site "appropriation" by the Romans, set up shop, make your custom mods and re expand a newly labeled empire with old tech. adapt, repair and "improve" , empire a go go.

The Emperor's palace in Japan, megalithic blocks are built in portions of the structure.

The overriding point, advanced geopolymers SHOULD NOT exist. Not in great antiquity, and they should have barnacles all over them underwater, not Teflon perfect. If we don't have the tech now how did they? How can we identify it? Next time you're driving down the road, stuck in one construction lane while the overhead bridge is being completely redone, ask yourself why doesn't it last like an ancient geopolymer.

Chapter 10

LETS RE-BUILD A SUPER ADVANCED ANCIENT SOCIETY AAAND MAKE IT FALL DOWN

SUB CHAPTER MATERIALS PART TWO: NOW LETS RE-BUILD A SUPER ADVANCED ANCIENT SOCIETY...AFTER WE TALK FOUNDATIONS : (

Wow, genetic control of your body. A society with Elongated skulls, cutting genes at whim, engineered soil, engineered plants and animals, advanced cloaking buildings, healing centers, geopolymers, Cymatic polygonal construction, cutting any material like butter, control of scalar waves, frequencies, connections to the earth, and imagine a Mozart that composed for a society of synesthesians. Disaster and catastrophe planning for millions of years of civilization. We don't have the whole story about an ancient advanced society that had gene control, we are gonna paint a picture of what this society could physically look like, lets back it up and talk foundations...(not Asimov unfortunately)

MATERIALS PART: BOTTOM: BOTTOMS=FOUNDATIONS

There are these broken and shattered megalithic structures of buildings all over. There are similar components like cymatic polygonal constructions and keystone cuts all over the earth. Other common building themes include building on lay lines and accounting for toroidal and magnetic fields. There are many indicators of a large scale society occupying the whole world. At least one Pyramid Society.

What could this society look like? We have covered many different pieces of technology and a scale based on ancient mining tailings that could have been huge. We are going to start at the bottom. The bottom being the Foundations. Everywhere on earth, Polygonal foundations.

It is important to have a crash course in construction. Ask an anthropologist to discern how to build the Empire State Building, or an archaeologist to build a laptop computer. We are just beating the remnants of a dead horse now. I feel like a stain where the carcass is all that is left.

Here is the first thing about construction, lets say it's a single family three bedroom with what many people don't have, a basement. Some areas you can't build a basement because it has a high water table or you are on bedrock. Maybe a lava river. Well unlikely. So when you dig out a basement you have to hit below the frost line in areas that have cold winters. Then a frequently forgotten step is to pre-compact the soil. You can manually tamp it or with a machine with a gas engine tamping till the ground the soil or gravel material becomes tightly packed. It helps a building be and continue to be level. It would be very interesting to dig below the foundations of these walls and get a core sample to see if the foundation of earth is pre-compacted. If it is, to what degree? Did they use a hand tamper? A hand tamper is usually a heavy, flat metal plate. It is weighted usually about 12inx12in attached to the end of a broom handle. You walk around and tamp it on the ground over and over and it slowly packs all the dirt, rock, whatever is below the tamper tighter and tighter together. This makes it harder for water, freezing or bugs, or anything to loosening this area. Upon this we will place the walls for the building. As the earth shifts the dirt or rock below the building is set harder by the compaction. It can keep the building from sinking or listing, like the Titanic. Have you been in any old homes, even 30 year old homes, many are built in developments built on former wetlands, or sand. They sink and usually because the building's foundation is sitting on un-compacted soil. There are areas in America where a basement is impossible because the water table is so high it would just flood. There are other old homes that just aren't square anymore. Just stand in grandma and grandpas 100 year old home at look across even a 12x12ft room and see how the floors can drop 2-6 inches in one direction while in the other they drop toward the center of the house and there is a big hump in the middle of the floor. You can do the marble thing and toss marbles and see what direction they end up. Basically most foundations are dug, footings are made but rarely is the ground below the foundation walls ever pre-compacted.

To build a foundation the right way, you dig down, preparing for a foundation doing a pre-compact with a machine tamper on the dirt first. A machine tamper is bigger, 2x2 ft, gas powered and run along where the walls will go and pre-compacting the dirt or sand or clay whatever first. Then a layer of rock generally referred to as class five is laid in about 12 inches deep, then pact down to 5-9 inches. As the class 5 layer is packed, more and more class five is added till the compaction meets over 90 percent. To check level, a long 5-6 ft level is placed on the class five and or a string is staked in the ground along the path of the compactor and it's declared "level" at some point. Now the forms are built, if the building is to be poured, then walls of plywood must be built and along the base for the concrete to be poured into to create the foundation walls. If you're pouring a foundation building it with concrete blocks, through the compacted soil long steel rods are placed along the center of the foundation wall. Then eventually when the forms are up, they pour concrete down the middle of the forms filling them to the top. The steel rods stick out of the top of the pour adding strength within the foundation walls and creating an attachment point for the walls of the pending structure. These could be wood walls or metal. The steel rods would be threaded at the top and a wood plate would be held down on the foundation wall. The foundations could be 8 ft. to maybe 60 ft. It depends if the building is to be a commercial or residential building. Or maybe a skyscraper. Building a foundation is simple yet due either to laziness, or an assumption that it isn't that complicated, steps are missed. If you don't have a very old home, many states keep contractors on the hook for 10 years from the date of construction for structural issues. If you'd like to pay for a couple core samples, it is likely that your foundations may or may not have been pre-compacted to 90 percent.

Foundations are this important. In this advanced world, had they just taken a shovel, and started setting stones, this would be what we expect from an old civilization right? So the walls are heavy wouldn't they just weigh the soil down? Well yeah, but just like anything you see in a small home, due to earthquakes, shifting plate tectonics, they would move. Causing them to fall over, tip, tilt, break up, crack, generally and ultimately breaking down.

Should we start noticing that frequently overlooked technology of the Great Pyramid of Giza with a foundation that hasn't moved in possibly 50,000 years? Or any other polygonal walled foundation building, or Baalbek. Baalbek is a wreck, the completely miss matched walls above the trilithons. The foundation of Baalbek where the 1200 plus ton bases are do not move, much. To the point, what is the layer under the block doing? As in was it pre-compacted. What material did they use, how many layers of material did they pre-compact?

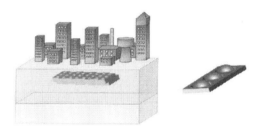

FIG. 1. Schematic, not to scale, representation of a seismic wave shield consisting of a periodic array of split-ball resonators placed underneath the foundations of a large civil infrastructure. Such inertial resonators shield wavelengths much larger than their typical size thanks to low frequency stop bands associated with local resonances.

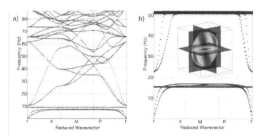

FIG. 2. Band diagrams for an elastic wave propagating within a periodic structure (1 metre in sidelength) made of concrete (host medium - with density ρ = 2.3x10³ kg m⁻³ and Youngs modulus E = 17x10⁹ Pa) and inertial resonators (of diameter 0.74m) connected to the propagation medium via a steel (density ρ = 7.870x10³ kg m⁻³ and Youngs modulus E = 200x10⁹ Pa) ligaments 0.02 m in diameter and 0.03 m in length (left figure) and same with ligaments replaced by a coating with rubber property (a polymeric material with density ρ = 1.2x10³ kg m⁻³and Youngs modulus E = 1.1x10⁶ Pa) (right figure). Vertical axis is the Bloch wave frequency (Hz) and horizontal axis the Bloch wavenumber (m⁻¹).

I do not know of any research into this area of any of the polygonal buildings, or the pyramids till the paper we have already discussed published just in April of 2019. The Seismic Paper, "Role of Nanophotonics in the birth of seismic megastructures". This incredibly important paper discussing the geophysics and civil-engineering applications in the decameter scale. Engineered soils and invisibility cloaking on a meta city scale is just a piece of the paper's content. Part of the paper dives into soft soils around mega structures like Greco-Roman amphitheaters and their abilities to negative lensing and cloaking creating a negative refraction. Deflecting earthquakes and other negative frequencies. It wasn't a matter to just "level" a building for a long time, but to "set" the sub layers throughout a whole city to absorb and or distribute energy across all the soil. It therefor isn't just the foundation that was important, but all the sub-soiling across the entire area of occupation, including growing plants!

Here are a couple mind blowing points. Did the big walls that we have been looking at not just on a sturdy foundation, as the paper discusses could the buildings like in Bologna, Italy act to cloak the buildings and people against earthquakes and other vibrations? Could they also gather, harness and amplify positive or desired waves? Here comes another point, were the trees above ground resonators also? Were the great sequoia engineered in the terra preta and chernozems soils to do the same nanophotonics and invisibility cloaking for metacities and people? The roots of the trees would be "buried mass Resonators just like the studied Greco-Roman foundations, working with other subsoil components to send through obelisks stone balls from the trees frequencies and waves. How is it that these great forests even lasted where they did in California except by accident? Pando, is an incredible organism. What if those massive trees and entities like Pando in the past were designed to listen to the programed soil, determine the center and movement of the sub surfaces of the earth, predict and send the information like all the plants and trees that were the above ground resonators as the paper suggests to the earth grid network. These ancient structures were part of a huge cloaking and resonating frequencies network? The relations of "natural plants and trees" to mega structures is one thing, the relationship as large natural resonators and "natural" cloaking devices is another layer currently unexplored but creeping into the picture. There are very large foundation blocks.

Looking at these ancient structures and to comprehend their original size and foundation is paramount to "seeing" a site. Not what you want to see which is what you get every time a site is found and it is always described as holy, ritualistic and that is the only reason to build in the past. Everything is ceremonial. Well it isn't. Period. The soil compaction and the type of dust is relevant at a site more than ever. Back in the early days of archaeology they threw the bones and items from a site to find beautiful statues and "art", now they are building beautiful stories about pyramid cities and sites with clearly longer histories than the Darwin timeline.

Stonehenge, Carnac, France, Libya, Siberia and all over we are looking at incredibly weathered stones that were likely party of super structures. Structures that have disintegrated and all that remains are ancient high technology resonating foundation stones and soil. At any point these ancient structural "beams" could have been repurposed re-built and used by later cultures. At a minimum they could have been set back up right in their original locations and the subsoil technology still in place. The research for seismic metamaterials is a new field. Bridges, dams, homes are repaired, additions are made, things continue on but it is daunting that the grains of the earth will need study.

Things are adapted right out of their original uses and worse, they become so romanticized that they become holy, mystical, magical. The historical majority of researchers have been so concerned about about putting the shattered pot back together. That pot was from the society that turned an engine fan into an incense bowl archeologists call it the Schist Disk.

Look today at existing new construction, mixed use, commercial residential, it's incredibly popular to build rental business on the first floor and residential on the second through 8 or 10 floors made entirely out of wood construction. If the entire building went unoccupied for a few hundred years, the structure may only have the concrete base. If you build cymatic polygonal foundations, you end up with spaced pillars, Carnac, France, Stonehenge, Machu Picchu, etc...

OLD FOUNDATIONS OUT OF PLACE AND OUT OF TIME

Here we have megalithic trilithon sized blocks under king Solomon's temple. Unknown but incredibly similar to Baalbek, Lebanon. Notice next to the guide the shape of the lowest rows of blocks. They have a protruding pattern similar to the blocks on the corner of Baalbek and similar to megalithic stones on Malta and many other academically established places that should not have the same style constructing. As usual looking toward the top of the photo you see that stones are small, mortared and a re-stacking. A site re-found and rebuilt by a later culture.

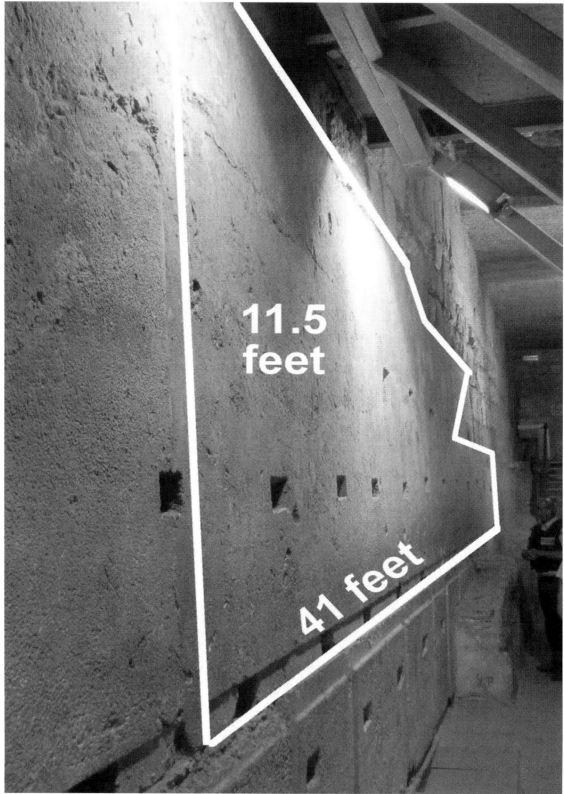

This stone represents one of many that are cymaticly connected in an incredibly large way. The technology in this coarse of blocks and lower, including the below ground soil and foundations material negates the establishment story of this temples post flood "original" build date. Like in Egypt, Japan, South America, the temple from this coarse up is like looking at a broken laptop with an abacus on top of it.

This is an interesting photo for many reasons, in the middle top of the trilithon itself there is a curve up. If you go back and look at the trilithons of Baalbek there is a similar curve with a fitting cymatic polygonal stone that matches the curve. It shows that crappy set mortar rows in this photo start at what would be even a higher level of destruction at this advanced megalithic site.

Large megalithic stones with perfect joinery on the base of the building. To the left of the man there is an extremely weathered megalithic block that appears to have seen as much rain as the Sphinx. The courses of block go up and are not consistent. They change and the mortar work is various in design ranging from stacked larger megalithic blocks, likely out of place, to overly mortared inconsistent small blocks. Masonry isn't done like this by an experienced mason. The work here has years of repairs but all of the blurring lines aside, studying the blocks from even this photo doesn't show a consistent method of building.

The weathering on this one stone alone is significant. Many questions come from this, this weathering is not consistent with the rest of the construction. With the significant sub-levels of megalithic construction at King Solomon's Temple shows a completely different level of construction below ground that was unknown till recently. How many places have foundations bigger and more advanced but have never been dug into? This is one of our most obvious misses including nano structures in meta materials in soil and surrounding dirt of foundations.

There are examples around the world that we have built our modern history and religions on. In the west, it doesn't get more famous than the Temple of Jerusalem. We only have a few cranes on earth that could lift megalithic trilithons and today only straight up and down. The foundation of the temple of Jerusalem is said to be built by King Salomon in 1000-586 BCE. However there is the Western Stone: weighing in on estimates of 587 tones, megalithic(ancient in design). The university of Wisconsin- Eau Claire, measured it out to be 44.6 feet long and 9.8 feet high and about 10.8 feet wide. The team is guessing at the depth to 5.9-8.2 feet. One of these stones doesn't fit with another. This is a block of Ashler stone that is one of many that make up "foundation" courses for the rest of the temple. You don't have to be an expert to know that a newer group built on something way more ancient. This base is likely high technology Seismic Metamaterial in design. The post flood culture that built their religion on this site in the last 12-13,000 years, didn't build first.

At Baalbek there are 1200-1600 ton blocks cut and moved. Well out side of what we can do today. In Gornaya Shoria in Southern Siberia are megalithic blocks that are over 3000 tons. The ancient human society that could create and work with these size blocks didn't do it randomly. Living on earth through many massive disasters over eons would leave a society wanting to create structures that would be unmovable depending on the disaster and could be repaired quickly after the disaster has passed.

This is an unknown site till recently, Gobekli Tepe is rewriting the history for standard academia. On the heels is the knowledge that Gobekli Tepe itself is only 5% dug up with many sites in the area being identified, still buried and as old. Here is Gornaya Shoria, what do you do when the technology siting unburied exceeds everything else seen on earth? Don't issue digging permits, avoid publicity but it is out. We are looking at some of the largest monumental achievements of our ancient ancestors.

Here are clear signs of the stones being stacked. One of the first ways standard academia likes to hide sites for themselves, their reputations, governments etc...is to say they are natural breaks. That this is not joinery of stacked stones, that mother nature just made square, stacked, cut shaped breaks and they just appear natural.

Just like the leaning unmoved block in the Baalbek quarry, here is another fallen or almost in place cymatic block. Research and investigation at this site will hopefully reveal if it is part of a fallen structure or if it was part of an install.

WHAT ABOUT SIBERIA?

Dr. Valery Uvarov Head of the Department of Paleoscience, Paleotechnology and UFO Research of the National Security Academy of Russia went to Gornaya Shoria in Southern Siberia. They investigated enormous megaliths and I hope his credentials put him in the "expert" wing like the father of geopolymers and he has confirmed, in his opinion they are man made. 3000 tons in size. Twice the size of Baalbeks biggest block that are still in the quarry, those are still estimated at about 1500 pounds. Gornaya Shoria is an area in Russia that was blocked from exploration during the Soviet Union. It is now open and the mountain reaches to over 1100 meters above sea level. They found many large megalithic stones and objects. Some measured 20 meters by 6 meters by 6 meters and appear to be megacymatic polygonally constructed.

Georgy Sidorov and a team was studying energy readings from these mega foundational walls. Despite no soil, the energy was so invigorating that trees were alive, tall and growing on the stone with no soil. Makes you wonder about terra preta and Chernozems, are they just for growing food. Sidorov said they had only seen 1 percent of what they surveyed. They found pyramids, above ground and covered in trees. Ancient as far as the research group could access.

Siberia, Russia is not alone in bizarre cymantic polygonal work. We have already mentioned sites that are sacred to the Greeks, on Malta, pyramids in China, there is matching foundational work across the globe. Of course we should talk about Giza again, look at the foundation, the "plaza" that people walk on, the size and scope of the stones that are what make the causeway, the walking area. Have you ever been fascinated by foundations this much? The facts are that the blocks are huge, set and polished and cut to laser fit on the concourse around the Great Pyramid plaza.

PLANES, TRAINS & GENERAL ANCIENT HIGH TECHNOLOGY SOCIETY, WHAT DID IT LOOK LIKE

All over the Earth in the ancient past, a well connected advanced international society of megalithic builders. Pyramid energy centers, providing power, communications and connected through circuits written into the earth from Nazca, Peru through Bolivia, Jordan, Russia, there world connected on terra circuits. Our, human race, with many genetically different peoples, because, having been here for millions of years they developed disaster contingencies which included genetic diversity. Cymatic technologies including healing centers, large auditoriums seating 1000's to tune cellular damage, protect against earthquakes and possibly just to gather for events. Obelisks, cast spheres, electrical geoglyph, pyramids and unknown structures, tuned the ionosphere to keep harmful and random vibrational/frequency energy from penetrating to our living environment. As we travel through space, the solar system, galaxy and universe encountering new waves of energy organized or random, the machines developed here canceled them out with Nanophotonics, invisibility cloaking and other scaler technologies.

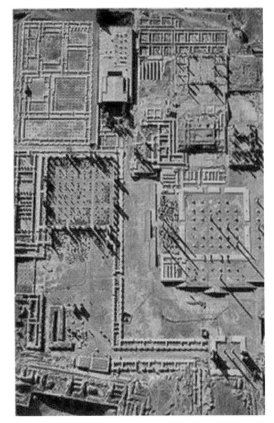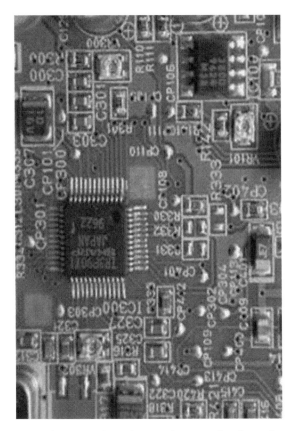

We are so behind till now that we hyper focused on the stones and we weren't ready to see how complex the society we once were we gave it away to aliens or slave masters to build big buildings. Making the earth into a giant connected circuit system, energy, communications network, safe zoned disaster areas and megalithic shelter systems. Not to mention artistic mediums we have never dreamt of. Here is our idea of a circuit on the right and on the left our ancient human ancestor's idea.

Communication was easy, our pineal gland, with it's ocular nerves, our third eye combined with the very nuclear fusion that flows in us now mystified as Chi Gong, was all part of our companion animals network. Like the Bible says pre-flood we all at plants. The vibrational and frequency energy was so vast, we used plants and animals to filter all the available information to know how and when to tune the atmosphere, tweak a treatment for cellular regeneration or know of a shift in the earth. Rebalancing and continuing to terraform developing new technologies. Communications around the planet was instant, easy and travel was simple. Hop on a ship as describe in the Vamana, ancient PAN/AM and travel anywhere despite being instantly connected through our collective consciousness. Need an extra boast to get to a communication to the moon or mars, stop in Aswan or Giza, hop in your reserved time communication chamber and speak to your off world friend.

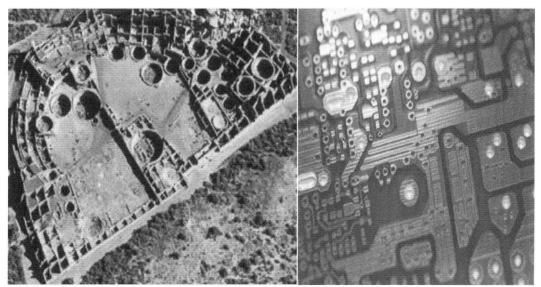

Now that we have knowledge of engineered soils and clear testing showing metamaterial engineering and cymatic polygonal construction showing clear cloaking and damping of vibrational and frequency canceling in large ancient structures, it's easier to see these "earth circuits".

Ancient satellites, possibly like the Black Knight, high in the atmosphere and watching for incoming interstellar disasters monitoring off world communications with our moon, mars and other satellite colonies. The installation points for earth power and antenna networks was easier, the coastlines miles from out to the sea from where they are now. 25 kilometers from Nazca the earth circuits connected cities, buildings maybe even airships. Large cities built with Metasequoia held homes 100's of feet in the air.

With Terra Preta, Chernozem and other unknown to us now engineered soils, they made the best, nutrient rich plants to feed our cellular regeneration program. It was a way to connect to the engineered planet. Engineered soils helped field energy of the earth flow and recharge the antennas, pyramid and energy centers and animals that each had there function. The soils were layered and engineered for our megalithic structures and cities. Providing wave cloaking and invisibility to earthquakes, weaponized scaler beams and foreign scans. Terra preta and chernozems help the plants, trees, molds, funguses to connect and communicate.

Building with forests of Sequoia and Giant Redwoods made wonderful cabins the size of mountains. Treetop fun houses were 1000 feet in the air. Material sciences and products from obsidian, crystal, wood, genetic in structure, stone, and nano structures produced useful appliances for daily living. Nano structures, incorporated into the small and large structure and in our DNA.

The human of our ancient day was experimenting with Denisovans, Neanderthal, humanity itself was customized. Blood lines and genetic lines within the human race had become specialized to their jobs. Some walked as Giants, living simply larger doing manual tasks, lifting tons instead of 100's of pounds. Trimming and maintaining large trees and structures were just easier at the heights these giants grew to. Some ancients customized themselves to work in small spaces and underground. They chose a smaller size to maneuver tight spaces. The ancients body customizations lead to putting on Kurzwell like genetic expression, customizing their bodies to adapt to their interests. There skin color, blue, grey, white, all sizes and shapes. Walking down the street the elongated skulled human opens the door for the grey, bug eyed alien looking human that is going to meet any mythological thing east or west has dreamt of in Greek or eastern myths. They developed what looks like alien appearances due to ancient technologies. There were levitation and other scalar machines not just for lifting heavy blocks but to shape beautiful wood structures the size of sky scrapers. Some tools were as small as the ancient nano parts found in Siberia with medical and other technology applications. Adapting their physical bodies to see inferred, dimensional space and bodies that can tolerate zero stops and turns in antigravity ships. Ancient humans were connected consciously, moving in the sky, space, ocean and land either physically or in consciousness. Bodies were genetically modifiable to any need over thousands of years.

The roads once lined with stone spheres, that were once floating, mounted and reflecting and distributing energies from the pyramids and other machines and structures. Massive networks of underground multilevel and fail safe structures built to connect them in case of disaster and war. With no effort, the giant machines of this society moved earth, built where and how they wanted. Terraforming as desired. Using the earth's natural power grid, building their own network with soil, gravel and chemicals on it to connect the planet.

The ancients walked with their companion animals that processed the waves and frequencies of the universe. The animals could feel and sense vibrations and energies and communicate with us also. While the ancients focused on other information, the animals processed the rest. The animals could warn us when something is off with the tuning of the planet or the ancients themselves. So much information in all the frequency and waves coming from the galaxy from the soil through the plants and animals all the information is scanned, processed and handled in these layers. For example, these animals can sense that we have come through a solar storm that has brought some off tweak of the ionosphere. Some people would become sick, maybe just crabby, worse violent, despite all the technology not everything rippling the either was understood. What field perturbation of the universe has disturbed the planet and touched some of the organics or magnetics of the planet throwing it off. Our companion animals would know this, "sense" this off frequencies. Maybe the ancient's plants, the very blades of grass in the yard are leaning in a way that their medical awareness group would process the negative frequencies that the earth was passing though. The developed cure was composing a new frequency song that could cure the effected. Gathering in one of their large stadium Greco-Roman style theaters for treatments and entertainment. The ancients gathered for them to sing a new song containing the vibrations and frequencies to cure the effects of this "negative" or unknown field perturbation while giving the rest of us a cool song to sing. The assumption that these stadiums were open air, while here in the ancient past, large meta-materials shaded the stadiums and blocked rain as needed.

It is quite possible that all cellular damage was repairable. It could have been a society that never died, except in extreme accidents, they lived and repaired themselves indefinitely possibly backing ourselves up in a collective consciousness. Our ancient ancestor's cities and countryside's were a gym. There was no "gym". Movement was throughout the the streets. One could walk, run swing through the environment. There was no need to go to a spa for rejuvenation. The air was cleaned and filtered as needed for the lungs, the buildings filtered the air from living filters like trees. The rivers and waterways were always a step away. Highly healthy ionized air was invigorated by water features that fell at frequencies for your best brain entrainment, or added highly mineralized particulates to the air as you walked down the street. As an example for advanced food and health, walking into an ancient coffee cafe to meet a friend, sitting down and by the time you do, the coffee you're both drinking would contain completely different nutrients. By the time you have sat down, the analysis of where your personal gut biome was would have communicated to the cafe what nutrients are needed for the cellular repairs and advances being done that hour for your body. No one in this ancient advanced society eats for just fun. The nutrients needed daily for each person is complex, and it is individual. Every food is customized for the individual. Food could be nano delivered and or eaten as a food but it would deliver specific building blocks to each person. Healing waves are in the air helping your cells stay. Walls deflect negative waves and frequencies while your very nano tech cloths do the same thing a Royal Rife machine does but without thinking, it's just in the fibers of your cloths working instantly with light. destroying out of tune and negative cells like cancer and bad viruses and bacteria. The walls, streets and all buildings deflect negative waves or absorb them and transfer them harmlessly out of the electrical, magnetic and positive fields of the intentionally designed ancient planetary network.

In the ancient efforts to keep watch on cataclysmic events after millions of years of disaster, a network was set up from the soil to satellites. Keeping constant vigilance through satellites, expanding to the Moon, Mars, and beyond. Our minds could travel, we had full awareness of our pineal glands, we could speak, hear, see each other and know. By tuning our planet, incoming galactic threats could be handled in different ways. With the moon to deflect asteroids, comets, and meteors like a baseball player. Building large and massive structures that could survive any catastrophe. Planning and knowing that through any unknown disaster, the physical structures of the planet ever vigilantly running the world would support us while we retreated underground or stay off world in a cataclysm. We built so big weather of any kind would not harm us. The buildings would never wash away, the roads and walls could sink to the waters and we would still be able to continue. Not shattered, not broken like in post flood times as separated peoples.

Together, as the society that we were. Our energy systems would kick back on tuning the atmosphere, cleaning and filtering would begin again and we would come out of floating, flying and underground locations to live on the earth again. The vast tunnels under Turkey, Jordan, Egypt, Africa and connecting as far away as England kept everyone safely connected when the planet surfaces was too challenging and damaged. The vast tunnels under Bolivia, Brazil, and Peru kept this ancient society to depths and temperatures that were safe while the world would reset in safe mode during and after a cataclysm. Accounting for vegetarian losses, animals and all levels of life, the full planetary system may have taken time to restart. Giant redwoods and sequoia may need time to regrow if broken or burnt after a disaster. The plants and animals would need to be grown or bread to repopulate effected areas. Terra preta and Chernozems may need re-grooming. The process to get the planet to run as a large scale terraformed machine again may require the physical relocation of a number of inhabitants. To regrow, rebuild, and develop a planet again could and would displace specialized populations.

The terrifying weaponization of a society that built with polygonal masonry foundations and of a society that could create waves and frequency that could evaporate every cell in a living body as well as dust a building. Burn, melt, change stone and all material alike to being able to agate any cell, any way. The limitlessness turned to a weaponization and bioweapons would be the worst of any nightmare.

THEN IT ALL FELL APART: THE RIGHT CATACLYSM

The terror of it. If the wrong thought went in the wrong person, with the right challenges facing a society that could think collectively, what would collective fear look like? Imagine the terrifying weaponization of a society that could cut the hardest materials on earth easily. Work on the cellular level. What diseases could they execute. The Hindu Vedas speak of nuclear weapons of the gods, but what about those small custom viruses? Just like limes disease. Only a society surfacing after a disaster so sideways and knowing they can't go back to what it was could for the first time, in thousands of years be capable of hurting each other indiscriminately. There is the possibility that extreme measures could be taken if they thought the population was going to turn on itself. Knowing the immortality is not maintainable with the machines like the pyramids deactivated, measures would have to be taken to restart. Nazca has a few buildings and structures connected and left standing, Bolivia, Jordan, Bosnia, Egypt, Australia, North America all with polygonal, wood, metal mega structures still standing but in shambles. A pineal gland communicating society comes to the surface and re-lands from the sky to know they all won't be able to achieve a global resurrection of the planet before they start actually dying. Communications with each other, the remaining plants, animals and trees sending off data as best everyone could for a global disaster assessment.

The day came, the limitlessness stopped. The crater in Greenland is one big example. 700 megatons, the air across the planet incinerating everything without warning. a heat wave, wall of fire, evaporating everything in its' wake. A 19 mile wide diameter crater in Greenland showing the outline of an insane impact. The buildings and megalithic structures of Egypt show signs of vitrification. This is where stone is super heated and then cools after a blast of heat, it's called vitrification. Even with warning, the impact was so big. All the connectivity of the planet gone. Animals, plants, all of it hit into unconsciousness and set to safe mode. This one mega disaster could be a challenge for any society.

The great gathering places of the healing amphitheaters are just that, amphitheaters. If the temperature on the surface cooled enough and the waters subsided enough, nothing that kept you immortal was functioning fully. What would the survivors do? Operating on the basics what would the animals do, what were they programmed to do in safe mode after millions or thousands of years of programming? The idea that advanced humans would continue to modify and reprogram or improve genetic programming is not far fetched. It's not a matter of just developing new genetic ways but predicting and preserving the system. In a safe mode situation, would the animals, in need of feeding, turn on each other? In turn what appears to be natural, they feed, higher communication functions are off, they sustain themselves till the over all system can be reset. The life waters, the pyramid energy centers, everything isn't operating as it should. As the post flood Bible command stated, eat everything. The system runs until everyone can get out and start putting the network back together in safe mode, but this is the worst disaster ever. To re-engineer from scratch would be such a monumental task. The encoding on the genes themselves allow for all the preprogrammed organic machines to go into safe mode and do what they do till everything can be rebuilt. Plants, trees and animals start to go wild and native.

The surfaces of the earth being flooded, muddled, heated and burned, the weather system and the tuning of the great pyramids are shut and shutting down. The protocols of hitting the underground cities, high mountain retreats, ships, everyone that could get to something does or dies trying in an event missed or miss calculated. During the impact people are simply evaporated, animals, tech. Just gone. Many of the operators, specialists, they die, the records might be available but the people that could understand, put the puzzle of this advance society back are no longer alive. The conscious network muted.

Meanwhile The simple tribal humans that live along side our advanced societies have now had 100's maybe thousands of years to inhabit the old cities while our advanced ancestors hid, survived underground or just came out of the ground and there just wasn't the numbers anymore to repopulated the city centers. Being handicapped in resources and population they retreated on the planet to areas that they could rebuild. The whole planet on its own, genetically, materially, functioning like a flickering fluorescent light that won't die.

Here is this formally advanced society, reappearing on a surface of a system that had millions or thousands of years of programming completely wiped. The tribes of simpler humans everywhere in their old spaces and or the extent they had repopulated may have been unexpected. While underground or off world they could have developed new technology, the requirement for the whole planet to be back in the system they had may have been irrelevant.

Factions of this society could be in disagreement on how to move forward. Some may long for the old world they once had but lacking the desire, or will or intelligence to recreate it. Some digressed to crown themselves "gods" over the tribal people that had moved back into the high technology population centers. The simpler humans they had always left alone on the planet are now wearing the ipads of their day as jewelry. Resetting cymatic polygonal construction into four walls and a legend.

Some of the advanced survivors may have gathered high technology and taught some of these simple tribal flood survivors the basics of farming. Now capable of "higher" living to begin tilling and farming, tribes could develop themselves in the ruins of these megalithic cities. Why teach these tribes? Imagine coming out of tunnels, despite having the ability to engineer food, animals technology, if the disaster that hit was so unexpected that it flooded, destroyed or greatly reduced the population of a highly advanced society, then a quick way to get food and have enough for your own growing population, would be to get the tribes to do the work. While you run around and try to get any surviving piece of technology you can find. Meanwhile, perhaps the thought was it was no longer time to live and let alone, these tribes needed to be brought into the fold and the planet was going to take thousands of years to build back. Why not raise these humans consciousness and build back the planet.

Other advanced humans may have been truly benevolent, upset with themselves, the accident that put them where they ended up and truly in pain over the plants, animals, the living world they groomed in waste. To crown it off, the simple humans, tribes or "lower" humans that they left to live in harmony. The more advanced humans could have given them mana so they would not kill or harm the animals. Perhaps they knew better than to do that. With the catastrophe upon the earth these tribes had suffered and died also. The advanced society had retreated to save themselves and these poor tribal people were decimated by this last world catastrophe. They did or couldn't do anything for these simple people during the event. The survivors didn't want to remove them, they were not violent and the surface survivors had made their way into the pieces of these advanced megalithic cities. Enough of the survivors technology had been wiped out, enough of them had died, they couldn't rebuild anyway gathering technology from their fallen cities was easy. The tribal people had limited or no exposure to this high technology. They wanted shelter, food, a sense of safety and community. The more advanced survivors gathered up what could be salvaged, they rebuilt away from these simple humans.

Over time, these advanced surviving ancestors retreated, developing new and different philosophies. The massive world wide society they had built and lived in for millions of years is gone. Some feel a life of isolationism is necessary. This group continuing rediscovering or recovering their technology also continued genetic research. They get genetic tech developed alongside their other high technology that sets them down new paths. Some, like the Paracus, reject the old ways, move to the coast of Peru from Crimea and start what is maybe the first commune. The elongated skulled Paracus, from their mummies, lived a simple life on the coast of Peru.

Our advanced ancient ancestors, possessing the technology with thousands of years behind them now started setting up research centers in smaller more remote locations, think Machu Picchu. The technology to genetically modify themselves as they wish or reengineer the planet is still in their encyclopedias but they might only have access to pieces of it. Having had the technology for 1000's or millions of years. They modified themselves to fit their new environments and new endeavors, big eyes makes seeing in low light better, perhaps inferred. Wave and frequencies, all visible. They develop ocular and physical bodies for new inter dimensional space travel. Perhaps Skin ton for the artificial light. Most important, the ability to travel and move in space and on a quantum level that would make looking the way we look not relevant. Not because they didn't want to look human, but because it was not a genetic structure that made sense for the g forces, space folding, or space travel, whatever they developed it was necessary to not have the physical structure that we have now.

VIBRATIONAL FREQUENCY MACHINES FAIL

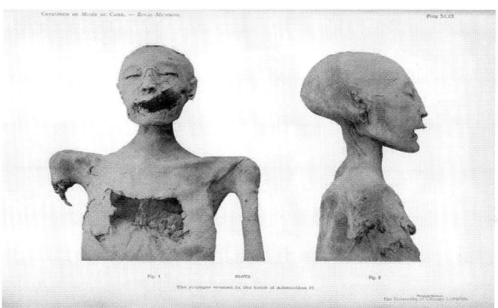

Here we have a clearly elongated skulled mummy. What if the sliver of truth, preserving the body for healing was once just icing the body if broken down to put into a healing machine when available. Eventually through the ages the only thing to remember was that preserving the body was important. The question remains if elongated skulls in other parts of the world when natural, were descendants or children of ancient advanced humans or intentional plants into normal daily routines of the rising masses of people from a post cataclysm. Intentionally living, reporting and or just "helping."

Imagine back in ancient advanced time the power of a vibrational frequency healing center like an amphitheater in Rome not working and broken down but the one in Bosnia still works. What happens when normally 50,000 people a day or an hour went to the one in Rome start walking to the one in Rome. 50,000 people pounding on door for an amphitheater healing center that can only take the existing local populations? People whom never died, never were sick are now that. Dying, bribing, rioting to get into repair what was once a simple cancer, an imbalance. Now people are dying, no longer equal. how much of the communication between people and their pineal glands have stopped, or have they just shut the door. How long before distrust, fear and panic would set in. Was it a couple weeks or hundreds of years in shelters shutting out the screams of their companion animals that they abandoned on the surface? Even though the animals were computer components to a living machine, they were each unique, did they beg to be let in to the underground cities? Were they still bravely giving information to their creators till the moments of their deaths? Did they succumb to the safe mode and start eating each other first? By the time we walked out of our shelters did we look at our former companions and just keep that connection closed, or were there no closing it, was it hard genetically wired and we just heard them scream to our souls while they were killed and killing each other for food. Was it just the tribal types, the loincloths on the surface, the tribes they had "left alone" to live their way in the jungles, deserts and wilds of the day, had they succumbed to the flood and started slaughtering our animal friends? Was it possible we just walked out of our shelters, looked around and so much time had past underground the ancients had forgot. They knew they could speak with these creatures and they could speak with us, but they just couldn't start the pineal gland or the external machines again to bring it all out of safe mode. They ate the animals instead and mystified it later for the rest of humanity so they could be ok. Safe mode.

Chapter 11

THEY FELL, WHO CAME NEXT? CONSPIRACIES, ARE THEY ASSHOLES?

We need more discernment applied to our advanced past. Sacred, mystical, special, these words applied to what should be a search and rescue of our advanced past, so advanced that it contains answers to our future medicines and other sciences. Don't be upset about the last 12,000 years humans have created epic myths and stories. We needed to live and die for something. If you have a post disaster faith, keep it. Just stop yourself of condemning or killing or maiming another if they don't believe what you do.

We have been left with more questions then answers, but good questions, questions that can drive research into our past and future in a more productive way. By going down the realistic rabbit hole that we were more advanced in the ancient past we can be more discerning in our analysis of our past and the facts in the ground instead of forcing the theories to fit dusty Victorians. We have evidence beyond a shadow of a doubt, that there was at least one incredibly great advanced society pre-flood. Potentially genetically in control of their own lifespan, possibly programming the planet and then what? Technology scattered to the ends of the earth, who picks up the first pieces? Perhaps the first germination of truth in the Greek story of Atlantis is that a great society fell. Who survived though?

We take it for granted that we would find a machine, we found actual gold and aluminum parts that are hundreds of thousands of years old. We assume that they would have an external device when the biology of all animals, humans, the energy of the earth and the ability to use it would look entirely different then our daily routine getting a coffee and working on a laptop. This is a location in Chernobyl. Note the walls, how fast the paint is disappearing.

The cars are quickly being engulfed by nature itself. The foliage isn't giving the elements time to rust them away. The road itself is being broken by bushes, trees, and other plants. It is interesting that there are roman roads, the Great Pyramid and the Nazca Lines themselves don't have these problems.

Cars are quickly becoming forest. Studies are now suggesting that Northern Africa which is now desert, was rich with vegetation as early as 5,000 years ago. In prior estimates it was thought the the Sphinx was in a tropical environment 28-40,000 years ago.

The exception is to become a fossil, despite finding 5000 new species a year, there is this broad brush stroke that is spoken to induce unnecessary fear, that 99% of anything that has ever lived on the planet is gone. We really don't know that.

Here are older cars that appear to be melting into the ground. Gold nano parts found in Siberia are survivors because they are gold, the stone megaliths and other stone artifacts have survived with their original purpose shrouded in terms like sacred tea light, sacred geometry, sun temple candle lighter.

If we look at a catastrophic event to an ancient high technology human culture like a giant cruise ship that crashed, we might understand it a little better. The bartender from the cruise ship may have lived and the guy who turned the satellite radar on and off died. The satellite tech died and all they have left is one machine that's got a manual that no one can understand, let alone a manual to rebuild a satellite! Then what? The immediate users of this technology could gather what is left, and start rebuilding. If at the time of our imagined cruise ship disaster, there was a large group of simpler human cultures creating a very hostile environment for the formerly advanced society all over the globe. Having invaded former ports of this one and only advanced cruise ship they are hostile to anything outside their understanding of the world. Now the massive Caribbean cruise ship with 5000 passengers has crashed to shore. They are devastated and there are thousands or millions of lesser advanced humans that are out to sacrifice them to gods know what. None of these tribes have seen anything more advanced then whatever they have thought of and it's not millions of tons of high tech floating metal with radar and satellite communications. Not to mention medical facilities, computers, plumbing and advanced machine shops. If a ship like this crashed, it would be a hodgepodge to collect the higher technology pieces out of this ship and the separation of passenger, maintenance man Vs. creator, software writer and manufacturer is a completely different thing.

The Paracus, in a theory had a violent end via the people being called the Nazca. The genetic anomalies showing clear genetic differences from ourselves today and the Paracus themselves. We can't currently identify this race of humans. Are they our more advanced grandparents or cousins intentionally not rebuilding the old way? Did the

Paracus become the Quaker's of their day only to be eliminated by the Nazca tribes? The Paracus genetic markers not being able to be identified as human as we know it, still doesn't paint a picture of aliens. It is very possible that the human survivors of an ancient highly genetically advanced society may have had different plans after the last cataclysm. They easily could have said no to what the survivors calling themselves the Annunaki were planning and got on boats from Crimea and sailed to new lands. They knew where they were going and they intentionally left to have a peaceful, simple life.

To entertain more conspiracies, could some of the more advanced humans that knew the Paracus and their retreat from the former highly genetically advanced ancient society object to them opting out so much that they had the Nazca eliminate them? The ancients being called the Paracus, with naturally born elongated skulls could have pre-flood, been the navigators and technicians they needed before the flood. When the Paracus chose to leave Crimea, start over, it was outside of what was acceptable and the faction that stayed eliminated them. Gathering up the local lessor human races and rebuilding something with formerly advanced humans calling themselves gods, or Annunaki or Ra. Instead of attempting to rebuild a higher culture on a mass level again they themselves digressed and disagreed on what to do post apocalypse.

Imagine gathering up everything you can from a beached cruise liner and heading into the hills that may be hostile to your presence. Not to mention in a shamble from what ever catastrophe had just beached your ass. Imagine having only one or two pieces of your past and having only manuals or literature to read. No pieces remain. Just the crystals and inanimate objects to a less advanced human who is in the middle of burning the next page to Tesla's either and magnetic theories.

Off the crashed cruise liner and where do you build again and defend your physical position while trying to rebuild? Produce enough influence to the locals and convince them you're a god maybe? Establish military security? Begin rebuilding without one machine that built your machines. How many people would need to learn about the technology to re-engineer it or the math?

Here are two views of an abandoned nuclear power plant. After one thousand years and more beautiful green moss, do the people in 5,000 years see even the hint of this structure for it's true purpose or through interruptive future archaeologists and after those many cultures have used it, does it turn into the following photo.

There is nothing wrong with believing that the human race is wonderful, beautiful, loving and kind... and asleep, but awaking. It is ok to dance and celebrate the last few thousand years of living. Anything that has been a thing for a thousand years to a human is important. We have placed so much meaning on the post flood myths, stories, and lore, we aren't seen the reactor. Archaeologists, with good intentions, put this site back together. People seeking meaning in their own lives and community come together giving more meaning to the site. The reality of what it really is requires practical human eyes that also know we were once great. Great before 12,500 years ago.

This is a current nuclear facility. How many years after a disaster is a new culture building it into a temple and celebrations for the moon are taking place? It is funny and deadly serious to stop sanctifying our past and looking at the realities.

273

Possibly 50,000, 400,000 or millions of years ago the advanced structures we know as pyramids and polygonal masonry existed. Disasters hit from time to time and they rebuilt, and it isn't until the final hit 12,000-13,000 years or so ago that they are finally smashed completely. Now what? Fragments of this past are picked up again. The alleged longevity of the ancient immortal technologies lost. The nuclear and energies knowledge gone to the masses of survivors. I think I am describing Thundarr the Barbarian. Look that up on the internets. There are either too few of them left or to many of the less advanced masses to overcome or secure an open city. Perhaps an "Atlantis" or many Atlantis's.

Trying to rebuilt now they hide, they slowly redeveloped their technology, perhaps in their now old tunnels and underground places. Places that are forgotten as they demo entrances and exits from surrounding humans, creating demons, monsters, legends to scare the tribes away. Those tribes, humans create rituals, religions, myths that they live and die by. The descendants of survivors are rebuilding and seeking out their old tech, mapping where they once were thousands of years ago. Even they don't remember where they were. Teams, theories are put together and they look for old technology. How do you come out of a bunker and locate technology that is buried maybe under tons of mud, sand and soil? Become a god, a visitor, show up and "help" them farm, help these simple humans with basic medical knowledge, farming, sciences. Use them to dig up your remaining tech?

What if it has taken the last 12,000 years to become what they once were. Carefully staying away from the masses and developing into what they once were but only through the awareness of where they once were and through re-engineering their past. What does that do if you aren't using the tech you lost? The tech and knowledge you had over the last millions of years? Wouldn't your philosophy change with you tech? Is it possible in staying away from the greater human population your ideas and morals change your decisions on how to interact with the tribes? All the people you left to reinvent themselves and their devastated existences from the flood, wouldn't they develop their own answers for what happened. What happens when the answers become something worth killing each other over. First for disbelieving and next for the "gods" satisfactions. When you are that advanced society that has left these tribes to develop beliefs based on your nudging of technology where does your responsibility lay? Over 12,000 years you showed up as a god every few years or influenced a storm cloud to rain, left, never came back thinking ya gav'em a good push in the right way. Maybe that society would morph good or bad based on the sliver of technology you showed up showed off and left with. Would it mater after 2000 years when you haven't shown back up, or to the Aztecs that thought the Spanish were their gods?

POT FLOOD PICK UPS

Advanced humans back in the saddle after the last cataclysm. Again or continuously, limitless, loving your planet, you come out of the bunkers and your ancient high tech home grown over with these squatter cultures. When you take off and fly around you avoid being seen. Perhaps now after a large amount of debates about how helping has gone in the last 5000 years, the record of "help" looks a little bloodier than they had planned. Perhaps if the world wide humans today see you fly at right angles stop mid flight and turn, it will inspire them in new directions of research? A debate amongst your people, do we reveal who we are, do we reveal pieces, do we stay the puppet masters?

CONSPIRACY

Secret societies for the last 12,000 or at least last 5,000 years of recorded history, what do they know? The various Cabals, the mystics, druids, Catholic Church, the power money new world order people? What do they all know? Thanks to human simplicity, almost nothing is the same. The ones that want to stay in power, manipulate the necessary buttons, the church can suppress any pre history, overlapping self interests of government nationalism helps bury Roman wrecks off the coast of Brazil where the history doesn't line up if Roman galleons are there. To secret societies that are really sure there is no Christian god, but think the lizard people they saw for real, once, a 1000 years ago are the true over lords of the hollow earth and have a secret lizard group. When in reality the very advanced humans that were well on their way to changing genetic code at will had found a more comfortable genetic code for working in the center of the earth or near it. It just happened that it was lizard like. Here we have a group believing in lizard people when it was just a convenient form for the work the ancients were doing. Like the countless aliens that are big black eyed, short white aliens. Perhaps that is the best human form to withstand phase shifted, right angle Mach 11 to faster than light travel. Maybe those big eyes are inferred and up screen genetic quantum screens allowing them interface to their ships, quantum calculations and communications to connect and process to their even faster or fully conscious brains. The body they pick to be in now is the one that works best to travel to Mars, interstellar looking or going to and from the former planets that we may have occupied pre-flood. Perhaps after 12,000 years, they have interstellar flight back but not as advanced as they once were. Perhaps the rediscovery isn't over for their own searches in our solar system for all the available technology they lost. Lost satellites, moon bases, moon bases around Mars. Or in the interstellar Kepler belts way out where and there.

It serves well for a lot of sheeple humans to worry about their own slow re-advance to leave the more advanced humans alone. There is no algorithm that helps them continue with us, the masses. We are left to the scientific unknown and the scraps they may feed the governments and religious institutions that have figured them out. Bribes to keep them away. Threats even. Essentially we are at the divergence of a single race. Their necessities mixing with a guilt, with a need to leave us to continue. It's mixed signals at a minimum

As an example, the Freemasons may not know whom this advanced human ancestors are, but they noticed the keystone cuts long ago in their infancy as a secret society. The masons may have noticed in a time where people are burned at the stake for religious decent that they had discovered something special. Their revelation of advanced stone work alone was a secret worth keeping even if they didn't know the source, it protected their trade. They delighted in secret knowledge and hid their symbols in churches as already described by the Da Vinci code. Does this mean they saw a piece of ancient high technology or does it mean they saw the whole pie?

Did the church identify that we were old, that possibly in the Vatican vaults there is physical proof of the antiquity of man, even old technology? They may not know what it is but they have it. Do they have an interest in engineering it? No, maybe, is it clear that they are interested in continuing the status quo, check their bank account. There are volumes that could be written on the Church and maintaining the power they have cultivated. Makes you wonder about Gobekli Tepe being intentionally buried. Our ancient ancestors, in the rebuild, with the advanced digging equipment or Colonel High Priest Mustard, with shovels and a crusade?

Are the minds that are starting to grasp the concept that we are older than written history also grasping that there are secret societies, yes. Decoding the money/power families that are running the countries doesn't point to our ancient past but it helps us understand the slow morphine drip of ignorance we seem to be on. It is a longer thing to read like The Creature from Jekyll Island and see what the money/power families are doing, then watch A Century of Enslavement, The History of The Federal Reserve. Directing the sheeple has been an obvious calling for the power money families of modern times. The idea that they are more conscious is not likely. Try Wim Hof or Stig's Breathology for 20 minutes. Connect your paleo-self and see how quickly your diet, exercise and consciousness doesn't truly elevate after you fucking de-mystify. The evil on us all is our amnesias. Those that know that there is more, but are willing to have "power" for a short 100 years on this planet to maintain their "power" represent some of the worst of our devolved humans. Which, to be fair to our great great great ancient genetically advanced ancestors, may be one of the reasons they let us kinda do our own things. Just like we leave tribes alone to stone people to death if they marry the wrong person from the wrong tribe and genital mutilations being done all over this planet as I write, our advanced ancestors leave us to our own. Some of our modern society let these atrocities happen while others are still practicing these disgusting immoral activities. All the time eyes stay off our ancestors that appear as "UFOS" or aliens. They are not aliens, they are us. We are them. They are kinda assholes.

WHY A-HOLES? LET THE BACKUP WRITE ITSELF

Your worldly society has fell to the worst of it. You have come out of the high tech bunkers, honeycombs, the off planet hiding in orbit, the moon maybe mars, and the earth is worse than a new hoarders starter collection. Every tribe you left alone while you groomed and tuned the planet has taken over all your populations centers, or you let them.

After millions of years of ups and downs, has there been such a fracture in the will or belief that the planet can be maintained that the decision is made to stay small, create or maintain technology that will sustain them but not using the planet the way they had.

Since the humans on the surface, including giants, small small people, the Paracus and all elongated people that chose to join the survivors on the surfaces were looked at as a new fail safe. No more would the big pyramid energy machines run, no more immortality for the surface dwellers, they can breed, live and die on their own. A self cleaning bio computer eliminating bad code or making redundancies. This time if the earth gets hit there will be a larger back up pool that includes their own formerly advanced people. The Paracus, the other races of humans, Neanderthal and Denisovans, all living and sorting themselves out. The animals losing their original function just replicate, unmanaged like the plants and people, their genes just start writing their own program.

Tribes are using crystal memory sticks as jewelry and pestles for corn and flour. The schist disk is now an incense burner, the pyramids are tombs. The lines waiting for the healing chambers are gone, mummifying replaces cold holding chambers that once got people tuned and fixed when there were lines and not riots at the healing centers. Now the pieces of technology are left are just being repurposed to oblivion.

What is the genetic safe mode that our super advanced ancient high tech great great great great x thousands grandparents are thinking? I am calling a total dick move....

Well, we left the tribes that lived in loincloths, ate bark and ritually mutilated themselves and their children alone, level one.

Well, we got some of the users of our advanced tech on the surface, they don't know how to make it but....lets let them figure their own thing out, they were the bartenders anyway. The question now is do some of these ancient survivors become the "gods" or the Anunaki? You could show up with a half functioning laptop and cell phone and impress everyone.

Why? Fail safes, if the earth is hit again, any combo of these genetics will live on. Why does it matter? Because the ancient backup of all DNA in all of them contains the living coding for all past humans maybe? For a fully restored earth. The most advanced of us think we are a control experiment on the ground, a test lab. A necessary fail safe they can turn their heads while we murder, rape, destroy ourselves and stay in complete agony over who and what we are. They are only doing it because the true history of the earth and humanity is millions of years older than we know of today. They turn a blind eye while we die, interacting out of guilt, intent or actual fairness, individuals of our advanced past keep showing up or talking to some of us. We would never know who they are. Show up as a reptilian, a grey, a hobbit. We would believe if they "descend" from the sky and only meet with the militaries, or abduct a few of us and they make it really obvious to us, they are alien, but they aren't, they are first class dicks. How would you react to find out your entire life was a lie in that they created your faith, to push you toward awareness of quantum connectivity, that your thoughts do affect water to each other, but otherwise your actual faith in the god of your choice was a lie. They did it to just make the planet a little more stable and all the torture on the earth between religions could be justified simply because it was better than when the flood had just ended.

How would you feel to know your immortal now? Look at how we live, how vengeful would we be on our 100 percent brain using great ancestors that reveal that they are our human ancestors and thought we should be left to die, fight and commiserate in case the planet had another reset. Some of us would make it in another disaster. We had repopulated the planet, we live about 80 years that ain't bad. Maybe they thought, why help them more, the genes will carry all, we can restore them all when the whole planet will get just conscious enough to bring everyone back. Meanwhile over the last 5-12,000 years tribal humans have been murdering their neighbor for being of the wrong faith, but shit, it was fixable with a gene switch and a frequency change to the planets programming.

Show up in your hi tech antigravity ship, look and sound alien to your former selves, who's gonna know? As far as today's human consciousness goes, the "power elite" controlling with their incredibly low functioning mortal selves, money, religion, they thought they were happy. How mad would you be to know that a simpler disclosure of our true history could put us on a path of full recovery, connection and immortality. I would be pissed. We are killing each other over believing in the right fruit or god vegetable, we are warring over nothing, borders that don't raise our consciousness, mystifying consciousness techniques. How many times have our great ancestors showed up in an effort to help and or to really slow us or hinder us from remembering? Sending us down another now historical slaughter of ourselves to erase our own forward progress. This is the "alien" that is ourselves, it's worse than an alien from another planet. Can you imagine an alien showing up to this miss managed shit show after the last or one of many cataclysms? There could have been a hand shake or an exchange of information.

Have you seen the YouTube video 240 that will change your life? Essentially showing the entire universe full of life but we are the most interesting planet? Inter dimensional beings come from all over just to watch us eat, fuck and die?

....or worse, our asshole relatives are just masquerading as aliens as we crawl out of our amnesia and hopefully won't remember who clobbered us?

SACRED, EVERYTHING IS SACRED

First and most important. We all have our beliefs, our true life experiences, some unexplainable and others clear as day with deep spiritual meaning. Whether birth, death, a spiritual retreat, a near death experience, there are uncountable ways we connect to a spiritual realm. Some have passionate beliefs that their way is the only way while there are those that have joined tribal like beliefs in a natural world and it is best that we live closer to the natural world. There are the beliefs of the atheist and the the non believers of anything. Good for everyone.

Just like the archaeologists that came from a pre 21 century view of the earth, the desire to imprint "sacred on forms of the earth that we observe today, is just an interpretation. It is abundantly clear in what we have of a fossil record is a fraction. When we apply our early understandings of this world in the past the theories prevailed as science. Instead of pointing to a new truth, the theories deleted facts in the ground and staring at us in genetic information and physical remains of buildings with many cultures building on a single site. When the Paracus are in your face, just say it wasn't me.

Currently we have alternative history researchers using buzz words like "sacred geometry" sacred shaman medicine, ayahuasca or peyote to go on vision quests to visit the spirituality of ancient sites, it goes on...We are at a point in history that it just isn't that these things are or are not sacred the issue is we have labeled them before we understand them. We are just starting to realize, hey, we were pretty advanced, looks like history is amiss. As we have already been discussing in this book, things are always labeled an "Enigma" a one off, a "first of its kind". Oh, how did we get that pyramid or megalithic stone in place without satellites or machines. Well maybe it was aliens and we have spent years putting those labels on and dancing in fairy costumes at Stonehenge.

Here is the final shroud placed on our past, everything is sacred, and mystical. Every culture that has been sitting on top of an ancient site or can legitimately say they have been in a site for 1000's or just hundreds of years can claim it's sacred. Then we have this research where Gobekli Tepe is found, it's sacred, Stonehenge, sacred, pyramids, sacred, this is starting to sound like Shaggy again, "it wasn't me."

You don't describe your IPhone as sacred. Or your laptop, or your car, or your watch or the location of Chernobyl. Is Chernobyl sacred, if 1000 years in the future they are doing yoga at the center of the old reactor, is it sacred? Maybe for the yoga people, even if they show genetic connections to the people who built it. It's just a nuclear reactor. DO you see the danger in labeling something sacred at this stage of our realizations about our highly advanced past? Sacred geometry...

Let's look at the Chernobyl example first, if you're worried about offending a group of yogis in 900 years that have been at the Chernobyl site doing yoga, how long or much further do you get to dig at the site when they say the concrete floor of the reactor is the holiest of holies and the desecration of the sacred waters beneath that is the legendary waters of God and creation?

Key stone cuts and rebuilds. We have discussed this with cymatic polygonal masonry, there are keystone cuts in the stones connecting them.

Investigating ancient sites are simply problematic on every continent. Ancient finds in the United States, are re-appropriated to burials after being claimed "native peoples". Based on our ever growing understanding of modern humans being well into a fog of disinformation about the past, more appreciation has to be there in "native" cultures that claim residencies in the last even 3000 years because occupations are going so far past that we have to dig and discover them all. A complete human record and evidences of pyramids, mounds, geo works and channel systems in the United States pointing to an ancient past must be made known and researched. These remains can not be claimed by a recent post-antediluvian tribe till genetic information is tested, mapped and better excavated. Don't the more forgotten "native" people deserve a voice? Because they are even deeper, in the ground, their lives don't deserve recognition?

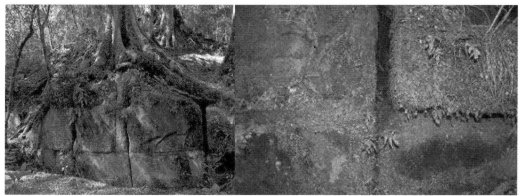

Here are two megalithic walls in New Zealand suffering from one of the deadliest threats to our human past. "Sacred" sites that "belong" to the natives. The modern idea that there were separate cultures all over the earth made it easy for a local indigenous to the post flood world to claim that these or other ruins are theirs. This could have been true if history had happened the way Darwinists said. It will be uncomfortable and necessary for indigenous people to know that the earth was once part of a global nation and sites have to be looked at that might have been given to them as theirs when in reality it's even older and may have sat for 1000's of years with out being occupied. At a minimum don't all ancient people deserve to be remembered?

The Maori of New Zealand are the natives of New Zealand. There are megalithic walls all over the island. Can't dig at them because it's holy to the descendants of the Maori. Cymatic polygonal walls lay half buried and can be seen in documentaries. They are very curious structures.

Some of the worst examples are in Israel, There are certain zealots, that don't want any research even into biblical time periods, archaeologist get interrupted or shut down at tells. The zealots claim the archaeologists are disrupting holy sites.

A couple huge dangers in truly revealing our past, ONE: makes people nervous, worried and defensive about their religious beliefs, (also makes those in charge of those beliefs worried about their powers). TWO: no one in recent history can save face, everyone has it part wrong and they don't give out degrees for part wrong and questioning things yet. The other issue is the sciences we are re-discovering is so complex that it looks almost mystical. That is how vibrational medicine and IPhones can look sacred to a tribal people that work with sticks. Or to people who believe in magic. Sound energy, sound technology, and magnetism is so complex that it would look wizardry to move a megalithic block by floating. Aliens did it. They thought, lets get them three blocks in and take off, they will be wondering for years why. Lol. Instasnapbookchat. Haha.

By stamping it "Holy" or "Sacred Geometry" there is this desire to stamp some kind of mystical intangible meaning that we can't grasp yet on our ancient high technology. We know spirituality is real. Even in the early stages of research we feel that some honor is done to this "spiritual" higher being, or existence that we give gratitude to by acknowledging it as sacred geometry. That is not what is happening. It is keeping a fog on an old laptop design. We are making a hymn out of an ancient MRI ultrasound machine.

DEMYSTIFY EVERYTHING-STOP MAKING YOUR SIDEWALK SACRED

It would help shift the paradigm if we related to what we see by the true function of the structures. We find structures and label them what they might be as we reverse engineer the tech. Not, the temple of the sun WTF in the A!?!?

That already sounds better. Temple of the sacred holy cow...lets tip it and get on.

There is a dialog in documentaries, books interviews that are creating a dangerous following with creating new mystical ideas on research work. When you hear "what were the the ancients trying to tell us with sacred geometry???? " They were saying the same thing your gas gauge does when it says your close to empty ...NO ONE is trying to tell you anything. The tank was empty and the Smartphone needed a recharge, it wasn't a sacred recharge, just a charge.

We need to constantly in every way not fall into a modern trap of the alternative histories. Erich Von Daniken has done amazing things by opening our eyes to an alternate explanation of the Ark of the Covenant and identifying for us that our holy recent ancient past is filled with high technology. He is looking through and demystifying the faiths of legends and time and looking at the clues. It helps clear a path to look at the material we are digging up and reverse engineer it.

We have another group of people who have built up stories of their experiences and mixed it with modern movies, stories and culture. This is the group that has now mixed, religion with the belief that there are aliens and that there is a group of aliens on earth living amongst us. This group believes there are aliens and they are multi dimensional and have continued over 60 years to build an alternative story living amongst us. They believe genuinely that there is a need to rule earth, that there is this large drama around these alien races that need gold, to use us as slaves, that they are multidimensional beings that are really obsessed with earth and some aliens are good and others are bad.

Yes, this is slightly repetitive, there is too much to absorb. The idea that our relatives are here, still advanced, still calling this home and just ancient versions of us. They are us. We are them. It isn't that we are part them. We came up as a race, made our way, fell and some of us are reading this book and watching Netflix later, while other ancient humans are traveling inter-dimensionally and it's getting harder to hide. The disclosure we are looking for isn't to point the finger at power families or governments or secret societies, they all wash away when we are awake again. There is nothing more powerful then our conscious selves in this world once repaired, we will all be super.

Chapter 12

NEW ARCHAEOLOGY: IT'S A RESCUE MISSION NOT A RESEARCH MISSION!!!!

All the genetic information, our quantum consciousness and a simple thing like water, is revealing our past was significantly different than what it is now. A highly advanced human race fell, the remnants or Phoenix of those people rebuilt themselves and maybe helped the survivors of the tribes outside of this advanced society start again. Because there are UFO sightings and specifically the admission by the United States military just this year in 2019 that they have been tracking UFOs and want the public's help, we know that there is something outside of what we know to be modern man here. We assume alien and UFO means out of this world, when the more likely story that these are our own relatives that have left us on a planet in safe mode. We have killed ourselves and each other over that feeling of who are we, scratching at it so hard we founded secret societies, religions, governments, traditions on the idea, while all along we know, we don't know.

We have enough facts now. We have the videos, pictures, genetic information and real self experimentation that is reactivating powerful human abilities to know that the world has is a great missing, human society. The technical achievements are laying in front of us and within us as we eat and breath.

Let's start adding up the technology involved to analyze surfaces, there is x-ray photoelectron spectroscopy, scanning electron microscopy focused with energy dispersive spectroscopy. They analyzed the surfaces and sub surfaces.

These are some of the techniques that would need to be applied at sites and surfaces of large megalithic structures. Quantum computing is just around the corner, it would not be wasted to take LIDAR and start speculating on the programming of blocks, rubble and stones that could be reassembled in their original ways with the help of quantum computing. Quickly coming is going to be the ability to decipher the rebuilds of ancient cymatic polygonal constructions and the dust under the buildings. Everything has a side, even if it is dust, unless a quantum particle, buildings that have been dusted may be rebuildable.

LIDAR and satellites can be added to a growing map available online and in book format to all. Online, daily scans could publish all the latest scans and LIDAR images. Groups already responsible for analysis could be speculating on what the maps say, not how they feel about a fertility goddess or how sacred the secret is.

These are two mining tailing piles. These are current and obviously not natural. What happens to tailing piles of a society that cuts 1600 and 3000 ton blocks. Works with cymatic polygonal stones, pillars and statues of any tonnage and can move them 1000 of miles? How big would their mining equipment be? What would ancient high technology mines look like vs the mimic cultures and tribes of the post flood world, the ones really wearing loin cloths...?

Mega mining sites. We have pits all over the earth for open mining. When you build on the scale that this ancient advanced society did they left huge piles of tailings. They mined on a level that was way outside of our current grasp. We have spoken of 800, 1000, 1600, even 3000 plus ton stones. Cut and moved, they didn't try making a few and quit. Ancient quarries all over the earth have ancient saw cuts that are thinner than the blades we have now. There are many current open mines, that create slag, run off, material that after it's been sifted, crushed, run through, gets dumped away. The mine itself has stepped cut sites making them look like giant amphitheaters, as they are tapped out they leave very distinguishable signs of having been mined.

This is an old gold mine. Water canons and other modern methods were used to create this current very natural look. How many years could have past that the geology of an ancient quarry or mine of any kind could or would be gone? Worse, what if this ancient society mined something out of the earth that we have zero or currently untraceable amounts of. Could there be something more valuable then our idea of known minerals?

This is the type of water cannon that would be used. It was called a water monitor, it blasted off the walls and rock itself into slurry that could be crushed, sifted, washed and searched for the precious minerals that were desired. This is the device that would make the hills and valleys above in the last photo. In the background you can see the height of the mine. The tree line is high and in the distance it would appear a "natural" cliff despite being turned into what you see by man.

The art of archeo-mining maybe a field that will be incredibly valuable for reverse engineering and pointing to our high technology ancestors former work locations. There are sites in Antarctica that look like large mined areas. There are signs the Grand Canyon was a mine. Our citizen scientists need only to look at Sylvie Ivanova and her documentaries on ancient megalithic mining. The work is brilliant and the sheer scale of this ancient society would leave what today would appear to be "natural" formations or mountains. To not look at what appears to be large scale tailings and mining of a forgotten ancient society is a big miss right now. Gravel could indicate the types of stone built with that may only be left in foundations or "field" stone walls in a 3rd world country. The stones could be devastated cymatic polygonal walls. There is an unlimited amount of research to just begin. There are ancient quarry sites in China that are massive and ancient. Well before China was China.

Multiple water monitors are working to get material down to head into a sorting machine. The appearance in the distance of a large "natural" canyon is forming. Is it more than possible that the canyons we visit now on our camping, hiking, and climbing trips are remnant mines of our ancestors in a time where the equipment worked at a scale unimaginable today?

Multiple water monitors are working to get material down to head into a sorting machine. The appearance in the distance of a large "natural" canyon is forming. Is it more than possible that the canyons we visit now on our camping, hiking, and climbing trips are remnant mines of our ancestors in a time where the equipment worked at a scale unimaginable today?

Another "canyon" being created from mining. This land scape will be undistinguishable to a natural canyon. Here the work has been done with water. There is a massive drum wheel and Hoist, capable of lifting 25 tons safely to the right of the men. Generally, a drum wheel and hoist is made from redwood and metal.

Water cannons work on multiple levels. How would we be able to look at ancient mining sites that are as old or older than our Cuban pyramid let alone see them if the the ancient mine sites are 2000 feet below sea level.

This is a drum wheel and hoist crane. These cranes have been in operation over 150 years. They are generally made from redwood. In the last photo above you see a 4 ton cut block being moved. To keep the hoist from breaking from the weight of the blocks, the square metal frames you see up and down the hoist are bolted through the redwood trunk, while the metal rods run the length of the lift all to insure the beam itself doesn't twist, splinter and come crashing down under the block weight. Engineers made it a four to one ratio. The lift can manage 25 tons safely. It will break at 100 tons. It could break after 25 tons with the wrong movement. Now imagine 60 diameter 380 ft. Redwoods, cut and ready to lift 1200 tons.

Moving forward in archeo-mining, we have to re-evaluate areas we deem "natural". Look at these shear walls of the Grand Canyon. Water doesn't weather in straight walls. Below you will see a working stone quarry with metal wheels and hoists.

Above we have a working mine, the depth is staggering. Where do you look for a society that is mining and building at the scale they could build pre-flood?

These are different mines, what would the weathering appear to be after 5 or 50,000 thousand years in timeline to our Cuban timeline?

The erosion here could be compared to any mining site. The abandonment combined with 1000's of years, weathering, and multiple world wide disasters would leave their mark in this canyon. It would not negate the start, pause and restart of ancient high technology ancestors mining out this area creating canyons after eons.

Man made mining tailing piles at different locations.

These are tailings and other wastes from mining that are being taken back by nature. These are not the only things that would be taken back. Below, in order, a rusting crane, two pieces of a drum wheel and hoist crane, 11.5 ft granite cutting blade (diamond tipped)

Italian made cutting wheel with diamond tipped saw teeth despite the size of the wheel, the hole that has light shining though it is the maximum cutting depth. There are many larger cuts in ancient megalithic blocks.

Italian cutting wheel and the teeth where the diamond tipping cuts the stone.

This is an old wood crane and parts to a "newer" metal crane, just like the one moving the 4 ton block on page 289.

The equipment would change over the years as our ancient ancestors improved their own processes today's cutting equipment has a variety of appearances and machines for the same attachments.

As we look back at ancient quarries, we see ancient blade over cuts that are thinner than the equipment we can make today. We don't have site on the equipment but billions of tons of material show up and are all over the earth.

Smelting and casting machine. The trains on page 307 are dumping hot liquid metal and stone tailings over a temporary rail line, staining and changing the side of the hill. In some cases causing brilliant colors like in the the Rainbow Mountains.

Waste from ore processing needed to be dumped. An area not desired to be mined in would be located and the dumping would begin. To the point that railway was built to and from the dump site to be cost effective. This process left toxic and not natural mineral deposits.

These are "natural" color variations in the cliff sides. It doesn't appear much different than the rail ways dumping off the cliffs on page 307.

When you go to the southern rim of the Grand Canyon and you will see off in the distance to the right of the Sky Walk, a vary curious and locally famous formation on the sides of the hills. The second photo shows it closer. There is an Indian princess kissing a horse. If you look again at the smelters above perhaps much further back it was something else that left that staining. Let's look at some more natural and known mining waste sites...

These are man made dumping grounds from tailings to unwanted cooling metals and minerals separated in the forging processes.

Simplified world mining map

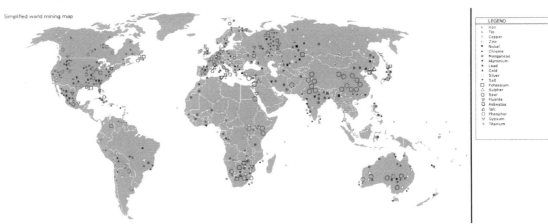

The map is known modern mining. The shapes of the stadium is "natural", discerning our past mining's will be difficult but what they could have been mining could be very different than what we are mining now. Their methods could have been similar or vary different. Look at this rope below, it's been made with diamond dust, the rope is actually a blade. It slices though stone like a wire in a block of clay.

Wim hof speaks of demystifying. We know there are shadows of truth in our post flood life that have those truths in them and likely in our genetics. What about some of the technology showing up in our last twelve thousand years, going round robin connecting it to the Anunaki then back to Sumerians then back to a more recent society or cult. While touring an old quarry I was able to get an amazing detailed description how they would move large tonnages after cutting them away from the rock beds, they would drill at angles into the block. Below you can see keys that are fatter at the bottom and narrower at the top.

From cutting a hole in a stone, the keys, approximately 15 pounds each would be placed into the holes and thinner metal shims placed between the two so they would open the bigger keys to fill the fatter bottom of the drilled hole. Then a hook like the one below would pick up the multi ton block

Here is where, after thousands of years and no use for keys 15 pounds to even larger and smaller depending on the quarry cuts, we have a tool. If there were no more machines, needs for meta material and nano structures in soil, what could a tool like this become?

This is what may have happened to a forgotten tool

This is a boot scraper. It was explained by this quarry veteran of 43 years that the foremen hated mud in the office. They would drill out a block and place exactly this kind of metal into it. Smelt it in and scrape their boots or have hell to pay for tracking mud in the office. No archaeologist could know that. This block, this one piece might as well be an ankh.

SOME THINGS TO DO:

1. Change your words- no more it's the first, isolating a dig or society by saying its the first, was it on the shipping lane for an Amazon order or the Fort Knox of its day

2. How much have we dug up? 1 % 5 % or all of a location. How many cultures can we identify have reoccupied a site, are there any post flood cultures that we may not know of that could be identified from this dig unknown to us. Could it help further identify a known squatter culture and help us lift their defacing of our more ancient past.
Prior to drawing a conclusion have we dug the whole site up....?

3. Has LIDAR and Sarah Parcak and Global Explorer satellite system identified the under surface and deep tunnel systems that might be present?

4. MATERIAL CHECK, are there geopolymers, is it really an ancient concrete, is it grown rock, is there anything special about the assembly of the stone?

5. Organics, has there been a point to mass cultivation, is this complex part of pre-flood history cultures and is the soil evidence of mass food production like near the lost city of Z?

6. Does the site fall on natural Earth Energy lines? Has there been testing of the megalithic structural bases, buildings, ruins, etc...is there a magnetic element to the stone, is it polygonal, is there inferred, is there a sublayer to the earth showing a deposit of Iron, or any other element that makes it unique including the soft or compacted soils around it?

7. What do the locals say, what are their myths, what parts of the site are holy, what in the area which could be near but seemingly onsite related. In reconstructing energy relays, could the site that is "holy" near the found site be the remnants of ancient technological sites. Per se an old Chernobyl

ArcheoAstronomy, Archaeo-Acustics, Forensic Archaeology, Archeo-Cymatics including Archaeo-cymatic constructions, Archaeo-gentics and Archeo-quantum technology. These are some of the sciences along with Archeo-genetics that will help us keep backing out and seeing our past. In our present, we need to continue to develop self experimentation, brain entrainment, relationships to light, water, the energies of the earth and the safe mode we are operating in.

TIMING AND MONEY

"It's gonna take plenty of money, to do it, to do it right now"

George Harrison, the Beatle himself

Yes, money, our past is all of our past, no matter who's feet it lays under or what government "owns" that land, not being allowed as a global world to re-discover ourselves as quickly as possible should be outlawed. Money should be government or United Nations mandated for the fastest recovery of our past for all our sakes.

Private individuals, museums, professors, governments withholding access to all archaeological information must be outlawed. Full access to all world citizens and digitization of information to decipher the human search and rescue is paramount.

We are digging up the cultures that have taken a much older or in some cases a multi-layered squatter cultures civilization and lived within, on top of, near or with their own religion and life on a higher technology. This has blurred and marred the original site with 12,000 years of human societal graffiti. The science points to much older structures but they don't fit into what we research currently to get on National Geographic.

We argue and go at digs as if it is simply a philosophical debate, while if we dug as if it was 9 miners in a collapsed mine, or a recovery of a crashed plane we would have gone at it quickly and CNN/FOX would be there night and day. Around the clock efforts would be made to uncover the miners. We are killing ourselves and living in a non stop question, who are we, what's the point? We are in shut down, safe mode. We need to quickly and forensically including all fields, archaeologists, geologists, physicists, and laymen, like the citizen scientists that are working with Global Explorer dig, discover, experiment with and collect obvious megalithic sites technology. Knowing that there is an advanced buried plane that is the origin or at the layer of our best tech that has been turned into a mobile for a loin cloth tribe or for their tiles on their huts or still laying in the jungle buried is unacceptable.

ROCK CUT RUINS

In Turkey, the Middle East, South America and many other places there are rock cut ruins. There are estimates that the caves could support over a million people in some locations. Labeling it "a mystery" is not what our most advanced and prestigious schools should be claiming as their answer to accepted dogma.

Petra has many rock cut formations. Again, credited to a Greek area yet the stone being cut in is more ancient. It is easy to re-appropriate an old building and make it a tomb, like a catacomb. Were they originally for the dead, or group sleeping blocks.

The site is often visited for the pillars at the "treasury". This is the spot you have seen in Indiana Jones movie with Sean Connery. What many people don't know is that it is approximately 7-13 miles long of rock cut development. It shows substantial weathering and the rock cut ruins are cut in multiple stories along the cliff sides. These were square well cut buildings. Where is the quantum computer to analyze the dusted remains and vitrified stone?

Near the famous treasury, the famous picture of Petra that is the treasury has two rooms under it, well near it, that are over 300,000 cubic sq. Ft. And another that is through the next door way, which is another 300,000 cubic sq. Ft in size.

Rock cut ruins require the same skill as the cymatic polygonal walls. The great amphitheaters and stadiums showing cloaking and solid acoustic properties, the abilities of these places to receive waves and frequencies goes un-researched completely.

We are constantly digging up eoliths and neoliths, so why can't they be more, just older? It would be more effective to bring in Physicists, Geologists and search and rescue crews than anthropologists to debate what to do with any find that stays buried for 50 years after finding it.

Why isn't there structural engineers? Physicists, forensic researchers, that only in the last decade, have realized that the soil around a body has chemicals and indicators of the buried that can be analyzed. Sifting out the bones and pottery is elementary. All sciences

327

must see a site. Max Uhle goes on about finding things, that the archaeologists, stick rods in the ground to hook or bang on a piece of what is buried and if they fish up some cloth they know they may have found something. Our research has to go beyond these elementary techniques.

The map of our globe is tilted. We are not rotating the way we did, our land masses have changed and there are 2000 meter deep and likely deeper ruins that need investigation. The genetic history of all living things is incomplete. Assumptions are the last thing we need and the baby and the bath water do not apply to the established theories. They suck. How is that for big words.

De-mystifying the past, becoming aware of our high tech past, sharing our awaking super powers and re-applying our growing perspectives against what we find will lead to our future. Our ancient ancestors are here. They walk amongst us, they clearly fly above us. They interact with some of us and we are not clear if this is in our best interests. What we are discovering is that we can be much more than we have devolved too. That our giant brain isn't a pre-gift by evolution. Hey, you'll grow into it, here's an extra brain. No, we need to hit all the breakers. Connecting to this planet is connecting to ourselves and a high technology we were likely responsible for.

Whether our ancient high tech ancestors want to reveal themselves to us in the open or not is one question. Whether we would even appreciate or understand why they left us to re-emerge on our own is an actual mystery. One we are on track with our very DNA to remember. Starting with the facts that we, humans have been here for millions of years is necessary to accept that we were capable and so advanced that we could live through planetary disasters and shifting continents. In the remnants of our DNA and our cymantic, genetic, and soil engineered past lays our remedy for amnesia. The continuing exercise of our quantum consciousness and self experimentation will allow us to know the truth. We have ancient relatives that don't want to come to Christmas, one day we might show up to their door and invite ourselves.

Made in the USA
San Bernardino, CA
04 August 2020